Praise for *The*

"With insight and empathy, be tackles all the questions you and practical blocks to writing but are too afraid to ask. Offering tips on everything from conquering procrastination and impostor syndrome to productively receiving and using criticism, *The Intuitive Author* offers practical guidance that I wish I'd had when I was starting out—and am grateful to have now, as a bestselling novelist. Every writer of every skill and experience level needs this book on their shelf."

—Stephanie Storey, *Los Angeles Times*-bestselling author of *Oil and Marble* and *Raphael*

"With this book, Martin offers what's too long been missing from writers' shelves: a guide to the emotional, personal, and yes, even spiritual aspects of navigating the writing life. This book is a balm for the writer's soul in the best possible way: practical tips, reasoned exploration of what it means to be both human and artist, and guidelines for making the writing life work in any given moment as well as for a lifelong creative journey. Reading this book is like sitting down with a wise creative coach over a cup of your favorite hot beverage and receiving generous measures of encouragement, wisdom, practical advice, and motivation, all in a well-organized, thoughtful manner."

—Sharon Short, author of *Trouble Island*/Jess Montgomery, author of the Kinship Historical Mysteries

"Writers need honest guidance on what it takes to sustain a publishing career, but it can be hard to offer that honesty without amplifying writerly anxiety and negativity. Tiffany's wise approach is one I wholeheartedly applaud: prioritize resilience in the face of new and old industry challenges. Every writer is going to encounter trouble, and Tiffany shows that it's how you respond that matters."

—Jane Friedman, author of *The Business of Being a Writer*

"Tiffany Yates Martin provides the perfect balance of hard-to-hear truths and honest-yet-hopeful experience that every author needs to make their dreams of being a professional writer a reality. *The Intuitive Author* is a much-needed resource, filled to the brim with wisdom and tips that every author needs to know. It should be required reading and belongs on every author's bookshelf."

—Amy Collins, literary agent, Talcott Notch

"Writers: Read this book. *The Intuitive Author* is the chiropractic realignment your hopes, dreams, and writing goals need. What a relief for your career!"

—Therese Walsh, editorial director of Writer Unboxed and author of *The Moon Sisters*

"Tiffany Yates Martin's *The Intuitive Author* is the book equivalent of a wise best friend whispering in your ear, 'You've got this.' It's the first writing book I've read that doesn't focus on craft or the professional side of writing but on the writer, helping each of us to figure out just what we want out of our career and how to make that happen. Publishing is a daunting, mercurial, kick-you-in-the-crotch industry, yet Martin—with wit, empathy, experience, and grace—teaches authors how to gain agency and autonomy in a business that often feels out of our control. This is a truly unique and valuable book that will help you joyfully slide into the driver's seat of your career and, dare I say it, your life."

—Erin Flanagan, Edgar-winning author of *Deer Season*

"This book is the best friend that every writer needs, but few are ever lucky enough to find. You may never have met Tiffany Yates Martin, but she certainly knows you—and deeply understands your writer's soul. This is a wise, compassionate and inspirational book that you will read, reread, dip into, and treasure for the entirety of your writing life."

—Peter Cox, founder, Litopia Writers' Colony, the net's oldest community for writers

"For anyone who dares to embark on a writing career, *The Intuitive Author* is required reading.... As an author and editor to successful writers, Tiffany has witnessed firsthand the radical changes in the business, the emotional anguish, and what tools writers need to pack in their arsenal. Her latest must-read is the companion to carry you through the battleground. She dives inside the complicated ups and downs, the necessary resiliency and risks, and the courage and stamina needed to survive. No one has their finger on the pulse of this business more than Tiffany Yates Martin.... This book will be an eye-opener for many, but it will also inspire and ignite your creative flame in the best possible way. Guaranteed."

—Rochelle B. Weinstein, bestselling author of *This Is Not How It Ends*

"What Tiffany Yates Martin offers in *The Intuitive Author* is as practical as it is inspirational—a guide to figuring out what's important to you as a writer and how to hold true to those things. The highest praise I can offer is that after months of being stalled, it got me writing again. Writers: This is a must-add title for your writing desk."

—Amy Jones, editor-in-chief of *Writer's Digest*

"*The Intuitive Author* is a writer's must-have, a true keeper, but it won't live on the shelf with all my other writing books—it'll live on my desk where its inspiration will always be within easy reach. If you're serious about both surviving and thriving as a writer, you need this book."

—Bestselling memoirist Rachael Herron

"It's not an exaggeration to say that Tiffany Yates Martin is one of the most influential support people in my writing career. To think that you, too, can get her levelheaded and experienced advice on how to develop the confidence and agency needed to navigate the unpredictable landscape of publishing is a true gift for any writer. Don't sleep on this book."

—Ann Garvin, *USA Today*–bestselling author of *There's No Coming Back from This*

THE
intuitive
AUTHOR

How to Grow & Sustain a
Happier Writing Career

TIFFANY YATES MARTIN

THE INTUITIVE AUTHOR
Copyright © 2024 by Tiffany Yates Martin

Published by FoxPrint Ink LLC

All rights reserved. No part of this book may be used or reproduced in any manner whatsoever, including internet usage, without written permission from the author, except in the case of brief quotations embodied in critical articles and reviews.

Book design and production by Domini Dragoone
Author Photograph Olympia Roll of Korey Howell Photography Group
Cover photos: tree © AnaWhite/iStock; rainbow © enjoynz/iStock

Although the author and publisher have made every effort to ensure that the information in this book was correct at press time, the author and publisher do not assume and hereby disclaim any liability to any party for any loss, damage, or disruption caused by errors or omissions, whether such errors or omissions result from negligence, accident, or any other cause.

Paperback: 978-1-950830-09-1
E-book: 978-1-950830-12-1
Hardcover: 978-1-950830-13-8
Audiobook: 978-1-950830-14-5

Printed in the United States of America

For the creators,

who connect us.

Contents

Introduction 1

PART ONE: FOUNDATION

Chapter One: What Is an Intuitive Author? 9

PART TWO: WRITING

Chapter Two: What Is Your Wendy? 33

Chapter Three: Finding the "Right" Way to Write 39

Chapter Four: What's Your Authentic Voice? 47

Chapter Five: Pay Attention to Your Progress 57

Chapter Six: 8 Lessons on Writing
 (Learned from Home Improvement) 67

Chapter Seven: Writing Enduring Stories
 and Your Artistic Legacy 75

Chapter Eight: The Power of "No" 81

Chapter Nine: When Will You Be a "Real Writer"? 87

Chapter Ten: Giving Your All for the Few 97

Chapter Eleven: Why You Can't Rush Your Process 105

PART THREE: ROADBLOCKS

Chapter Twelve: When the Demons Come for You
 (and They Will) 119

Chapter Thirteen: Impostor Syndrome............................. 133

Chapter Fourteen: Perfectionism and the Fear of Failure........... 141

Chapter Fifteen: Comparison and Competition..................... 151

Chapter Sixteen: If You Feel Like Sh*t, Sit with It.................. 165

Chapter Seventeen: Overcoming Procrastination.................... 171

Chapter Eighteen: "Writer's Block"—or Getting Unstuck
from the Wall of WTF... 179

PART FOUR: FEEDBACK

Chapter Nineteen: Assessing Writing Feedback: Criticism,
Commentary, and Critique.................................... 193

Chapter Twenty: How to Handle Feedback—
and What to Do with It 207

Chapter Twenty-one: Rejection, Criticism, and Crickets............ 223

Chapter Twenty-two: What Rejection Letters Do and Don't Mean... 237

Chapter Twenty-three: Knowledge Burnout and
Information Overload 247

PART FIVE: CAREER

Chapter Twenty-four:
Caveat Scriptor: When Creators Become the Customers...... 263

Chapter Twenty-five: Advocating for Your Writing,
Your Career, and Yourself 273

Chapter Twenty-six: How Do You Value Your Creative Work? 287

Chapter Twenty-seven: Build Your Community,
Not Your Network.. 297

PART SIX: LIFE

Chapter Twenty-eight: The Wisdom of William Shatner 307

Chapter Twenty-nine: Give It a Rest 313

Chapter Thirty: What Are You Working Toward? 321

Chapter Thirty-one: Reclaiming the Creative Spark
in Troubled Times... 329

Chapter Thirty-two: Lessons from an Unexpected Wedding....... 341

Endnotes.. 346

Acknowledgments... 351

About the Author... 355

Introduction

Why I Wrote This Book

In my thirty-year career in publishing I've learned something about pursuing writing as a career.

It's not just about writing.

In fact I'd venture to say it's not even mostly about writing, at least when you factor in all the other elements involved cumulatively in creating a sustainable, fulfilling long-term writing career. Writing is the heart of it, true, the source and the nexus of everything else involved, and writers must master the craft of storytelling and good writing. But today's authors who pursue publication must also be expert in marketing, publicity, platform building, and technology. They have to understand contract law, graphic design, copywriting, and sales.

But those considerations don't factor in what I call the "squishy skills" of writing, the ones that enable authors to pursue their craft at all: How to persist through rejection and daunting competition and market vagaries and writing dry spells. How to find a writing community, and why it matters. How to fit writing amid the many other obligations and demands of life. How to vanquish the demons who storm your psyche, fill you with self-doubt, and derail your writing.

It was all these other aspects of writing that began to define the blog posts I started writing for authors in 2020, during the pandemic, when writers suddenly found themselves locked down at home—a situation that should have sounded like author nirvana, great swaths of unspoken-for time to pursue their craft.

And yet the reality looked more like people crammed together in a confined space or painfully isolated in solitary confinement, all trying to maintain some semblance of real life; working and schooling from home amid fear, chaos, and uncertainty, nerves stretched taut; too many distractions—or far too few; and no toilet paper or hand sanitizer. What I heard from authors during that time, over and over, was that they couldn't create.

I started the blog to help address some of those areas and others where I saw authors struggling, my very first post fittingly about impostor syndrome, one of the many demons common to authors at least at some time in their career.

As the blog evolved over the years it also addressed the "hard skills" areas of writing, but more and more I found that the "squishy skills" posts garnered the most reaction and interaction with a growing writing community who found the site. More and more I saw the need to address those kinds of challenges of the writing life with the same kind of practical, actionable approach I brought to my work as an editor, my teaching, and my writing about craft.

Creating a successful writing career isn't about how much money you make from it. Webster's Collegiate Dictionary defines a career as "a profession for which one trains and which is undertaken as a permanent calling" that involves the "pursuit of consecutive progressive achievement." That describes every author I've had the privilege of working with. When I use the term "writing career" in this book, I mean it in that purest sense: as a calling authors consistently work to master in pursuit of progressive achievement—not whether it's your main source of income.

Creativity is a basic human impulse, a core aspect of our full well-being, the peak of Maslow's famous hierarchy of needs. It can take countless forms: art, gardening, cooking, knitting, scrapbooking, glassblowing—and, for those of us called to it, writing.

But the creative life can also be a harsh mistress, a pursuit filled with challenge and discouragement and doubt. If we want to create a writing career we can enjoy all our lives—whatever that may look like for each of us—we have to learn to navigate all these speed bumps.

That's why I wrote *The Intuitive Author*.

I've worked as an editor in the publishing industry for many decades. I've known authors who built long-term careers and those who flamed out fast. Those who crashed onto the scene with a splashy debut and then struggled for years to match the success of that first book, as well as those who slowly built up a head of steam on a career where every release garnered more and more readers.

I know authors who have weathered every conceivable challenge in the industry, from being unable to find an agent or publisher, to losing their agent or their editor at their publishing house, to receiving little to no marketing support, to having their incomes vary wildly over the course of their careers. I've seen them navigate blocked access to their social media accounts and all their followers, releasing their books at the beginning of a global pandemic, and battling AI-generated impostors of their work. They've suffered poor sales, bad reviews, shuttered publishing houses, and plenty more challenges, setbacks, and frustrations that are part of the roller coaster of a writing career.

And I've been on both sides of the page across the spectrum of the publishing business, working as an editor with major publishers, small presses, and indie authors, bestsellers and beginning writers. As an author I've traversed nearly every publishing path too—Big Five publisher, small press, and indie/self-pub—with six novels (under a pen name) and two nonfiction books for authors, including this one. I've worked with many hundreds of authors on literally thousands of stories, and in that time I've learned what separates the writers who endure from those who fall away; those who find meaning and reward in their careers, and those who feel discouraged and depleted by it and eventually give up.

What successful authors have in common is this: They know how to navigate the ups and downs of a business in which content is commerce and yet key aspects of their career may be outside the creator's control. They have a deep understanding of themselves and what drives them. They're clear-eyed about the business and know how to separate it from their craft. They know that ups and downs are normal in any creative career, and they've developed tools to productively cope with the most daunting challenges of their trade: rejection and criticism, motivation and productivity, self-doubt and loss of faith.

I've spent my career finding ways to help authors past these pitfalls, and in *The Intuitive Author* I want to share those lessons and insights I've gleaned along the way.

How to Use This Book

The Intuitive Author is the culmination of thoughts, insights, and suggestions gathered from more than three decades working with authors that do not fit neatly into categories of craft, culled from my blog, keynote speeches I've given, and conversations and correspondence with authors. The methods are also based in my personal experience and framed through that lens. My approach in writing them has always been, "Come into my living room and let's talk writing."

Inspiration and insight for how to create a satisfying, long-lasting writing career can be gleaned almost anywhere: from interviews with creators, podcasts and profiles, books and movies and TV shows, and everyday life experiences. I draw on all of these in this book.

It's my hope that these strategies will be helpful to writers in developing the über-skill of a sustainable career: resilience. You can use the book as a reference manual when you're looking for advice on a specific topic, or just read through chapter by chapter, as a daily handbook to creativity.

The Intuitive Author offers tactics for navigating some of the most common and intractable challenges of a creative career, and how to build a meaningful, rewarding writing life that will sustain and fulfill you for a lifetime.

Part One
FOUNDATION

Chapter One

What Is an Intuitive Author?

What made you decide to become an author? For many writers it's a calling, a passion. We may grow up as insatiable readers, infused with a profound love of story and the written word. We've likely done writing of our own in some form, whether snippets of thoughts and images and ideas, or compelling scenes, or short stories; kept a diary or journal; or even just relished engaging in eloquent correspondence. We love writing and storytelling, we've immersed ourselves in it for much of our lives, and one day we decide we'd like to make a career out of it.

But launching a writing career isn't like many other careers, where you gather the skills and experience required for entry, find a job in your field, and work your way up an established hierarchy.

- In most careers you get a job description and know what to expect and what is expected of you.
- Most careers have specific, delineated systems for training and advancement.

- Most have clearly established support and infrastructure.
- In most careers you're likely to steadily advance if you develop your skills and are reliable and conscientious.
- Most careers run on merit and hard work as you earn your way forward and climb the ladder.
- In most careers, pay is commensurate with experience, and your salary is likely to grow across the span of your career.

Writing careers offer almost none of that. The paths to becoming a writer are as unique and varied as every individual author, and no one really knows what works; one author's route to massive success might leave others stalled out, dead-ended, or stranded by the side of the road. There are countless outlets for learning your craft, yet they vary wildly in how effectively they may prepare you for an actual writing career. Skill, talent, and hard work are no guarantee of advancement: Success is mercurial and subjective, and can change on a dime with tastes and market vagaries. And money? Many authors struggle to make any at all from their creative work, let alone a living wage. If you do score a huge payday with one book, you might be offered dwindling compensation for subsequent ones, no matter how good your work may be.

In other careers, you might pick a field based on practical, concrete considerations: ample opportunity for employment and advancement, stability, financial remuneration or other perks, like paid time off, insurance, and retirement benefits. None of that exists in a writing career.

Authors rarely consider any of the factors in launching one; we're often just following a love for story and the written word, dreaming of the heights of success despite daunting odds.

That approach might *feel* intuitive, but really it's more impetuous, and it isn't likely to get you where you want to go. It's like spending your life using and enjoying computers, and then applying at Microsoft for a C-suite position.

When I talk about creating an intuitive writing career, I mean the same thing I do when I talked about an intuitive approach to editing and revision in my previous book, *Intuitive Editing*, which is to say working from the inside out. With editing and revision it means finding the heart of your story and growing it organically to tell it in the most effective, satisfying way, rather than rigidly following an external system or dogma and trying to cram your story into that mold.

In your writing career, an intuitive approach means something similar. There's no one path or right way to create one, any more than there is a single "right" way to write.

Creating an intuitive writing career means basing it on what you want and what you value, and taking the reins of your own career despite working in a field where so much of your success hinges on factors outside of your control.

That sounds like a contradiction, an impossible task. But it isn't. It's a skill like any other, one that I've repeatedly seen the most successful and enduring authors develop, and it's one you can nurture and develop as well.

The intuitive author builds their career by starting with their own goals, motivations, and values in deciding what kind of career is right for them, on their own terms. They create and sustain a calm, confident, joyful sense of agency and autonomy in constructing and conducting their writing career.

That can feel impossible in the current publishing environment, where writers may have little power over so many elements of the process, which is why many get discouraged, frustrated, or give up altogether. But taking charge of your career is simply a matter of going into it clear-eyed, knowing the environment and what to expect, and developing the tools every author needs to deal with its many challenges.

Though it may not always feel like it, writers are in control of our own careers to a much greater degree than many of us realize. We are the engine of them, and the captain of the ship—as long as we take the helm. That means mastering the core skills this book is based on, and the first necessary step is to understand the environment we're creating them in.

Strap in, friends—it's going to get bad before it gets better, but let's just rip off the Band-Aid.

Accepting Publishing Realities

Many writers pursue this craft with an ultimate intention—or at least the dream—of publishing their work.

That doesn't encompass all writers: Some are lifelong journalers who find fulfillment simply in recording their thoughts in a private diary. Some write memoirs of their lives intended solely for themselves or their loved ones. Some find an outlet in a personal blog, or in writing exercises and classes, or simply sharing what they've written with a handful of their most intimate circle.

All of those paths are valid. Creativity is its own reward and can be its own purpose.

But if you do intend to pursue a professional path for your writing, it's essential to consider the realities of the current publishing market—facts that can feel a little daunting or even depressing. But knowing them and truly accepting them is the foundation of creating a sustainable and satisfying career—one where you are at the wheel of the ship, not clinging to a dinghy being buffeted about by the waves.

- As of the most recent stats available at the time of this writing, more than two million books are published every year—in addition to the hundreds of millions of titles already published and on the market. That's your competition for readers' eyes and wallets.
- Advances in traditional book publishing seem to be trending downward in recent years, despite the occasional flashy

six-figure deal for much-hyped debuts, averaging in the low five figures for newer authors (sometimes the very low five figures), and decreasing for even established ones without a blockbuster sales track record. The days of publishers nurturing an author's career as it builds seem to be a relic of the nostalgic past. More than 75 percent of authors will never "earn out" their advance—meaning that's all the money they will see from publication of their book. Those advances aren't paid in a lump sum, but spread across three and lately sometimes more installments over a period of often more than a year and even longer.[1]

- Most writers don't make a living from their writing. According to the Authors Guild's most recent survey (2022), median income for member authors surveyed was just $2,000 from their books, and $5,000 total counting all writing-related income. Those figures go up only modestly for full-time authors: $10K from books and $20K including all writing-related income. Self-published author income averaged $12,800 from books and $15,000 from all writing-related income.[2]
- Marketing support is decreasing, with authors expected to shoulder more and more of their own publicity and marketing responsibilities and attendant costs, and often to develop a large platform of their own.
- Artificial intelligence large language models (LLM) are usurping the industry, with outlets and publications that once relied on writers increasingly using AI-generated writing to replace them; lawsuits and regulations to safeguard authors' rights currently patchy and unresolved at the time of this writing; and a great deal of uncertainty over AI's long-term effects on the writing market.

Now, you may be the exception to these bleak statistics. It is not out of the question that you will become the next *New York Times*–bestselling author whose book is adapted into an Academy Award–winning film who makes boatloads of money that you count in your mansion in Beverly Hills.

However, you are only slightly less likely to win the Powerball, or be struck by lightning, or get eaten by a shark. (These are true stats; I looked them up.)

If we put the same stock in those likelihoods that we do into our dream of major publishing success, we would bankrupt ourselves buying lottery tickets, and never go out in the rain or swim in the ocean. So why do we base an entire career plan around such an unlikely eventuality?

In a perfect world, every artist finds their audience and is paid well for their art. But this is not that world. If we are planning a career in this field anyway, we have to know that going into it.

But don't despair. Here's the sunnier flip side of current publishing realities:

- Writers have more opportunities than they've ever had. It's easier to query agents, easier to submit to publishers, and there are vastly more places to do so: Hundreds of literary agents represent authors in every genre. While the Big Five publishing houses still control the bulk of the U.S. book market (80 percent),[3] in 2021 there were more than 74,000 privately owned publishing establishments. Nearly 3,000 of those are publishing companies listed in the Publishers Global directory of American publishers—just in the U.S.! Other countries also offer unprecedented direct access to publishers, an estimated additional 20,000 of them.[4]
- Independent/self-publishing has democratized the industry and given authors more power than ever before to create and viably distribute their own books, to reach readers, to maintain those

connections between books, to build a following, to get their books into libraries. Imagine trying to do that pre-internet, or through snail mail, or schlepping books around in the trunk of your car as your only real distribution options. Imagine trying to do it pre–indie publishing, with expensive "vanity presses" your only option to print your books and no real distribution other than direct hand-to-hand sales.
- It's easier to write, with scores of tools and apps available to authors to help organize, brainstorm, create, structure, format, dictate text, and more—some of them AI-based, turning this powerful technology to authors' benefit. Authors have access to services and professionals never before widely available, like top-notch editors, designers, publicity experts, book and writing coaches. There are more sales outlets for books and it's easier than ever to buy and read them. There are more opportunities for publicity, with the explosion of Goodreads and blogs and podcasts and social media, and it's easier than ever to access these outlets directly.
- You have a variety of avenues for reaching readers. You can publish traditionally, small press, indie/self-publishing, or hybrid press. You can create your own legitimate books and put them in many of the same markets as any of the Big Five. You can sell directly to your fans. You can talk to them every single day, at the press of a few keystrokes.

The reality of the current publishing business is that there is beautiful, bountiful, unprecedented choice for authors in today's market, all these many paths available to you to pursue your craft and reach your readers. *And* that as with any increasingly complex environment, there are also more challenges.

If you truly accept and know all the business realities of publishing, good and bad, that frees you to create a career plan that is sustainable for the long term.

Taking Control of Your Career

Reclaiming our autonomy and agency as authors starts with reframing the way we think about our writing careers and what constitutes success for us.

That coin has two sides: business and art.

Relative to the business side, despite how much may be beyond your ability to influence, there is much that you do have a say over. You get to determine when you send your work out, and to whom, and what publishing path you want to take—if any. You get to decide what professionals to hire and when, how you want to find and reach readers, and how much time and effort you want to expend on those efforts. You have control over all those choices relative to the business of writing.

What you don't have control over is the *outcome*. You can't influence whether agents or editors will accept your work, or whether readers will buy it, or how it will be received and reviewed. No matter how brilliant your writing may be, art is the most subjective and mercurial of businesses, and often what makes one book a smash bestseller and another a flop or just lost in the slush pile is no more than chance or timing or luck or the right connections.

But you *can* control your own efforts and output, shifting away from defining your success or worth based on outside attainments—the process, not the product. You have complete control over what you write, how you write it, when, how often, what you do with it—all creative decisions about your work itself that *you* get to make.

But, like characters in our unedited stories bumbling around in circles and into dead ends because they don't have clearly delineated goals and motivations, authors may flounder in their careers because they fail to concretely define what they really want or look at their true reasons for wanting it. Identifying your own motivations and goals hinges on three core elements:

KNOW WHY YOU WRITE

Established authors I work with often tell me that the freest they ever felt as writers, the most they ever enjoyed it, was before they published or when they were between publishing contracts. That's when they didn't worry about deadlines or expectations or their platform or marketability; they just worked from the pure creative impulse that made them want to become writers in the first place.

But amid the chaos of the publishing world, it's easy to lose sight of that initial spark, our passion for the art and craft of writing: creating stories and worlds we dream of, exploring the vast reaches of our imagination, learning and honing our skills, expressing our inner selves on the page.

Those satisfactions come from within you, rather than hinging on outside forces or opinions, and are attainable through your efforts. Staying connected to your core "why" lays the foundation for agency and autonomy as an author, so you never feel like a beggar at the table hoping for scraps to be tossed your way, but rather a working artist consciously building your own creative career.

KNOW WHAT YOU WANT

But most of us didn't get into this field because we wanted to sit in our attic retreats and write for the sheer love of it, for no one's eyes but our own. It's human nature to want to share our creative work and find an appreciative audience. It's human nature—and practicality—to want to be paid for it.

That starts by defining what that means for you. For instance:

- Do you want to write full-time and make a living from your writing?
- Do you just want to augment your finances with writing income?
- Do you want the exposure and perceived cachet of being traditionally published?

- Do you want to have more control over your books and career and indie-publish?

These are just a few of many possible paths. Whatever your specific goals, what does that practically look like? For instance, how much money do you need to make from your writing to do it full-time? If you choose a traditional publishing path, what are advances like on average? How likely is it you will sell through and make additional royalties? Or how much can you reasonably expect to make on a small-, hybrid-, or indie-publishing track, where advances may be even smaller or nonexistent and profits widely variable? How many books will you need to publish each year given those estimates to make what you need to make to sustain a full-time writing career?

What does *that* look like? How much time is required for writing each book? How much for editing and revision? How about marketing? What does *that* look like in practice—a forty-hour workweek, broken up into writing one manuscript while editing another, and also marketing and publicity and platform building? Fifty hours? Sixty? And are you factoring these expenses, where you must carry them yourself, into your net yield?

When books become your main product that provides your income, your business model requires churning them out regularly, without fail. And market fluctuations are out of your control: Does your business model allow for "dry spells" if one book doesn't sell well, or advances drop, or you lose a publishing contract, or you fall behind in production of your stories?

When you consider what your goals actually mean and entail, do they still sound enjoyable to you? Is this what you had in mind when you dreamed of making your living writing?

Maybe it is. But maybe it isn't, and you realize that in fact when you say you want to write full-time, what you really mean is you *do* want to be Emily Brontë writing in her attic aerie, untroubled by the chaotic realities of the business or the world, simply living as a pure artist. Or that it's enough to write part-time, buying yourself creative freedom with your "day job" the way so many authors do, even bestsellers.

And maybe that's already within your reach.

This is why it's crucial to pinpoint goals and motivations concretely and fully—for ourselves just as with our characters. Your stories will never come together if you don't, and neither will a rewarding writing career.

KNOW WHAT YOU VALUE

Even though it may feel like it, art is not life.

Early in my creative working life, as an actor in New York, I was on vacation with a boyfriend when my talent agent called with a huge audition for me. I told her I was out of town and could the production company see me in a couple of days when we flew back, and she said no, I needed to get on a plane immediately and show up for the audition the next day. When I refused, she dropped me as a client.

Signing with a talent agent is as challenging as garnering a literary agent, but I didn't regret it then and I don't regret it now. My art is important to me, but my life and the people in it are more important.

Knowing what you value in your life is key to creating a sustainable long-term career that will give you joy and satisfaction.

For instance, I'm a big fan of safety and security and control. I've always known I wanted to be able to afford a certain lifestyle for myself, which includes a comfortable living, a home of my own, being able to pay my bills without undue stress. I also value autonomy and freedom, financial and otherwise. I want to decide what and to whom I give my time. Because I knew those things were important to me, it dictated how I handled my career as a creative. Whether I was working as an actor, a freelance journalist, or a novelist, I've always had a "day job" to supplement that income, be it waitressing or temping or copyediting.

Not everyone feels that way. I knew an actor who was perfectly happy couch-surfing on his friends' sofas because he wanted to concentrate solely on his art and he didn't care that he didn't have a place of his own or much money. That worked for him, but it wasn't right for me. You have to think about and determine what *you* value and what is important for your life and the way you want it to look—in its entirety, not just artistically.

Notice that my "day jobs" were ones that offered me many of my values: a certain amount of freedom and autonomy and choice. A decent paycheck. Even the career I kind of accidentally built out of it—as a full-time freelance editor—ticks all of those boxes. I was buying the things I value, but I was also doing it in ways that met those values.

Your day job doesn't have to be a necessary evil for survival in the world. It's your freedom, your ticket to pursue your art without the fetters of being dependent on everyone else's opinion so that you can continue to do so.

It empowers you and it liberates your art.

You may not currently have a day job that you love, and that's okay. But I encourage you to look for one that you at least like, that fulfills some aspect of what you enjoy. That's why I began working as a freelance proofreader and copy editor for the Big Six publishing houses (back in the olden days), to support my acting doing something I enjoyed more than waiting tables.

This job is not where you serve your time until your ship comes in. It *is* your ship. Approaching it that way allows you to create a writing career that incorporates your bill-paying career, if they're different. You might look for ways to earn money that incorporate your creative passions—as a freelance writer, for instance, or a copywriter, or a teacher.

And you may surprise yourself by discovering that one of these pursuits reveals itself as your truest passion. I realized eventually that editing was what I loved to do most, my calling—more than acting, even more than writing—and I've built an incredibly satisfying lifelong career from it.

But besides the joy of pursuing your art and the potential of making money from it, if that's among your goals, what else do you value for a full and meaningful life? What—and most important, who—matters most to you? Your partner? Children? Pets? Your family of origin? Your family of friends? Your community, writing and otherwise?

What does that look like to you in your ideal life? Do you want time every day to devote to those people, to nourish yourself and these relationships? What does that mean, *specifically*: twenty minutes of meaningful conversation? Shared activity and enjoyment? More?

What about your other enthusiasms and interests, where do they fit in? Is regular exercise important to you, or being in nature, or hobbies and other pastimes? And by the way, do you put weight on doing these things perfectly or professionally? Or do you enjoy them for their own sake, for the pleasure they bring you? We don't expect to make a career or a profit from any of those kinds of interests. Yet we may dedicate hours—many happy hours lost in flow—to the pursuit of them. This isn't time "wasted." It's time spent in dedication to something that gives us joy, that allows us to express ourselves. Writing doesn't necessarily have to be a paying career to be fulfilling either, or to be worth dedicating yourself to.

Based on *all* your values, what does success mean to you? What would feel like enough?

I remember when I first left acting and started writing, but had also realized how much I enjoyed editing and needed it to fully utilize another region of my brain. I told myself that my perfect life would be if I could write in the mornings and edit in the afternoons, with freedom on evenings and weekends for the people and other pursuits I valued.

I was initially imagining myself as a massively successful novelist doing so, but then I realized one day that that had been the structure of my life for quite some time, and still is. Between my morning writing and my afternoon editing, I pursue creativity and storytelling all day long and it pays my bills. The rest of my time is mine for my husband and family (including my very needy dogs), my friends, and all my other interests. And that feels like the attainment of every goal I could ever have wanted.

Treat Your Writing Career as a Business

So now you know the setting: the realities of our industry. You know your motivations: your "why." You know your goals: your "enough." You know the stakes: what you value. Once you define these parameters, what do you do with them?

They become the basis for how you build your writing career. They allow you to make decisions and create a life that fulfills you.

Now you have to create the plot: the actions you will take to reach the goals you desire, within your control. That means treating your writing as a business and as a career, and honoring your right to pursue it whether or not it's "profitable."

HAVE A PLAN

Once you've defined what you hope to achieve in your writing career, determine what you need to do to attain those concrete goals.

Create a mission statement and business plan—an actual written one that you keep. Make a flowchart, a bullet list, a spreadsheet, whatever works for you to delineate the steps on the path that are necessary to achieve your particular defined goals.

That likely starts with creating a writing routine and treating it like any other firm commitment—like a job. Writers write; they don't just talk about writing. Schedule your writing time and honor that. Keep learning your craft to hone your skills, as you would in any other field you want to master and succeed in.

If your goals involve your stories reaching readers, pinpoint the avenue(s) you want to pursue and learn the steps involved—and then put them into action, creating a step-by-step, concrete plan for that too.

You wouldn't dream of trying to launch any other business without a researched business and marketing plan. Treat your writing career the same way—and have a budget for your time as well as your finances. What are the markets for selling your work? What do you have to do to be competitive in those markets? What do they pay—is it enough to live on, or how much of it will you have to do to make your desired income? Is that feasible/sustainable? How, exactly? If not, how will you supplement that income, if you need to? Make a specific, concrete plan for soliciting and attaining paid work—and follow it.

There are many excellent resources for researching and developing the business side of your career. For a solid place to start I highly recommend publishing-industry expert Jane Friedman's comprehensive book *The Business of Being a Writer* (in an updated edition as of spring of 2025) and her expansive website (www.janefriedman.com), and publishing entrepreneur Joanna Penn's Creative Penn podcast, blog, books, and website (www.thecreativepenn.com).

ADJUST WHEN NEEDED

Periodically revisit your mission statement and tweak as needed. You are not stuck in the rut of the things you may have wanted in the past. People grow and change, and their goals must evolve with them.

Changing track in your focus or goals doesn't invalidate what you've already done; nor does it mean you've "failed." It's simply reevaluating what you want and what you need *now* in order to continue to find fulfillment in your career.

Although I have been working in the publishing field as an editor for more than three decades, in that time my business model and focus have undergone fairly extensive shifts: from starting as a proofreader and copy editor in New York to moving into developmental editing.

From focusing mainly on the editing work itself to diversifying into more speaking, teaching, and writing as well.

Conducting a regular review of what I want for my life and my business has resulted in an ever-evolving mission statement and business plan, and subsequently an ever-growing and evolving career.

No matter what level you're operating your writing career on, it too demands regular attention, maintenance, and upgrades. When is the last time you examined your goals for your writing for the coming year, five years, ten years and beyond? When is the last time you questioned the path you're on to see whether it's still the one that matches your current values, goals, and commitment level?

When is the last time you considered the projects you're dedicating your time and energy to and whether they're still where you wish to devote your focus? Have you been working on a story that's begun to feel like a slog? Ask yourself why.

Does it still match the passions that animate you? It may be that you're simply stuck in a frustrating part of the writing, a stage so common that it might as well be an official part of the creative process. Sometimes you just have to persist and struggle through those briar patches until you find the path past them.

But if that animating spark has gone out and you no longer feel the same ardor and drive for a story you once did, it could be that your focus or goals have simply shifted. This isn't the project for you right now.

It doesn't mean it's lost forever; every one of my "books in the drawer" has eventually found its way into publication. It just means that maybe the time is not now. And now is all we have for sure. Goals are important and they can motivate and focus us, but none of us knows what the future will bring. The life we're living is the one we're living *now*, and if what we're doing isn't fulfilling us in the present moment, why are we doing it?

Make a habit of regularly examining your intentions, desires, and objectives for your writing career, say at the beginning or end of each year or some other regular interval. If we don't stop and assess our motivations, goals, and values periodically, we fail to take into account that we change as humans. Our priorities may shift, our minds may change, our perspective may evolve. If we're still operating under old assumptions, we're no longer creating a career meaningful to us in the present.

In your regular evaluation look at the business side of your writing career as well. Have you always dreamed of traditionally publishing, for instance? Think about the current state of publishing and the market and what it requires of you and the time frame involved and honestly assess, in specific, concrete terms and in depth, whether that still matches your goals.

I worked with one multipublished author recently who was determined to publish traditionally what he felt would be his final novel. But he'd come to realize he didn't want to wait for the sometimes eternal-seeming process of submission, production, and publication. He wanted to get that story out *now*, on his own terms, so he changed tracks and self-published—not because he's giving up his dream, but because he refuses to, and has decided that while his goal may be the same as far as getting his work into the world, the means by which he wants to do it have shifted.

Do the things you once thought you wanted out of your writing career still apply to what you want now? The answer may be yes, but the only way to know for sure is to examine your premises and your desires and your goals and see if all factors are still the same or you need to do some pruning, uprooting, and replanting.

And yet even with a business plan, dedication, hard work, education and experience and contacts and every other element of pursuing a successful writing career, so much of it may be out of your control. Some of the best stories I've ever read never found a wide audience, or even a publisher. Some blockbuster titles are so unreadable to me that I can't even finish them.

This is a complex, ever-shifting business. Do everything you can to set yourself up for success, but continue to revisit your goals, your motivations, the realities, and your values—your definition of success, on your terms—to keep feeding your soul.

That doesn't mean you don't dream. Our wildest dreams can sustain us and help motivate us. But it does mean shifting away from defining the attainment of those dreams as success. Away from defining our success or artistic validity based on external metrics rather than internal satisfactions.

Define your success not as what will make you happy, but as what can you be happy *with*? It's a subtle shift in thinking that keeps you from waiting for some holy grail before you can enjoy your life or your career.

Stay in the Game

It's such oft-repeated advice for writers that it's a cliché, but the secret of creating a successful writing career is persistence. And the main tool to be able to persist in this chaotic, challenging business is resilience.

And the way to create resilience is to remember that we are not our writing. We are not our writing careers. Our validity is not dependent on the performance or popularity or perfection of our creative output.

It can be hard to hold on to that in those literary dark nights of the soul, when we may be beset by self-doubt, discouragement, even despair. For all the practicalities and concretes a successful writing career entails, it's still a profession based on creativity, that most personal, subjective, and vulnerable of human impulses.

It's these "squishy" areas of a writing career that can be the most profound stumbling blocks to creating and sustaining one.

- When we doubt our talent, our skill. When we look at the pages we were so proud to have written yesterday and find them to be dreck today. Or when we stare at a blank page knowing we have nothing meaningful to fill it with, or harshly judge every word as we're writing it, and our creativity and confidence grind to a halt.
- When we're neck-deep in a hairy revision and we just know that the whole idea was garbage in the first place, and there's no redeeming it.
- When we submit our work to agents or editors and receive rejection after rejection—or almost worse, silence, as if our work were invisible and doesn't matter.
- When our release makes only a ripple in the vast publishing waters and then slowly fades from view.

None of those things has any bearing on the worth of our stories, or of us as their creators. Our creative output has inherent value because *we* instill it. We don't exist for our writing—our writing exists because of us. As long as you pursue it—on whatever level is meaningful to you—you are a writer.

Knowing your "enough" also means knowing *you are enough*. We have to know—foundationally know—that we have worth, intrinsically and independent of any need to "earn" it or prove it or measure it by external metrics.

Building a creative career is a big, complicated, lifelong journey for many of us. It has peaks and valleys. There are times we may feel ten feet tall and bulletproof, filled with creative fervor and flow, the Muse kissing our foreheads and the writing feeling almost effortless, every word utterly right and good.

And there are times when we may be filled with doubt, beset by the demons of perfectionism, or impostor syndrome, or competition, or just "not enoughness." When we're stalled out with procrastination or creative burnout. When we feel like we have to earn our ticket to ride day after day after day—and that most days we're failing. These valleys amid the peaks are so much of what a writing career can entail that they have their own mythology: the grim specter of the frustrated author paralyzed by "writer's block"; the tortured artist futilely seeking comfort or escape or inspiration in alcohol or drugs or a profligate lifestyle; creatives driven to madness and despair by the frustrations of their art, like poor Vincent van Gogh and his unfortunate ear.

These challenges can derail your writing career as surely as can the failure to define your goals and make a clear plan to achieve them. Sometimes even more so, because they strike at the very heart of what inspires and motivates us to pursue a creative career.

At those times, when you need to reconnect with that animating spark that will sustain you, it can be helpful to conduct a little mental check-in I've used throughout my entire career in both editing and when I was a journalist and an actor: If somebody told you that you would never hit the heights you dreamed of, would you continue to do what you're doing?

If you can answer yes—right now, wherever you are in your career—then you already have all the ingredients for creating your own success as a writer.

Asking myself that question is why I quit acting. It's why I stepped away from writing fiction. The inherent rewards of these pursuits no longer felt fulfilling to me if my career never advanced.

But so far every day my answer to that in my editing and teaching career is a big yes. Maybe one day I might realize that even this work that *does* feel like my truest passion isn't anymore. Maybe I'll find something new that is.

Or maybe I'll just keep at it—keep showing up, keep doing the work, keep feeding my soul and looking for the people I connect with over that potent purpose I feel.

Maybe, when you sit down to work on your own creative career, day after day after day, you will too.

There's a Southern saying about being a guest somewhere: that you should leave a place a little better than you found it. I often think about that regarding the legacy of my life and creative work. It guides many of my choices in what I dedicate my time and energy to: I'd like to leave the world a little better than I found it after I'm gone.

I think a lot of us may feel that way about our creative efforts. It's something we hope may add something good to the world and live on beyond us.

With all the challenges of a creative life, it's one of the noblest pursuits humans can have. Writing sheds light where there is darkness. It brings us a greater understanding of ourselves and one another and the world. It connects people and brings them together. It makes our world warmer and brighter and more hopeful.

These things matter. They're essential to a fulfilling life not just for ourselves as creators, but for all souls touched by the power of creative work.

🍃 🍃 🍃

These core ideas are what we'll explore in the rest of this book. Developing the skills involved in each of these areas will help you build a fulfilling, satisfying writing career, one you can sustain for years, for a lifetime. These skills become tools you keep in your author toolbox, using what you need when you need it to fix whatever problems arise—and they will. They always will.

Knowing how to handle them when they do is how the intuitive author carves their own path and builds an unshakable foundation for a happier writing life.

Part Two
WRITING

Chapter Two

What Is Your Wendy?

I have a neighbor I know only as Wendy, and I only ever see her in one place: standing in her front yard either just staring out at the street or occasionally doing things like laundry, with her washing machine pulled out on the front yard.

Wendy, who looks to be maybe in her thirties or so, slender and blandly pretty, sometimes blond and sometimes brunette, is also something of a fashion plate. In fact one of the reasons she's a highlight of many of my mornings when I pass by her house is seeing what outfit she has on that day. It's generally seasonal and sometimes oriented to the holidays.

Near Christmas, for example, she looks especially magnificent, wearing a red velvet full-length robe lined in snowy white fleece, like the most elegant Mrs. Claus. Sometimes she wears more fanciful outfits, like a tulle-covered fairy costume complete with wings, or in the summertime a little bathing number and an inner tube. One day she showed up in a wedding dress.

Many days I will take a picture of her current sartorial splendor (she never minds it) and share it with friends, who don't fully understand what's going on with Wendy but find her as entertaining and engaging as I do.

I'm told the neighbors have mixed feelings about her, some finding her creepy just standing there all the time, some thinking she devalues the neighborhood, but others, like me, absolutely delighted with her.

Oh, Wendy is actually a mannequin. Did I mention?

I was speaking with her mother, or roommate, or whatever you'd like to call her one day about her outfits and how much I enjoyed seeing Wendy on my dog walks every day, and we talked about her history with Wendy the mannequin.

Her mother, whose name I am embarrassed to say escapes me in my fascination with Wendy, told me that she found Wendy at a garage sale and had to have her. I don't remember why Wendy ended up in the front yard, but her mother told me that soon she was enjoying dressing her in outfits from her own closet.

After a while that morphed into buying and making bespoke outfits specifically for Wendy, and then customizing her for the seasons. A lovely chandelier found its way into the front yard over where Wendy keeps vigil, classing up the joint a little bit. Moving the washing machine out was inspired, the result of her mother replacing hers and asking the deliveryman to leave the old one behind. Because mise-en-scène.

I'm a little bit in awe of Wendy and her mom's efforts with her. I often alter my route to make sure I go by and check out her latest situation. Wendy makes me smile. Sometimes I get fashion ideas from her.

This to me is what creativity *is*. There's no purpose to it for Wendy's mom; she just enjoys it. It brings her delight, makes her laugh, and seems to have the same effect on many of the other neighbors—including me.

I think it's easy for writers to lose sight of their own initial spark of simple joy in the act of creation—the pull that first drew us to want to create stories in our heads and put them on paper to share with other people. The impulse to share them on a broad stage is understandable, but so often that gets mixed up with the commerce of creative products, which can be the most brutally random business

WHAT IS YOUR WENDY? 　**35**

The many moods of Wendy...

model that, like so many businesses built around art, often profits the artist least of all.

I've written about the difficult path of creating a writing career. I talk to many successful writers about theirs. I don't discourage anyone from wanting to create a paid career from their writing. I do too.

But I do think it's important to stay in touch with the real reason we do it, or at least began to do it, which had very little to do with remuneration. Few of us go into this career hoping to make our fortune. (If you did, please allow chapter one to gently disabuse you of that romantically far-fetched notion.)

Wendy's mom doesn't make any money from her efforts with Wendy, obviously. She simply takes joy in dressing and staging her and presenting her to the world—at least that small part of the world that happens by her street.

There's something so pure about that that brings delight to me as well. And isn't that the truest, most foundational purpose of our creative work?

Wendy reminds me to stay connected to that root reason for why I create—because I love it, and it fulfills me, and the idea of *not* creating would rob much of the shine from my life. Every time I pass her, she brings me a flash of delight.

I like imagining my creative work having a similar effect on readers—people whose reactions to it I may never see, but to whom it brings a moment of joy, or insight, or comfort.

My first book for writers, *Intuitive Editing: Creative & Practical Ways to Revise Your Writing*, came out in May of 2020, in the midst of a pandemic that was upending every part of people's lives across the world, and I didn't know what to expect. Would the book make a ripple? Would it reach authors at a time when so many were struggling to create amid the chaos? I didn't know.

But what I did know—down to my soul—was why I wrote it: I am passionate about how editing can transform a story and bring it to life, make it more closely match on the page the author's vision for it in her head, and I wanted to demystify what can often feel like an impenetrable swamp of revision. I wanted to gather and articulate the techniques and insights I'd formulated and honed from working on thousands of manuscripts.

I knew that I had a ball (for the most part) creating it, that it inspired me as I realized exactly how much I've learned from the authors I've been privileged to work with over the last thirty-plus years, and that it was rewarding to feel as if I was giving something back to the writing community. I knew that writing the book made me a better editor.

The day I finished the manuscript and set the wheels in motion for publication, I told my husband something that made him do a double take: "If I die once this thing is out there," I said, "I'll be okay with that."

I didn't mean I was "done" in life or had a death wish (although when the zombie apocalypse comes I do hope I go in the first wave). I was trying to convey that this was a long-held dream realized, a passion project that meant a great deal to me. When my time comes (not for a while, I hope), I'll go feeling I left something good behind. If a single author reads the book and finds it helpful, if it makes them feel they know how to be a better writer, to better serve their art and express their creativity, then maybe I'll have left the world a little bit better than I found it.

That sounds grandiose—but it's why I wrote the book. And knowing that on a foundational level is why I'll continue to write, regardless of how my books sell. I love editing, and I love helping authors.

Knowing that to my core takes away a lot of the angst writers often experience. It frees me to write what I want to write, the way I want to write it. It frees me to continue to love doing it—instead of using writing (or not writing) as a whip to make myself feel inadequate or untalented or discouraged.

Why Do You Write?

What is it you want from your writing and your writing career, or what does it give you that feeds you in some essential way? If you hope for James Patterson–level success, more power to you—but at least you'll go in knowing how narrow that part of the bell curve is and you're *informed*.

And if publishing superstardom is the only thing that means success or fulfillment to you in your writing career, maybe that's something to take a second look at, knowing how unlikely the chances of it are. If you don't achieve that goal, will your life and career feel like a failure? That's a lot to put on your creative efforts, almost guaranteed to shut down the very part of you that feeds that creativity. If that remote possibility is the only outcome that will make your writing efforts feel worthwhile, perhaps it makes you reconsider whether all the challenges, hardships, and frustrations of a writing career are truly worth it to you.

But maybe you find out that you write because it feeds your soul… or because you want to affect the world even a little bit, even through impacting perhaps just a single reader's life. Or maybe you write to tell yourself stories you aren't seeing anywhere else, or to allow your imagination to stretch its legs because your moneymaking career doesn't nurture that part of you (and that's totally valid—we all have to survive, and a day job that pays the bills and allows you to pursue your art in your free time is an honorable thing).

Maybe it simply nourishes your creative spirit to dress and stage a metaphorical mannequin in your front yard for the enjoyment of the act itself, and the delight it may bring to others who enjoy your creation.

But know your reasons—know them to your marrow. Because writing can be a tough road, friends, and when the going gets slow and difficult and depressing and you feel you're slogging it all alone, that reason is the spark that keeps your engine running.

What is your Wendy?

Chapter Three

Finding the "Right" Way to Write

One reason I love interviewing writers for the How Writers Revise feature on my blog[5] is the chance to get to speak to so many different authors about their writing, editing, and revision processes. And what I see, over and over, is how widely they vary.

- Sharon Short (also writing as Jess Montgomery) writes what she calls a "clunky and murky" first draft, because "drafting is my least favorite part of the writing process." Erin Flanagan also grits out a "crap first draft" so she can then revise it into what she calls the "better draft" stage, then the final-draft polish.
- Steven James pantses out his first drafts, asking himself at every turn four specific questions that help him find the story as he goes—but he doesn't move forward in writing each next scene until he's painstakingly polished the preceding one.
- Lisa Barr can spend years researching and plotting a story before she starts writing at what she calls "a grandmotherly

pace" that results in a fairly complete and clean "first" draft that then just needs fine-tuning, a process echoed by the late Leila Meacham.
- Stephanie Storey writes multiple entirely different drafts to determine which story she's telling and from what perspective, and only then embarks on the editing and revision phase. "I have loads of sand to play with" at that point, she says, "so if I'm working on revisions and I think, 'You know what I really need? Blank,' well, 90 percent of the time I already have that idea, paragraph, or scene written in one of the other versions."
- Laurie Frankel sees little division between writing and revising; she leaves herself "free to draft as messily as I will" by making dozens, sometimes hundreds of editing passes of her stories as she goes.

All these authors have achieved success by most writers' standards: major publishing contracts and bestseller statuses, critical reviews and broad readership.

So which one of them is doing it "right"?

Writers tend to love learning writing: studying other authors' work, reading hundreds of articles on craft, lining their bookshelves with craft books, signing up for workshops and courses and conferences and panels. (It's one reason I have a job.)

With this craft we love so much, we want to learn how to do it *right*.

But what does "doing it right" mean when it comes to a creative, subjective pursuit like writing?

Some authors participate in the monthlong frenzy of NaNoWriMo (National Novel Writing Month), for example, and love the incentive and the satisfaction of simply getting words on the page, regardless of how sloppy that draft may be.

For them, breakneck first-drafting may help them push through the resistance of regular life's time constraints or that nasty little critical voice that might ordinarily freeze them up if they didn't just plow ahead with their creative impulse and "vomit it up" on the page, to borrow one of my favorite phrases from the marvelous *If You Want to Write*, by Brenda Ueland (one of the first books I ever read in my own quest to learn to write).

Having a deadline and parameters motivates those writers to get the words on the page, because once they have something to work with, they know they can develop it into the story they envision.

But some authors may get frozen up by the relentless pressure to churn out words regardless of how sloppy. For them, it's impossible to move forward in the story if they know that what they've already written isn't complete or airtight. Everything that follows rests and builds on that foundation, and they could no more keep building on a broken or incomplete one than they'd try to construct a house that way.

Others, like me, may fall somewhere in between, shuddering at the thought of the kind of pressured, free-for-all writing of NaNo or the no-holds-barred "vomit draft," but also prone to shutting down if the critical "editor brain" steps in too soon or too heavily as they're finding the story in the drafting stage.

Which way is right: pantser or plotter? Vomit it up or edit as you go? Or something in between?

That's up to you. Finding what works best for your writing is part of the process of developing as a writer.

The writing process is not only different for each author, but it may vary with each project. When people ask me how long it takes me to write a novel (under my pen name, Phoebe Fox), I always joke, "Anywhere between nine months and fifteen years."

Except it's not really a joke, because it's true: One of my books came together in under a year, vomited merrily onto the page; my last one aged in a barrel for a decade and a half, painstakingly crafted line by line, over and over and over, till it was ready.

Building a writing career isn't just about learning craft. It's about learning *your* craft. How do you work best? What does each story require? If you're struggling or floundering, what do you need? To get out of that critical editor brain and just puke it up, damn the torpedoes, knowing you'll fix it in post, as we used to say in the film biz?

Or have you stalled out because you got lost in a detour, wound up at a dead end, or didn't know what trip you were taking in the first place? In that case, maybe you need to go back, slow down, carefully lay the groundwork for the trip turn by turn.

Learn voraciously, ceaselessly. Even after thirty years as an editor and more as a writer, I suck up craft books and articles and classes like mother's milk—not to learn which way is "right," but to broaden my perspective and understanding, to gather tools to put in my toolbox that I can offer to writers in my editing and choose to wield as needed in my writing, and in the way that works best for me.

But not every author will need every tool for every job. Having them ready to hand while you're working is a big part of mastering your craft—but it would be absurd to try to use them all, exactly the way others do, for each and every project.

When writers get hung up on doing it "right," they're chasing some amorphous idea of perfection, as if they believe that once they master all the right tools and techniques, success is guaranteed. But they may never examine their central flawed premise: that perfection is possible—or even if it were, that it's a desirable thing for their creative product.

A friend of mine sent me an article about a recent trend in celebrities pursuing an absolutely perfect smile, and a cosmetic dentist on TikTok who's gained a viral following by analyzing celebrity teeth and reporting on who has veneers.[6]

Leaving aside the admitted concerns over publicly judging people's appearances, this story hit a chord with me on several levels, particularly what feels like society's current obsession with perfection.

Here's how that may manifest with authors:

- Writers who dream of writing, but can't seem to get started out of fear of not being good enough, or intimidation because they worry they can't compete with other authors, or "lack of ideas" (in quotes because you are a human and as such you are teeming with creative ideas), or "lack of time" (in quotes because if we want to write, we will find the time, even if it's only snatched moments in the shower or dictating on our dog walks, while we commute, or doing chores).
- Writers who write and rewrite and revise and edit and do it all over again, working on a manuscript for years—not in the healthy, building-a-story way that some require, but rather doubting and belaboring every scene, line, nuance for not yet being good enough to submit or publish.
- Writers who start countless stories, but never finish any.
- Writers who lose interest in a current story every time a shiny new thing pops its tiny head into their mind.
- Writers who are experiencing "writer's block" (in quotes because I maintain this is not a thing, just an obstacle to our creativity that always has a specific cause, one we can hurdle if we only diagnose what that is and address it. See chapter eighteen, "'Writer's Block'—or Getting Unstuck from the Wall of WTF").
- Writers who have so diligently followed whatever craft system has resonated with them that their story may be technically "perfect," but they've stripped out the originality and life that make story stand out.

And so many other permutations of perfection paralysis.

Writers are as susceptible as anyone to wanting to do things "right"—perhaps, as sensitive creatures forever baring their tenderest and most vulnerable parts, even more so.

But trying to tell ourselves, "Don't get hung up on perfection," is almost impossible in a society where its messages are everywhere: in ads, in social media, in filtered and Photoshopped selfies, and rampant in the media we consume.

Instead, maybe we should look at what "perfection" is and means, and reconsider whether it's a valid value at all.

Perfection is an impossible standard. There is no such thing as a "perfect" anything, because the assessment of perfection requires some objective, uniformly agreed-upon standard that's impossible to define.

For instance, Chris Pine's face is so freaking perfect in my estimation that *it hurts my eyeballs* to look upon. I don't want to like it, because I am a fan of quirky, unique looks, and for God's sake, his face is like a Michelangelo sculpture come to life, but I cannot look away. It's not even real, right?

Yet a friend of mine and I have long disagreed about this assessment. She finds this face meh in the extreme. (Side note, however: When she met the owner of this face in person in a coffeeshop in L.A., she said she was struck entirely mute by the sheer chiseled beauty of it, so there you are: Perfection is subjective not only from perception to perception, but situationally.)

When the definition of what is perfect can't be agreed upon by any two humans on earth, why would we set ourselves up to pursue a goal that can't possibly be reached—one that doesn't in fact exist?

Perfection strips away originality, voice, and authenticity

One takeaway from the article about Hollywood dental work, to me, is the fact that in almost every case of before-and-afters, the perfectly white, perfectly uniform, perfectly aligned smiles of the "afters" result in something just ever so gently creepy and disturbing, like Ross after his extreme teeth-whitening incident in *Friends*. Our minds perceive that there's something wrong and unnatural about perfection; it's why AI-generated and CGI-altered images always feel a little "off." We may not be able to pinpoint what's weird about them, but we sense it.

But more than that, perhaps because it's an impossible standard, impossible to achieve, the pursuit of perfection usually winds up denuding its subject of its unique, individual features that make it a standout. Specifically I see this with authors when the pursuit of a technically "perfect" version of their stories through following some perceived expert's writing formula or dogma has rendered their manuscript flat, lifeless, and homogenous.

Can you imagine Lauren Hutton's iconic face with a "perfect" smile? Or Tim Curry's lascivious lips and mouth in *The Rocky Horror Picture Show* if he had a featurelessly uniform set of choppers (or for that matter Patricia Quinn's iconic ones in the opening credits)? Or Steve Buscemi's ruggedly fascinating features around a boring set of homogenous Chiclet teeth? A "perfect" set of veneers would alter something fundamental about these people and their uniqueness and memorability.

Perfection is boring as hell.

Of course, that itself is a completely subjective assessment—which is the point—but even if most people can agree on what constitutes perfection, by the very necessity of having to appeal to "most people," perfection aims for the broadest possible tastes. And that means avoiding the more interesting, memorable features that may draw in the most fervent appreciation in a smaller subset.

You often sacrifice individual perceivers' assessment of quality in the pursuit of quantity when you pander to universally agreed upon standards of anything. Everyone can agree: Perfection is "nice." It's "lovely."

It's milquetoast.

Give me the face I can't forget, the smile that comes from inside and reaches the eyes and hits my heart and tells me something of who that person is, not the sanitized, homogenized one someone purchased at the dentist from a catalog.

Give me the piece of art that engenders a powerful reaction in me, not a tepid appreciation for the artist's painstaking adherence to the principles of painting.

Give me a song that gets inside me and hits a powerful chord and liquefies my innards, not one that faithfully follows classic chord progression and structure.

Give me the book that sucks me in, that transports me, that wrings me out and leaves me thinking—and feeling—for days, weeks… years, not the one some media outlet or award board has hailed as "the most pulsating, lapidary voice of our generation."

Give me a story that speaks powerfully to something desperately personal and unique in *me*, because it represents something desperately personal and unique in the author. Give me that connection of imperfection.

Don't try to write a perfect story. Don't try to present exhaustively developed characters whose every life experience you've faithfully examined and developed and recorded in an exhaustive character bible, a plot you've fit into the mold of someone else's definition of how to do it right, a story whose elements comply with every "rule" of writing you've read.

Write the story that feels right to you. Make it the best you can. Consider your reader enough to make that story as readable and complete and engaging as you can—but not to the point where you're trying to make it all things to all readers and homogenize it to bland, perfect veneers. Let it reflect *you*: your voice, your aesthetic, your style.

Even if that's not "perfect." Trust me, it'll be a lot more interesting than if it were.

Chapter Four

What's Your Authentic Voice?

I'm obsessed with the *SmartLess* podcast. Started during the pandemic lockdown by three real-life best friends—Jason Bateman, Sean Hayes, and Will Arnett—partly as an excuse to regularly see each other, the show quickly gained popularity, with millions of listeners and often topping the podcast charts. Every week one of the three invites a "mystery guest"—usually an actor or other high-profile public figure—whom the others don't know about ahead of time.

Because there's no time to research or prepare, it generally winds up being an hour of four people casually chatting as if they were alone in one of their living rooms—and it often results in startlingly candid conversations about deeply personal issues, like Robert Downey Jr. discussing his time in jail, or Dax Shepard talking about his addiction and recovery, or Julia Louis-Dreyfus sharing hilariously inappropriate personal gynecological information. Because the hosts are clearly close friends and are all so quick-witted—as are most of their guests, often friends of theirs—it also yields some of the best banter you're likely to hear.

And all this is what makes me love the show so much—it's just *real*.

Real is powerful. It's the reason for the old showbiz adage never to do a scene with animals or children: because against a completely natural, authentic being, "acting" looks artificial.

And it's why the most memorable stories stay with us: Not only do the characters become real to us, but the author lets her naked soul, with all its glory and gunk, onto the page, and we sense it. It creates an exceptional intimacy between us and the story.

We know the difference between a real connection with someone and the surface exchanges that make up so much of our daily lives, from casual encounters to social media posts to even the perfunctory habitual conversations with our closest loved ones that can result from years of putting up battlements around our tenderest and most vulnerable places.

In my work as an editor I frequently see authors skim past some of the most potentially rich, impactful moments of their stories, or gloss over the depths of emotion they might mine out. Why would we as writers neglect to fully squeeze all the juice from the characters and situations we've so painstakingly created?

My hypothesis is that, just as we may do with our personal relationships, we unconsciously keep protected those most naked parts of ourselves, the ones that can be windows into our most unguarded selves. The ones that may make us dive deep into uncomfortable or painful places.

Yet that, so often, is where you'll dig out the most flawless diamonds.

Writing Real

This morning I wrote a fan letter to an author whose latest book I adored (I do this a lot), delineating exactly what I loved most about it. As I wrote I noticed myself searching for the perfectly worded phrasing, the most powerful descriptors to convey my level of appreciation for her writing.

Each time I caught myself drifting away from what was simply authentic and real, I kept stopping to ask myself, What's driving me to write this?

My most genuine intention wasn't to impress or forge a connection with the author, or to write an expertly crafted review of her book, or entice her to let me feature her in a future interview—though all those would be side effects I'd be happy to achieve. My truest intention was simply to express my honest feelings and reactions to the story she created.

That kind of unvarnished sincerity might not be perfectly polished, but it's *real*, and the reader senses that. We usually know when we're being snowed (just check out the average advertisement, political propaganda, or social media humblebrag). And we know how it feels when someone is open and honest and true with us.

The hard part is that being real requires letting go of a little bit of control...dropping that veneer of protection around our truest selves that keeps us from risking judgment on what's most deeply personal and raw inside us. What if we're genuine and it sucks? What if we're utterly real and people hate it—not just our writing but our honest *selves*?

But that's the risk. That's what makes art both hard and sublime: the exhilaration and terror of tearing off the facade and showing the world what's *true*.

Digging Down to Authentic Voice

What's real, authentic, and true often stems from—and creates—one of the areas of craft I most frequently hear authors struggle with: voice. What is it, how do they find theirs, does it differ from story to story?

Part of the problem is that the term "voice" is used broadly in writing, referring to the narrative perspective of your story, how your characters speak, and also to the author's sensibility that permeates the pages: that thing that makes a story by Toni Morrison or Kent Haruf or Ann Patchett instantly identifiable as theirs.

In the context of writing authentically we're referring to the latter definition of voice: your artist's voice as the creator of your work. This can often be the hardest type to pin down because it's ephemeral. The author's voice should never draw reader attention away from the story and characters, but rather infuse it, enhance it.

Voice isn't something you create; you already have it. It's simply something you learn to free. Rather than look to manufacture or artificially construct your artist's voice, how can you strip away what's keeping it from finding its way naturally into your work?

WHAT IS VOICE?

In a *TED Radio Hour* episode called "The Artist's Voice,"[7] four artists in varying fields talked about this key element of their art.

Within their wildly differing stories was the common thread that each discovered their voice as they began to find and define themselves in the world, to realize what mattered to them and what they had to say about it.

Sometimes this happens organically as we get older. As we gain comfort and confidence inside our own skins and have the proverbial "fewer fucks to give," the inhibitions, fears, and self-consciousness that may have once papered over our authentic voice fall away.

But you don't have to wait for the freedom of age to excavate yours; we can find ways to dig down to our truest core and determine what we have to say and how we want to say it.

The key is to stop defining voice externally. So often we as authors, as artists, may unconsciously parrot the voices of the stories and authors we love most, that speak to us, unconsciously mimicking or trying to follow someone else's blueprint of what strong voice should be.

But there is no "right" definition of voice, and identifying another author's version of it doesn't necessarily help you find your own.

Instead of trying to create your voice from the outside in, explore *inside* yourself and honor your own unique perspective.

But you can't free your voice without knowing what that perspective is, so let's look at a few key questions to start your journey to the center of the artist.

Who are you?
What makes you, you? In the TED show I listened to, each artist felt a strong connection to the parts of their background that most defined who they became as a person.

Film director Jon M. Chu (*Crazy Rich Asians*) is a first-generation Asian American son of immigrants from a large and close-knit family he says were raised to always be mindful of how they were perceived in the world, but also to find and pursue wholeheartedly what called to them. He grew up downplaying his Asian and immigrant heritage in his career, but later came to fully claim it in both his life and his art.[8]

Poet Lee Mokobe grew up transgender in South Africa under apartheid, where there isn't even a word in the Xhosa and Zulu languages for "he" or "she," only labels of traditional gender roles like "young man," "old lady," "grandmother." They remember being stifled and rejected for expressing their authentic self before they began to assert it.[9]

All our formative experiences are key to who we become—like the backstory and the "wounds" you give your characters that shape who they are in your stories.

Try defining yourself in a few words or brief phrases and see what feels most intrinsic to your identity: Is it your background—where you're from or how you were raised or the traditions and norms of your faith or cultural background? Your interests or career—artist, accountant, avocational gardener? Your role in your family or with loved ones—daughter, mother, brother, friend? Something else?

What matters to you?
What are the ideas, themes, causes, beliefs that matter most to you? What value system defines the way you live your life?

See if you can sum up in a phrase the core of what drives you: your urge to be of service, for instance, as a helper or teacher or friend; or your desire to right society's wrongs; or the push to make your mark in the world. Digging out the core values that drive you is often a key to discovering your voice.

Choreographer Camille A. Brown loved the power of African American social dance to unite a community, and started an online dance school to use the power of her art in fostering joyful social connections.[10]

Poet Amanda Gorman was driven to write by her urge to identify and speak out about political and social issues, and by her personal mantra that informs all her poetry: "I am the daughter of Black writers who are descended from freedom fighters, who broke their chains and changed the world. They call me."[11]

Chef Gerardo Gonzalez left the New York culinary scene to head the dining program at a resort on Grand Cayman, where he had carte blanche to fulfill his vision of reimagining the role of food in connecting cultures, people, and disciplines.[12]

Our creative work is about more than simply telling an entertaining story; artists use their powerful, singular perspective and voice in their work to *affect* people: their emotions, their worldview, their ideas, their thoughts, their beliefs, their assumptions, prejudices, blind spots. You can't deeply impact a reader unless you know what matters profoundly to you and infuse that into your work.

How do you express yourself?
I don't mean how you intentionally craft your prose—but rather that organic, automatic voice in you that is an intrinsic part of what makes you, you.

Every person expresses themselves in their own way. It's an amalgam of all the factors of your life: your family, where you were raised, your education, your background, your interests, experiences, ad infinitum.

Voice isn't something we invent fresh or from whole cloth; we "borrow" from all the influences in our life to form our own unique voice. We're all working with the same pigments but they combine in each of us in a different way.

Your job is to find the way the combination has truly become yours, not something you're trying to mimic or something you saw or heard someone else do successfully. How do you express yourself in the privacy of your mind? How do you dance when no one is watching?

Camille A. Brown talks about learning traditional Haitian dance for choreographing the Broadway musical *Once on This Island*[13] and then telling the woman who taught her not to expect to see those actual dances verbatim in her work. She honored those original rhythms and moves but expressed them in her own "voice" as an artist. Amanda Gorman writes and speaks her poetry in distinct rhythms with unexpected rhyming patterns.

Voice is more than how we phrase things. It's how we *think* them, the patois that comes naturally to us as a result of all our influences, that comprises the way we communicate. It's our reference points, the mental and emotional connections we make, the meanings we assign, the Byzantine paths our minds may forge whose routes and detours are ours alone.

Listening to podcasts is a wonderful way to start paying attention to those differences in how people express themselves in a medium where you can isolate their literal voice: the words they use, their phrasings, rhythms, tone, the music of their language, the unique way they may look at the world.

Keep noticing those same things in yourself. Keep asking yourself questions to circle in on these essential areas in claiming your voice.

And keep letting yourself allow all the richness and depth and uniqueness that is *you* to spill onto the page in your writing.

How to Get Real in Your Writing

Every time you sit down to write—whether fiction, nonfiction, or even an email—try starting by reminding yourself not what you want to accomplish or what impression you want to give or how it might impact readers, but what's motivating you to want to write this in the first place, what you want to convey or express. It may not come out finely polished, but that's what editing is for.

Or if it's easier, do it the other way around: If you find yourself defaulting to tired clichés or emotional shortcuts in your early drafts, just go with it. I often set off this kind of empty or overused verbiage in brackets, my signal to myself to go back later in revisions and dig deeper, explore more authentic and original descriptions and emotions.

Look for where you've taken easy shortcuts. If you've used general descriptors, for instance, to simply label reactions—"devastated," "heartbroken," "shattered," "furious," etc.—see if you can go deeper, put yourself into that situation and imagine what it might feel like: viscerally, emotionally, in your most raw and real places. Put *that* on the page.

Consider the trite tropes you may unconsciously have parroted. How many times have you read of a single tear trailing down someone's cheek? How often have you actually "swallowed back bile" or vomited from an upsetting experience? Admittedly I'm not Everyreader, but when I cry it's rarely so poignant or pretty as a lone tear, and the only times I've had to fight throwing up are when I'm ill, in a turbulent flight, or cleaning up something horrific that came out of one of my dogs' orifices.

Maybe these phenomena truly happen, but even if they're as common in life as they seem to be in fiction, overused phrases like these have become clichés, void of meaning or any real emotional response in the reader.

Empty descriptions like these are shortcuts writers have seen so often in stories they become an automatic default setting for describing reactions, rather than taking the time to sit and imagine experiencing what characters are going through, and how that might feel and look.

If you've defaulted to letting external or physical responses stand in for the truer reactions that prompted them, see if you can keep pushing through to what's behind those externalizations: If "tears fill his eyes" or "her fists clench" or "their brows draw downward," what's causing those physical reactions, exactly? What might specifically, concretely be going on inside someone that could result in those responses? Put *that* on the page.

Maybe you feel a character's disgust really is like swallowing back bile, but can you find a more authentic and original way of conveying that reaction? How do *you* see it? What do these emotions feel like when *you* experience them? How might it affect *you* to go through something like what your character is going through—and how can you convey that as straightforwardly and truthfully as possible?

This is what brings a story to life, sets it apart, gives it truth and power and voice. This is what turns readers into fans: that they can count on a favorite author to give them an authentic experience, to plunge them into a story and characters that are so genuine and true they feel real and stick with them long after they turn the final page.

Authors too often fixate on making their prose perfect or pretty. Don't worry about that. Make it real, genuine, true. It's vulnerable and scary and naked…but that's what creativity *is*. And it's what creates that most powerful effect of story: making your reader connect, believe, *feel*.

Chapter Five

Pay Attention to Your Progress

Several years ago I brought home a dog from the Austin Animal Center, where I worked as a volunteer, with whom I'd fallen rather quickly in love. From the moment we met, Gavin was calm and kept all four feet on the ground when I went into his kennel, staying gently focused on me—traits I always look for in a new dog. He was responsive and sweetly affectionate.

I brought him home as a foster, because the shelter was overcrowded and they were desperate to place animals, but I think we all knew from the get-go that that was a fiction.

As was Gavin's calm, modulated demeanor, I quickly discovered.

I knew, of course, that animals could act differently in the high-stress, unfamiliar environment of a shelter, but I expected it to be the other way around: that their behavior might be *more* excitable and unpredictable in that environment. Gavin, though, was apparently holding it all in till he felt more secure and settled...when he decided it was safe to let it all out.

He'd evinced house-trained behaviors at the shelter, but at our house he started peeing inside, always in one certain spot. He'd been marked as a "green-dot" dog at AAC, meaning he'd been assessed as fairly docile and without problem behaviors, so any visitors to the shelter could go right into his kennel without needing assistance from staff or volunteers. But once he settled into our home he became wary and defensive with anyone who wasn't us.

While he'd trotted obediently alongside me when I took him out of his kennel at the shelter, on walks in our neighborhood he nearly yanked my arm off lunging after anything that moved: cars, scooters, bikes, squirrels, leaves. He was a scavenger, nose constantly to the ground like a truffle pig, and I had to watch him constantly because he would eat literally anything he found. A partial list: mulch, dirt, beetles, rocks, trash, roadkill residue, deer poop…a bunny (we shall not speak of that dark day).

He ate a dog bed. *Ate* it.

He was…not quite the dog I assessed him to be in the shelter. And he was not like our previous rescue dogs, who'd come to us pretty WYSIWYG and low-maintenance.

But he was *our* dog now.

So we took him to trainers—several of them. We finally found the right one (Austin's gifted dog-behavior specialist Tara Stermer of K9 Workingmind) and I started working with Gavin every single day, not just on the specific program she laid out for us, but in nearly every activity we did. Walks, backyard playtime, games, feeding, and even relaxation time all became opportunities to shape his behavior.

We saw improvement from our very first session with Tara—and ongoingly—but periodically we got frustrated. *Why* wasn't he consistently calm and nonreactive like our other dog? Why did he always push every little boundary if we weren't vigilant? Why did he sometimes have sudden setbacks and revert to his old ways?

Gavin, we decided, was Gavin, and he could be a handful.

Training Your Writing to Behave

Some stories come on like Gavin, presenting themselves so perfectly you imagine you'll just need to transcribe the idea flowering in your head and *poof!* Bestseller.

And then come unexpected problem behaviors: Dead ends and roadblocks. Meaningless detours. Stalled momentum. Wrong turns. No matter how much you revise and rework, your story just won't come together.

You get discouraged. Maybe you think about giving up. Your *last* story wasn't this hard, right?

But the steady, consistent work of honing, developing, polishing, working toward shaping a manuscript into the story an author hopes it will become can take time, and results aren't always obvious at first. It's an incremental, cumulative process, just like dog training or learning any other skill.

Slowly I started noticing how much progress Gavin was making. His marking behavior inside the house has long been a thing of the past. He's much more comfortable and even affectionate with strangers. Once a relentless beggar who'd nearly topple us while we cooked, lunging for any tiny crumb that fell on the floor, now he plants his butt on his rug just outside the kitchen and simply looks at me if something drops off the cutting board, until I give him permission to take it.

On walks, if a kid buzzes by on a skateboard or a passing dog barks and pulls toward him, rather than lunging Gavin looks up at me for praise or a treat. If he goes barking after someone on the sidewalk passing by our backyard, most of the time he turns immediately around and comes trotting back to me the moment I say, "Stop—come back." He knows a panoply of commands and loves nothing better than eagerly executing them and always learning more.

Don't get me wrong—he can still be a real pain in the ass, and he hears it so often the poor dog probably thinks "Dammit, Gavin!" is his name. Gavin gonna Gavin, and his training is a work in progress.

But little by little, without my entirely realizing it, he's turned into a damn good dog.

Progress Takes Persistence

Like dog training, writing is often not made up of giant, sudden measurable strides forward in achievement or ability. Rather, you work like the tortoise, not the hare, honing your capabilities day after day by being consistent, patiently showing up and doing the work.

Again and again and again.

That regular work—whether it's daily or a few times a week or any other consistent schedule—isn't always easy, and it isn't often glamorous (witness me fighting for calm on the fifteenth time Gavin keeps getting up from a "stay").

And it isn't always immediately satisfying or even appealing. More often than not I look at training sessions as something to get through that I don't always enjoy doing, even though I'm always happy afterward to have done it (sound familiar, authors?).

And while I sometimes have breakthroughs with Gavin where I see he finally gets it, most days I don't see or feel a difference from the previous one as far as progress. Practice at anything has incremental payoff, usually by small measures at a time.

But...if we learn to take the time to step back now and then and *notice*—how we're feeling, how challenging a certain skill is for us compared to how it used to be, the caliber of our work—that's when we see the progress we've made.

It's important to do that in any area, but particularly in creative pursuits, where progress is so often gradual, not sudden; steady rather than dramatic. Otherwise it can be easy to feel disappointed, get frustrated...even give up. I remember not long ago feeling disheartened that Gavin hasn't turned into the calm, perfectly behaved Lassie I fantasized about, while watching him play one day with a friend's puppy who actually *was*, even at just a few months old.

But, as my friend pointed out, not that long ago I wouldn't have trusted Gavin to play well with a strange puppy at all. I wouldn't have been confident that if I called a firm, "Stop," to curb whatever behavior was concerning me, he would, and consistently does.

We've made measurable progress with slow, steady, consistent work…one tiny increment at a time.

Progress Doesn't Mean Perfection

We're inculcated, particularly in American culture, with messages that exhort us to do something a hundred percent or not do it at all: Go big or go home. Give it your all. A job worth doing is worth doing right.

That's certainly been a governing principle of most of my life, and it's often at the root of a host of the demons of our collective psyche, among them perfectionism, where an A—or, God forbid, a nice competent B or C—isn't good enough. Only first place matters and everyone else is just an also-ran. Winning is everything.

We want instant, perfect results, and if we don't get them it's so easy to feel discouraged.

It's why if you miss one workout at the gym it's so much easier to start missing more and more, until inertia gets you right back on that sofa in front of Netflix night after night. It's why we may break our diet and decide we've ruined everything, so we might as well binge on an entire half gallon of ice cream.

And it's why, too often, we don't make progress on our writing.

We're busy. Life is pressing. Crises come up. The people we love need us, and we need them. Who has a chunk of time to sit down and work on their WIP with any regularity? And if you lose steam or get derailed or can't get butt-in-seat every day for those long, productive creative stretches, what's the point?

But that's life. It's made up of all those obligations, responsibilities, distractions. That won't change, so if you want to make time to pursue your meaningful creative goals, then *you* must change.

That doesn't mean wholesale shifting your life to open up giant blocks of uninterrupted writing time. It simply means making space for progress—even if it's just a few minutes at a time.

In his bestselling book *Atomic Habits*, author James Clear suggests making it as easy as possible to begin instilling habits you want to incorporate into your life, like regular writing: Take just two minutes to work toward your goal.

It doesn't seem meaningful or effective. In two minutes we may still be settling into our groove in the seat and waiting for our coffee to cool enough to take that first sip and charge up the creative juices.

And yet.

Training Gavin happened in intervals of just a few minutes a day—setting him up for success, our trainer explained, while his focus was strong and he could achieve the goals I had for him.

Telling ourselves we only have to sit there and write for two minutes makes it pretty ridiculous to find excuses for why we can't spare that time. And once you're there, over that initial hump of resistance, you're likely to find a groove and write a little longer. You're not *limited* to two minutes; it's just your baseline requirement.

Two minutes will get you in the seat in front of your WIP. It will start to form a regular writing habit on whatever schedule works for you. It will result in words on the page. Maybe not by leaps and bounds, but by dribs and drabs, you will make progress.

You want to write. You have a story to tell—or many stories. You have a desire and a dream and a passion. You wouldn't be reading this book if you didn't.

Can you honor that for two minutes a day? Give yourself at least 120 seconds to dedicate to what is so meaningful to you, no matter how hectic or demanding the rest of your life may be?

If you can, you may find that without even trying, you've created an unshakable writing habit—one that may ebb and flow, but is always waiting for you...just two minutes away.

Measure Your Progress by What You Have Done, Not What You Haven't

Writing is hard, and it's a struggle more often than not. When you're trying to wrestle a plot, or do the hard work of character building, or scythe a path through weeds so tall you feel you can't see your way out, it's easy to wonder whether you'll ever get good at this writing thing. Whether you've learned anything. Whether you even know what you're doing at all.

But instead of focusing on what you *can't* do or *haven't* yet done, take a step back for a moment and take in what you *have* already achieved, how it compares to what you might have done a few months ago, or a year, or decades.

- Are you struggling through a story and wondering if you have the chops to finish it? Remember when you'd never even tried before and dreamed of doing it? Remember looking at that blank page when you first started? How far have you come since then?
- Perhaps you haven't yet signed with an agent or publisher, but have you completed a manuscript…or two…or more? Remember when you started that first one and wondered whether you could even manage to finish a whole story?
- Are you facing disappointing sales of your book, or have lost your editor or publishing contract, or are worried about the future of your career? Remember when you'd have given anything to publish your work…to reach readers…to get reviews…to do all the things you've already accomplished?

Writing isn't a journey with a destination or clear finish line. It's a continuum, just like mastering any other skill. There will be ebbs and flows, peaks and valleys, but if you're consistent and persistent then the arc will always bend toward progress.

Take time to appreciate all you've learned and accomplished to this point in your career. To gauge your progress as a writer by what you've achieved, not by what you feel you still lack. To consider your skill and talent not against others', but by how you continue to hone and develop your own. To encourage and support your own progress by the same standards you apply to your other writer friends.

There's a reason I refer to the bulk of the writing process as Revision Mountain: When you're looking up from the foothills, the summit can seem impossibly distant. Even as you take step after step after step toward the top, it can still seem so far away.

But if you turn around and glance back to where you started, you may be surprised to see how far you've come. And if you just keep your head on the step in front of you...and the next...and the next... you'll get ever closer to your goal.

My husband and I joke that our dog is "All Gavin! All the time!" And it's true—moderating his more...shall we say overenthusiastic traits and eliciting the behavior we want requires consistency and vigilance from us. Some dogs are like that.

So are some stories. I wrote my third book, *Heart Conditions* (under my pen name) in about nine months. I started my last fiction release, *The Way We Weren't,* nearly fifteen years prior. The former book came out in draft very close to the final published version; the latter went through countless revisions and overhauls. Every story is different, and takes what it takes.

I say this so often it's practically my tagline: The most important traits an author can have, both in their writing and in their career as a writer, are resilience and persistence.

This is a demanding craft and a tough business. There are rarely shortcuts. Success—whether that's turning out the most effective and compelling version of the story you set out to tell, or getting an agent or a publishing contract, or becoming a bestseller, or whatever metric you measure by—requires concerted, consistent, steady work. And like Gavin, it may never turn out quite the way you planned.

But I couldn't love that dog more. As challenging as he can be, every single day he makes me laugh. He looks at me like I invented everything good in the world, and I adore watching him go at life full-frontal, with his big goofy grin. He's worth every bit of work and attention and care we put into him—in fact all of that is what our relationship and life with our pets (and loved ones) *is*.

It's the same with your creativity. The process isn't a means to an end—it's the *point* of it, the journey itself, the experiences you have and what they build, how they let you grow. The truth is there's never an actual finish line (except for the ultimate one).

Write the story. Enjoy the process. Write another one, if it calls to you.

Don't forget to notice how far you've come.

Chapter Six

8 Lessons on Writing (Learned from Home Improvement)

Very shortly after I met my now-husband and we moved in together, I offered our services to help his mother tile a backsplash in her kitchen.

My then-boyfriend was not delighted with my generous dispensation of his time along with my own. He foresaw many long days driving to San Antonio to spend hours working on a complicated project he'd never attempted before.

"Nah," I assured him confidently, having recently (and quite competently and efficiently, I added) tiled the countertops in two bathrooms of the home I'd sold after we met. "Two days with curing and grouting too, a few hours a day, max, and I can do most of it on my own."

Reader, when I said this I believed it with all my soul.

What I did not take into account was that tiling a vertical wall is very different from tiling a horizontal countertop. I did not factor in the age of the house and its settling foundation that meant there wasn't a square angle or straight line on any of its walls. I failed to anticipate that my future mother-in-law would take my overly generous assessment of my tiling skills as license to add plans for an elaborate inset mosaic within the main field of backsplash tiles.

The project took two full weekends, working eight-hour days on top of our three-hour commute to and from Austin, and multiple visits to the tile and hardware stores for a seemingly endlessly regenerative list of items we (okay, *I*) hadn't anticipated needing.

Sixteen years later my husband has yet to let me live this episode down, and so when I recently announced that I planned to tile two recessed alcoves in our house, he was, shall we say, less than enthused.

And I, excited about my vision of beautiful, elegant decorative tile features, and having clearly learned nothing from history, said with great unconcern, "Don't worry about it—I can handle this one on my own. A few hours at most."

Authors, please take these important lessons every writer should learn about her own creative efforts from my abject failure to have learned them from my own prior tiling mishaps.

1. *Even with extensive preparation, you may encounter unexpected challenges.*

I spent days carefully prepping for the job so that I'd have no surprises when I started the actual installation, and it was going gangbusters at first, the sheets of decorative glass tile expediently gliding right into place almost all the way up to the arched top.

Where things abruptly came to a screeching halt.

I hadn't predicted how challenging tiling the shape of an arch would prove. I'd planned to cut the curve with my tile saw, but realized I couldn't measure the cuts accurately because of the indentation of the wall.

Even if you're the most meticulous plotter, stories and characters have a way of developing unexpectedly. You may find a route you'd planned to take doesn't serve the story, or a character doesn't want to do what you had in mind for her, or new facets of the story have popped up that dictate another path.

You can't force it to go the way you wanted it to if it simply doesn't work well for the story. In writing as in tiling, that leads to lesson number two:

2. *You may have to get creative to find new solutions.*

I wound up having to lay each tiny individual piece of glass tile one by one: measuring, judging the angle (different at every point of the arch), cutting with glass nippers, testing in the spot, recutting until it fit, and hand-sanding each edge before mortaring it in.

As your story comes to life on the page, you may discover new wrinkles, new obstacles, dead ends you never saw coming. The ideas you had in your head for the story may not quite fit the execution of it.

Take a different tack. Try something new. What's the worst thing that could befall your character right now? What advantage or resource could you take away from her?

Try something crazy. What's the most ridiculous plot development that could occur, or action you might have him take?

It doesn't have to be the right answer. No one need ever see your story until you're ready, and you can always change it, hone it, or try something else. Unlike tiling, story isn't set in mortar.

Eventually you'll find the right fit.

3. *It may get hard. Harder than you probably expected.*

The bottom five feet of the first alcove went just as planned and took less than an hour to tile. The top twelve inches of the arch took an additional five hours.

For a single arch. The second one gaped blankly at me, mocking my intention to finish both in a day. I just stuck with it, though, knowing the only way through was through and that if I didn't keep at it, there was *no* chance I'd finish the project.

You will come to parts of your story that are agony. Where you fear you will never find your way out of the maze, or that you've made such a hash of it there's no fixing it. You may wish you'd never bothered to start in the first place.

You're wrong—on all counts. (Except the agony part…there may indeed be pain.)

Grit your teeth, stick with it, and find a way through. This is a first draft—it's meant to suck. Just get something down on the page that gets you where you need to go. The magic happens in revision.

4. *There's a learning curve.*

Alcove number two posed the same challenges as alcove number one—but by then I knew what to expect and how to handle it. The second arch still took the bulk of the total time on the job, but it went much faster and more efficiently. (By which I mean three hours instead of six.)

Not only will your skill and knowledge increase with every manuscript you write, but even within those manuscripts, you'll find the lessons learned from wrong turns and dead ends give you more confidence and efficacy at handling subsequent snafus in the story.

Challenge begets mastery. If every story were easy you'd never grow as a writer.

5. *It's okay to have help.*

One of my friends wanted to learn to tile, so when I told her about my project she asked if she could come over to see me do it. I assumed she'd stop by, watch for an hour or so (if that), and then head on.

Instead she showed up for nearly three full days of work and dived right in to help: mortaring parts of the wall, laying some of the tile, running back and forth to the tile saw for cuts, helping to grout, and generally serving as my right hand. My husband chipped in on the second archway too, and their help was a big part of the reason that one went more smoothly.

That doesn't lessen the fact that I did the lion's share of this tile job and can be proud of it. Having help just made it much easier and more enjoyable.

Maybe you bounce ideas off your spouse or a writing buddy or your editor. Maybe they help you work out a thorny plot point or give you the key that unlocks a stuck story. Maybe they even offer a full-blown idea for a major part of the manuscript and help talk it through with you.

It's still your story. Let yourself enjoy walking part of what can often be the solitary journey of creativity with someone who makes the road a little easier.

6. *You may not finish when you think you will.*

I'd allotted two days for the installation. It took five.

But the deadline I'd imposed was an arbitrary one: The job didn't have to be finished "on time" except that I wanted it to be.

Many deadlines are mutable, even those that aren't self-imposed. I've worked in publishing long enough to know that there is almost always wiggle room in a production schedule. Indie pub offers even more schedule flexibility. NaNoWriMo's 50K-word goal is arbitrary, intended to encourage writers to sit down and pound out words, get the story on the page.

If these or any other deadlines or goals work for you, great. If you fall short, that's okay. You made a start; now keep going till you finish, however long it takes. Creativity is supposed to be a joy, not a chore, at least for the most part. The world won't end if you don't finish your story right on schedule.

7. It may not be "perfect" or exactly as you envisioned it.

My alcoves are flawed. Some of the grout lines are uneven. A few of the tiny pieces I had to cut for the fiddly little corners of the arch aren't quite right.

But you know what? It's fine. Unless you look closely you can't tell. And if I tried to chisel out those pieces, recut and re-mortar them, and grout them back in again, it might not make it any better. It might, in fact, make it look even worse.

I'd say with almost total confidence that every book you've ever loved has been reworked since its first draft…a lot. And even so, no book you've ever loved is "perfect." There's no such thing in a subjective field like story. And writers are constantly growing and evolving, so even if you think it's perfect at some point, if you reread it again years or even months later, you'll see areas you want to improve.

Let it go. The more you chisel away at it the more you risk losing what was working well already. And you keep yourself from moving on to a new creation, which will grow your skills even more. Because no matter what…

8. It will feel fantastic to do what you set out to do: whenever you finish, however it comes out.

How many times have you heard, on telling someone you're a writer, "Oh, I've always wanted to write a book!"

The truth, though, is that most people don't. Simply by virtue of practicing your craft you are already ahead of many people with dreams of creating who haven't made them a reality. And if you see a story all the way through and finish it? You're in an even more elite minority.

I get pleasure every single time I walk by my lovely tiled alcoves—not just because they're elegant (but oh, readers, they are!), but because I feel such pride and accomplishment in having done it. Those alcoves (and my mother-in-law's backsplash) represent a goal achieved, and all the memories of the many challenges I overcame in achieving it. I get to enjoy both process *and* product, even if they aren't perfect. They're good—and more important, they're done. They exist where before nothing did, thanks to my efforts.

Let yourself enjoy your own effort and the stories it yields, whether they're "perfect" or not. Two of the sweetest words in the English language are "the end."

Tell your stories, authors. Free them into the world to affect other people, and get to work on your next one.

Chapter Seven

Writing Enduring Stories and Your Artistic Legacy

I'm betting Francis Ford Coppola wasn't thinking about someone like me sitting in a theater watching his work half a century after its original release. But that's where I was the day of *The Godfather*'s theatrical rerelease, beyond excited to see one of my favorite films remastered and on the big screen—a movie I'd loved when I was much younger, already long after it had left theaters, watching my VHS copy over and over and over.

I've always found it hard to pin down why I'm so obsessed with this movie, as well as the excellent Mario Puzo book of the same name that it's based on. I'm not especially into Mafia stories, and the values they often glorify—strong-arm tactics, revenge, vigilante justice, violence—are not remotely my bag. In fact, I find them fairly antithetical to my personal value system.

And yet I watched it so many times when I was younger that I knew the movie shot for shot, even so many years later.

I lovingly berated my reluctant husband into seeing it with me for his first time by asserting with righteous pubescent fervor, "It's one of the greatest movies ever made!"

But I secretly worried that maybe it wasn't.

I wondered whether I might find that I'd changed so much from the melodramatic, emotion-charged teen I was when I first discovered *The Godfather* that now I'd find it overblown or ridiculously testosterone-charged (and no mistake, there's plenty of testosterone flying in this movie).

I wondered if, having learned so much about story and structure and character as an editor, I'd assess the film differently now—with a more educated, objective perspective that robbed it of the shine it had had for me for so long.

But I stand by my hyperbolic assessment. Five decades later this movie not only holds up, but it's as good as I remember—and haunts me as much. *The Godfather* is listed in nearly every "best movies of all time" list, regarded as a classic of the cinema, frequently used as a teaching tool, cited as a significant influence by major filmmakers like Martin Scorsese and Quentin Tarantino, and has inspired countless movies, TV shows, books, even video games.

What writer doesn't dream of her story (and everything is story—including nonfiction, memoir, poetry, song, even commercials) being an enduring classic that affects people for generations to come?

Focusing on that goal, though, is trying to hit an amorphous target that's too far out of range.

If you're fixated on your readers—current or future—you're no longer focused on *telling the story*. There's a time for focusing on the reader's experience, but it's later in editing, not during your initial drafting process.

Timeless stories present fully drawn characters that entice and invest readers in their journey, their actions and motivations based in universally relatable values, told with tight, rock-solid storytelling.

Time will determine how your story endures; this is not for the author to concern himself with. Your job is to write the stories of your heart that are real and alive for you *now*, with all the depth, texture, and skill you can muster.

But What If You're Not Francis Ford Coppola?

Now let's be real. Coppola achieved astounding success in his career. Not all artists will rise to those heights. Not most, if we're being honest. It's easy to talk about an enduring artistic legacy when referring to a screenwriter and filmmaker who is responsible for some of the most iconic and timeless stories in the modern cinematic canon, ones often listed among the greatest ever made: *The Godfather* both *I* and *II* (we shall not speak of *III*), *Apocalypse Now*. It's easy to sustain a creative career and follow your passions if you're revered as a master in your field and making big bucks while doing it.

But what if you're not? What if your creative career means dragging your exhausted self out of bed every morning an hour before your family wakes up to carve out a little bit of time to devote to your writing? What if it means working day after day through the challenges of storytelling, the limitations of life, and your own self-doubts about your skill and talent and whether your writing is even worth doing?

Francis Ford Coppola didn't start out at the top of his game. The first feature film he directed (and wrote) was a 1963 low-budget black-and-white horror film, *Dementia 13*, that released as the bottom half of a double bill with a Roger Corman sci-fi B-movie, to an ambivalent reception. Despite success directing the musical *Finian's Rainbow* five years later and winning an Academy Award for the screenplay for the movie *Patton* two years after that, Coppola was far from the first choice to direct *The Godfather*—at least eight other directors were considered before he was offered the job, and he was nearly fired during production.

But he persisted with his vision and his goals...still kept getting up to the plate to take a swing. And while he's had forgettable flops as well as cinematic triumphs, sixty years after he made his first film, Coppola is still working, still a towering presence in the film world, and still continues to have an influence on other artists, other movies, and on the American psyche.

Ernest Hemingway famously said that every person dies twice: once when we shuffle off this mortal coil, and once when our name is spoken on Earth for the last time.

Coppola's legacy is a towering one. His name will no doubt be spoken for many generations to come.

But *your* legacy will live on as well. Whether you publish or not, whether you become a bestseller or not, your creative work is what will survive you.

The *doing* of that work is so much of what gives our own life meaning and purpose and fulfillment in the time we have. But the *legacy* of it is what will define your life and who you are for those who come after you.

You Are Already Creating Your Legacy

I think a lot about legacy, and I think many artists do. What will outlive us; what impact might we make in the world after we're gone?

My mom and stepfather are not writers, nor even creatives in the strictest sense. But not long ago I started a writing project with them.

Periodically I send them questions about their lives when they were younger: who they were, what they wanted and dreamed of and loved, what they did, what they felt and thought, what their lives were like. They may write their responses or just talk through their answers and record them, but I'm slowly compiling them into a written record of who they are.

It's a way for our family to know them more intimately as people, not just parents. But I think it's also been rewarding and nourishing for them to think about these times and share them, to look at their lives through the perspective of who they are now and reflect on how their experiences shaped them. I think they both like the idea that in some way they will continue to live on for us through their words after they're gone.

And isn't that what we all hope for in our writing? Not only that we may find enjoyment and fulfillment and growth in the doing of it, but that our having done it may make an impact on someone else?

It may not be millions of people. It may be just a handful who read your words after you're gone. But how many people would you have to impact to make it meaningful to you? If you affect and connect with even a single soul, how many more numbers do you need for it to feel as if your words mattered?

What if those who are left behind look through your writing and think, *Look how they pursued what they loved*. What if they read something you wrote—anything, a story, a scene, a moving turn of phrase—and are affected by it, changed by it, moved? What if they think, as they reflect back on your life and your legacy, *What a life well lived*, and your passing is cause for celebrating how you lived?

I think most artists would love to achieve the heights attained by Francis Ford Coppola—money and fame and influence and adulation. But those are just the external rewards of living a creative life. Wouldn't it be lovely and empowering to realize how much of what makes a creative life fulfilling, the mark you hope to leave in the world, is already within your power?

Chapter Eight

The Power of "No"

Authors spend a lot of time and focus waiting for the yes. We hope for an unequivocal yes from early readers of our work, perhaps wait for a yes from an agent who wants to represent us or a publisher who might pay us for our work and help us get our books in readers' hands. We long for ecstatic yeses from those readers and from critical reviews.

So much of our business—of any creative business—is predicated on the creator getting the nod from those who will buy and consume it that it's easy to understand how writers might start to define themselves and their work by whether or not it comes.

And yet this is the mindset that keeps us dependent upon outside approval, defining our success by other people's opinions, awaiting these amorphous "others'" permission to pursue what we love.

The central idea of this book is about moving away from letting our careers revolve around the fulcrum of outside approval, and that means shifting our focus from waiting for other people's yes to validate or sanction our work, and giving ourselves permission to say no.

"No" is a powerful word: Ask the frustrated parents of any truculent toddler who's just learned it and realized that it gives them agency over their own choices, or their rebellious teenager using it for the same reason—to assert autonomy as the adults they are on the verge of becoming.

"No" puts you in the driver's seat. It allows you to take the wheel of your career and decide what path you're taking.

And yet it can also be one of the most terrifying words, especially in a career where so much hinges on the yeses. After sending out so many queries and persevering through the challenging process of finding an agent, how could an author say no when they finally get an offer from one, even if they aren't sure this is the best representative for them? Or how can they leave an agent they no longer feel is the right fit, knowing how difficult it may be to find a new one?

After managing to get their work published, how can an author who's being encouraged by their agent or publisher to change genres or even assume a pen name defy these experts and say no if those choices are not something they want, knowing that doing so may mean those people no longer choose to work with them?

When so much of building a career means getting your name out there and making people aware of you and your work, how can an author say no if they're asked to contribute their work or efforts for free, for the "exposure," if they believe they should be paid for it? How can they say no to launching into every social media site or ambitious marketing plan?

When reading about decreasing advances and increasing difficulty in selling their writing, how can an author say no if the money they're offered for their work doesn't feel like enough?

What you say no to is a big part of what creates the life you live—and this applies especially to your writing career. "No" shapes your life as thoroughly as "yes" does.

But there are good "no"s and bad "no"s.

My scariest "no" came on the verge of the publication of my fifth novel, when I realized I had lost faith in the small press that had published my first four books (as Phoebe Fox) and contracted for this one. Scant months before publication I decided to pull the novel from the publisher, eating the contract and in fact having to pay to regain the rights to the manuscript.

I didn't have another offer in the works. I didn't know if my agent would drop me after what could have been perceived as a highly unprofessional move. I honestly felt there was a very good chance that this decision augured the end of my fiction-writing career.

But it was a good "no." I felt as if I had lost control over a book that was important to me, which was not being handled the way I wanted it to be, and I deemed it more important to retrieve and own the rights to my own story and decide what became of it than to continue to barrel down a highway I didn't want to travel to a destination I didn't want to go to.

My agent supported my decision and agreed to shop the book around to publishers, and just a few months later we received a two-book offer for it and a second title from a major traditional publisher, which had been an important goal for me. Then we said "no" to their initial offer, and increased it by a third in negotiations—which more than covered my costs to buy back the rights from the small press.

Yet even if we hadn't received that offer, leaving that small press was still the right "no" for me. I'd already made peace with the fact that the book might never find a publishing home and planned to indie-publish it in that case. I'd already accepted that with those costs and the cost of retrieving the rights, the book might be a net loss. I'd already set my boundaries and honored them, and that made me feel I was creating my own career, not blindly accepting what I was given or following where I was told to go independent of whether it was what I genuinely wanted.

Even if I'd self-published, even if I'd reached just a handful of readers without the platform of a publisher behind me, even if it had ultimately cost me money, it felt right for my goals and preferences for my career to step away from what I knew I *didn't* want and toward what I did—to publish this story in a way that felt satisfying to me.

What You Say "No" to Shapes Your Career—and Your Life

Throughout my career as a freelance editor and speaker, I've built my business and reputation on being what I call "the yes girl"—the one publishers know they can call who will accept the project and get it done on time. The one writers' groups and organizations can count on if they need a presenter or keynote speaker. The one publications can offer assignments to who will accept and turn them in as specified, and on deadline.

But too many "yeses" means I work long hours, eating into nights and weekends. It means stealing time from other areas of my life that are important to me—my husband, family, and friends, my own creative work, time off and travel, personal projects, simple unconstructed downtime that's such a big part of charging the batteries.

Always saying yes has indeed helped me build my career—but what's it for if not all the rest? There's more to life than work and career, and I've begun turning down projects when I know I want that time for other things—or even no specific thing, just time for myself—which is much healthier than a "yes" would be.

I have a host of this kind of healthy "no" that has helped me shape a life and career I want:

- No to a "regular job": I've freelanced successfully for my entire career.
- No to judging myself by my creative output: I accept that some days' work is better than others, and that's fine. I know

how to make it better and have faith that I can, but I also know that its value and worth (and my own) aren't dependent on the caliber or quantity of the work.
- No to working on stories I'm not passionate about—as an editor or a writer. Part of shaping the career and life I want means that I want to enjoy what I do, every single day. And that means not taking on work that doesn't excite me, but rather holding open space for work that does.
- No when I don't want to say yes: I've learned to turn down jobs and other opportunities where the compensations—both monetary and otherwise—don't feel worth the time and effort they would require.

I say all of these "no"s consciously, deliberately, to achieve an outcome that feels right for my values, priorities, and goals. I'm learning to say "no" to overbooking myself with work and taking time away from my family and my life, and to give me the room to pursue other professional projects that I'm passionate about. To accept the potential risks and losses of my "no" when it fulfills other, more pressing values and goals. Those are good "no"s.

Bad "no"s are the ones we make out of fear, or self-doubt, or because of outside pressures or expectations:

- No to writing the book of your heart because it's not "marketable" or a hot genre or you're "too old"
- No to submitting or sharing your writing because you fear it's not good enough or there's too much competition
- No to the writing retreat or conference or class you were excited about because of guilt or duty or self-doubt
- No to asking to be paid for your work, or for more money or better terms, or for the agent or publisher you really want, because of fear that no one else will want you or you won't find anything better

- No to indie publishing to share your work because of some false idea of stratification or stigma in how you do so
- No to taking time away from your writing when everything in you is screaming for a break, because you "have to hit your word count" or because "writers write" or because you "have to get a book out"

This last point can be among the hardest. But sometimes stepping away even from something you love is crucial for creating a healthy, balanced life.

The great power of "no" is that it allows you to shape your life, to choose your priorities, to take care of yourself. To assert autonomy over your own creativity, your own career, and your own well-being. Use your "no"s positively and deliberately and without a scrap of guilt to reclaim your life—including your writing—from any definition but your own.

The only real authority to consult when deciding between "yes" and "no" is yourself: what *you* want, the stories *you* want to tell, the career *you* want to build, the goals you have for it that are meaningful for *you*. That's your North Star in determining which doors to walk through and which to contentedly walk away from.

Use your "no"s to give your "yes"es power and meaning, and to free you to consciously create the life—and the writing career—you want.

Chapter Nine

When Will You Be a "Real Writer"?

Not long ago, on a plane home from a writers' conference, I sat next to a woman who spent much of our flight on her computer studying and practicing kanji, a Chinese script used in the Japanese language.

At one point we struck up a conversation, and I asked her why she was learning it, wondering if it was for school or a job.

"No," she said. "I just want to."

I told her how impressed I was by her tackling what to me had always seemed an intimidatingly difficult language to learn, even though I love learning languages, and she shared some of her enthusiasm and enjoyment in studying it.

What neither of us did was dismiss it because she wasn't yet fluent or an expert. We did not denigrate her interest in it or pursuit of it because she was not a professional translator. It didn't undermine her joy or my admiration.

She simply enjoyed and shared with me her self-motivated, genuine interest in learning a complicated language, and I just thought it was impressive and inspiring that she was working with such dedication on a hard thing that was clearly of great interest and meaning to her.

Wouldn't it be nice if this were how conversations with others about our writing went?

And yet at the writers' conference where I'd just been presenting, many authors had joked about family and friends and acquaintances asking when they would finally get that book out, or were they making any money from their writing, or saying things like, "Oh, are you still working on that?"

I hear authors tell stories like this a lot. Or of being asked, when they tell people they meet that they're writers, how many books they have published, or whether their inquisitor would know them or have seen their books anywhere, and the disinterest or dismissiveness—or sometimes even denigration—they've received when the answers don't match someone's narrow view of what "being a real writer" means.

I wish this were an unusual occurrence, but it's not.

And bad enough that writers may receive this reaction from strangers, but how much worse when it comes from people they know, or those they love and who love them? That's an especially painful sort of diminution, one it's easy to internalize.

Worst of all when those belittling attitudes come from ourselves. I hear a lot of authors downplay or dismiss their own work because it doesn't yet meet some standard of legitimacy they've accepted: being published, being traditionally published, being a bestseller, making money, or whatever goalpost of validity they've assigned it.

I hear them talk about their disappointment in themselves. I hear them lose faith in their abilities.

Sometimes I hear them talk about giving up.

Too often authors are the first to make denigrating remarks about their own writing, diminishing it by what I call "just"-ifying their stories, their skills, themselves:

- "Oh, I'm just starting out with writing."
- "I just wrote two hundred words today."
- "I'm just partway through my story."
- "I'm just small-press/self-published."
- "I just write light, fun beach reads; it's not highbrow literature."

Do any of these comments sound familiar? Friends, that last one is pretty much a direct quote from me, more than once, about the novels I've written. Probably more than fifty times, if I'm honest.

In some ways I think this self-effacement comes from good instincts: to stay in beginner's mind and realize we are always learning—and there is always much to learn about our craft. That attitude is certainly more productive than its flipside: overconfidence that can shut us off to improving our writing and growing as artists.

But there's danger in talking about our writing in a disparaging way. Most obviously it sends us the message that our creative work isn't that important or worthwhile. It's just a lark, a silly little whim we pursue, but we're not kidding ourselves that we can stand beside the actual greats of literature.

We may also use "just"-ifying to beat anyone else to the punch, a defensive device to insulate us against criticism or disapproval: "You can't hurt me by telling me my efforts or my writing aren't good enough, because trust me, I already know it." If we're not trying to reach for the stars, after all, then it can't hurt to fall to Earth.

But that kind of self-deprecation can do damage to our creative efforts and to us as creators. It makes the one person who should always be our staunch champion—ourselves—into a constant critic. And that's not an environment conducive to giving ourselves the freedom to do our best work, to learn and expand our skills by trying big, and giving ourselves permission to fail big.

Modesty, Humility, and Pride

One of the reasons I think we struggle with talking about our own work is the societal stricture against pride, going all the way back to the Bible, where it goeth before a fall. We're encouraged to be humble and modest, which aren't the same things.

Modesty connotes downplaying skills or talents or positive traits you know you have, whereas humility can often evoke the idea of humiliation, abasing yourself and dismissing the notion that you could possibly have any of these positive attributes at all.

But that's not what humility is. Humility isn't the opposite of pride, as it's often presented. It's a facet of it. It's a realistic, human view of yourself and your own abilities, both your weaknesses and your strengths.

Rather than being opposites, pride versus humility, what if we were to think of them as *both* being important traits for nurturing our creativity—pride *and* humility (with all due respect to Jane Austen's perspective)?

That means having a clear-eyed view of your work and where there may be room for improvement and growth, while also allowing yourself to be proud of its merits and strengths. Without that how can we hope to improve as artists, any more than a child who is given nothing but criticism and disapproval can develop a healthy self-image and flourish? We have to create a safe space for ourselves as creatives where we have permission to fail, permission to grow.

"Just"-ifying also creates an external framework for how we evaluate our work, holding ourselves and our creative efforts up against others rather than evaluating them for what they are and how well they have expressed our vision. It judges them for what they are *not*, rather than what they *are*.

It's our internal judgment of our creative efforts that results in harmful "just"-ifying—the negative messages about it that we give ourselves.

But what if we replace those negative judgments with more positive interpretations?

- Instead of, "Oh, I'm just trying my hand at writing," what if you approach it as embarking on the first steps of a new artistic pursuit—how marvelous!
- Instead of "just" writing two hundred words, or whatever word count you were aiming for, you brought two hundred new words into existence that weren't on the page yesterday—isn't that extraordinary?
- Rather than "just" being small-press or indie published, what if you celebrate the fact that you brought your book(s) into existence? You finished a major undertaking, achieved a dream, shared your vision.
- What if you don't "just" write genre fiction; you give readers an experience, an adventure, a fun escape—how delightful!

We can allow ourselves to take pride in our work, openly and genuinely, while maintaining the humility that allows us to continue to improve it. One doesn't rule out the other; they work together to keep us pursuing the excellence we crave.

And we can take back the power to determine what gives our efforts worth and value by defining those metrics by our own standards, not anyone else's.

Whose Standards Are You Judging Yourself By?

The nerve I think denigrating comments hit on in writers, both from others and ourselves—and the part that may feel valid to an author—is the professional aspect of it. Even if we stay in touch with that original spark that made us want to write in the first place, many of us want to be professional writers, to be paid for it. To make a career of it.

That's an entirely valid goal. And to me it indicates something foundationally healthy and clear-eyed in our thinking: Our creative work has value, and we deserve to be paid for it.

It also indicates something wonderfully inherent in art: that its impact and power lies not solely in the creating of it, but the sharing of it.

But it's as if we don't believe we're "real writers" yet until we grab whatever external reward we or someone else has decided means we are: publishing, a paycheck, hitting some bestseller list. Until then we're wannabes. Amateurs.

"Amateur" has become a dirty word, implying an unskilled hack rather than a pro. But the root of the word is literally love—*amare*. An amateur is one who loves, or per Merriam-Webster, "one who is devoted to something."

I have met very few writers in my thirty-plus years in this business—at every level of their writing careers—who don't meet that description. We're *all* amateurs.

But even if you accept the connotation of that word as someone who isn't a professional at their pursuit, a hobbyist or aficionado… so what? Every artist you've ever admired started out that way. It's part of the journey—one that may take varying amounts of time and cover various terrains. Would you stomp out a seedling because it's not yet in bloom? Would you mock or dismiss someone's efforts to learn and improve at *anything* because they don't yet meet some standard of perfection or professionalism?

Accepting that standard bridles the soul—the root of any meaningful pursuit: the sheer love of it. The enjoyment of doing a thing for its own sake, like gardening, or cooking, or playing the piano, or painting, or rock climbing…or learning kanji.

Art is not commerce. I would venture to opine that when most of us were initially drawn to wanting to write, it wasn't because we were driven by the need to sell our work or see it published and on *New York Times* bestseller lists.

If we dig back to that initial spark that led us to put our thoughts and words and ideas and emotions and beliefs and perspectives on the page, I'm going to hazard a guess that it had more to do with a fervid love of language or story. Or that we wanted to give life to the vivid tales we wove in our heads. Or that we wanted to share with other people something we felt was important or elemental or fascinating—to connect with them.

Along the line we may have developed professional goals around our creative work, but that passion, that foundational spark, usually doesn't have much to do with some arbitrary external goalpost. Our writing comes from the truest place inside of us, and when we first start it's often for its own intrinsic sake, the joy and fulfillment creativity gives us, the interest we take in doing it. Kind of like my seatmate on the plane learning kanji.

And yet for some reason not only do others seem to dismiss the validity of pursuing this particular passion or interest if it hasn't crossed whatever Rubicon of professionalism they deem legitimizes it, but if we hear it often enough, I think we start to regard our own creative efforts that same way too.

I meet writers who will not claim the title of author because they're not yet published—even though they are the author of every word they've ever put on a page and every story they've ever imagined.

I meet writers who will immediately downplay their own progress and skill and achievement because they're new, or "only" write a particular genre, or haven't published, or haven't published *enough*, or with the right people, or for enough money.

Authors so frequently flog themselves with the "shoulds." They aren't writing as much or as well as they should. After X number of books they should be able to turn in a draft that needs less editing and revision. They should have more books published, or have higher sales, or should have gotten an agent or publishing contract by now.

The problem with "shoulding all over ourselves," as I've memorably heard it called, is that it unquestioningly accepts a metric for our assessment of our own performance based on some theoretical idea of what is "right" or "normal" or what the industry or other writers or some marketing guru or blog says constitutes success as a writer.

It defines our self-perception and our enjoyment of our career by an external benchmark against which we're comparing ourselves.

It's the equivalent of deciding that all dogs should be like Toto and imposing that standard on my dogs, who are neither small nor perky nor capable of walking off-leash without wandering away or going on the hunt for squirrels.

We often do it not just in our writing life, but in general—accepting arbitrary outside standards of beauty, our home and family lives, finances, our careers, even sometimes our ideology.

This puts the measure of our life's enjoyment and our own self-image in other people's hands: advertisers, social media "friends," Wall Street, colleagues, politicians.

Taking Back Your Own Definitions of Success

It's so easy for those external standards to slip in. To mindlessly adopt values for ourselves that may or may not fit our goals, our preferences, and our priorities.

- Do you worry about how many followers you have on social media, or how much engagement your posts receive, or how many newsletter subscribers?
- If you've published your writing, do you fall into the trap of measuring your success and validity as an author by the daily rankings, by sales, by reviews, by whether your publisher is happy with the book's performance?
- Do you find yourself slipping into behaviors and reactions based on unexamined subconscious standards for yourself that come from old childhood messaging or your own assumptions

and illusions, or other people's opinions—rather than consciously deciding what fits your own goals and values?
- Do you let your assumptions of what you "should" be doing as a good partner, good parent, good child, good friend, good employee, good pet parent, etc., push you into taking on more responsibilities and commitments than you need to, sidelining your own writing?

All of these goals may be important to you: to help your writing reach readers, to succeed in your work and pave the way to be able to do more of it, to spend quality time with the people (and pets!) you care about.

But if you unconsciously (or consciously) adopt external standards of "success" in these areas that aren't necessarily right for *you* at this moment, then you compromise your enjoyment of them for their own sake.

Just as it can be destructive and counterproductive try to fit ourselves into some standardized definition of what constitutes a "good person," we need to respect our own preferences and needs.

Every person is different, every book is different, and every author's writing career follows its own trajectory. When you find yourself scrambling toward some external outcome or beating yourself up for falling short, ask yourself whether the standards by which you're judging yourself are your own—or you're letting outside forces determine what's best for *you*.

Publishing is a subjective business, as is any industry based on creativity. Success is based on countless variables, mostly outside the creator's control: trends, gatekeeper tastes, consumer tastes, the market, the economy, catastrophic events outside *anyone's* control, like political unrest or a global pandemic or a paper shortage or a ship losing all the distribution copies of your new release overboard in rough seas[14]—countless variables beyond anyone's ability to predict or manage, least of all the artist.

All you can do is control the parts you can: Write—do the work. Create stories that mean something to you. Practice your craft and get more and more adept at it. Define your goals and figure out what concrete steps are required to achieve them, and then do those things to the best of your ability.

Ultimately what does it matter in your artistic life whether you hit some arbitrary goalpost that denotes "success" to the outside world? How does it affect the doing of the thing itself? Your work's intrinsic value? What it will have meant to you to have done it, at the end of your life when you're looking back on how you spent it?

Enjoy every step of the journey—and don't let anyone who crosses your path make you believe you're not in the right place yet. We are where we are, all of us, and every step is legitimate.

I recently read a quote I loved from Jesuit priest Anthony de Mello from his book *The Way to Love*:

"You must cultivate activities that you love. You must discover work that you do, not for its utility, but for itself, whether it succeeds or not, whether you are praised for it or not, whether you are loved and rewarded for it or not, whether people know about it and are grateful to you for it or not. How many activities can you count in your life that you engage in simply because they delight you and grip your soul? Find them out, cultivate them, for they are your passport to freedom and to love."

No one gets to define your freedom and what you love except you. You are a "real writer" already—right now—because you write. Grab that passport and cultivate your delight, authors. Let your writing grip your soul.

Chapter Ten

Giving Your All for the Few

One of our favorite local restaurants is called Pieous, and they specialize in—oddly—pizza, pastrami, and pastries. It's a frequent darling of area foodies and "best of" lists, and we probably eat there several times a month. There's always a fairly healthy crowd, many of them regulars.

The owners, Josh and Paige Kaner, left established careers and a life in LA and started this business when they moved to Austin to raise their family, having always dreamed of running their own restaurant. They use a sourdough starter for their crusts and pastries that's been in their family for decades, and they make everything from scratch every day, from the sauce to the mozzarella, as well as all their dessert and pastry offerings.

From the day they opened they've put in astonishing hours, and are constantly innovating new menu items that they bring samples of out to customers to get their input. They have a passion for their food and for this work—one they share with customers in a chalk-drawn "definition" of their restaurant's name that includes statements like "simply devoted to great food" and "sacred or devotional pursuit of turning simple ingredients into a divine meal," and "showing loyal reverence to great food."

Pieous has earned enduring local popularity and loyalty with a single location on the western outskirts of Austin. Josh and Paige do all this work for a tiny fraction of the food-eating world—but that doesn't seem to detract from their enjoyment of it, their dedication, and their constantly evolving craftsmanship.

Think about your favorite local restaurant, or artist, or musician, or podcast. Think about the satisfaction and joy you get from them and what they bring to your life.

Think of some of your favorite creative products, and the joy they give you. Your favorite book or film or TV show may or may not be a megahit. Mine are often niche-y little stories that barely made a blip marketing-wise.

Do you dismiss their value because they may not reach millions of people or have widespread name recognition?

And yet I think many authors do this with their writing. You create your stories and they may not get published, but your critique partners and writing group and family and friends have read and loved them. Yet that doesn't feel like enough.

Or you publish and your book never gains widespread traction with readers. But you've got a handful or dozens or even a few hundred reviews from people who love what you're doing, to whom it means something. Yet perhaps you feel the work isn't *really* a success if you're not topping bestseller charts or making bank.

If we ourselves can love and appreciate art that never finds a ubiquitously wide audience, why do we often feel that's not good enough for our own creative work? Why is a small audience any less valid or satisfying than a larger one?

Admittedly most of us get into this field not just because of our love of story, but because we dream of sharing it with others, as widely as we can. If we're honest, a lot of us probably hope to be major bestsellers, world-renowned, our books beloved by millions.

But if you've been in this business for any period of time (or read chapter one) you probably know the somewhat grim statistics. Not only is it astronomically unlikely that most authors will achieve those heights, but even moderate commercial, critical, and financial "success" as an author is achieved by only a small fraction of those attempting to make a career out of writing.

It's the same in a lot of creative fields—including cooking. The stats on opening a single successful restaurant are pretty daunting, let alone ballooning into multiple locations, franchising, and brand ubiquity—the "bestseller" status of the food world.

Yet here are Josh and Paige, showing up every day and giving their all to their restaurant, striving to create new recipes and perfecting existing ones. They worked diligently to attain an official VPN certification (Vera Pizza Napoletana) according to strict standards of traditional pizza makers required in Naples, Italy, one of few restaurants in this country to achieve that honor. Their pastrami and pastries were featured on an episode of *Diners, Drive-Ins, and Dives*.[15]

For a while they talked about opening other branches, new concepts, and I've even asked them about franchising. But for now this seems to be enough. Josh and Paige are happy doing what they love for a circle of superfans who are equally passionate about their creative product. They have found their personal definition of success, even at this relatively modest level. They're not waiting for their ship to come in or to garner the attention of millions around the country and the world. They're already happy doing what they love, day after day after day.

What Makes Your Art Matter?

I think about Josh and Paige a lot when I find myself getting caught up in a rat-race mentality, when I feel frustrated or disappointed with how my business is growing, or worry that I don't have the reach or platform that I'd like to have. When I fall into that mindset I can start to feel dissatisfied with what I do, unhappy and self-doubting about my own abilities. This is when my old familiar demons start to rear their heads: impostor syndrome. Perfectionism. Comparison.

I think about how hard Paige and Josh have worked from the day their restaurant opened. I think about the palpable joy that is always evident in both of them whenever we come in, no matter how busy they are, even during the pandemic, when they had to pivot their entire business to takeout only (and incidentally, retained every single employee on salary). They are following their dream every day, even when it's hard.

When I think about this in my moments of dissatisfaction and inadequacy, it reminds me why I do what I do, and that I already love doing it, day after day after day. Like Josh and Paige, I'm pretty much always baseline content and fulfilled by the work I do. A bigger platform would be nice, and it can be a long-term plan, but defining my success by that prevents me from enjoying the work that made me want to do that in the first place. It prevents me from relishing what I'm *already* doing, what I've *already* accomplished. It undermines that enjoyment and my confidence and faith in myself, and turns my passion into a flog to beat myself with.

This morning I walked through my house looking at some of the artwork in it that regularly gives me the greatest pleasure.

This painting was created by an author I worked with, Amulya Malladi, who took up acrylic painting as a hobby and "sells" her work in exchange for donations to various nonprofits.

I fell in love with this one—inspired by one of her books I especially loved, *The Copenhagen Affair*, and it hangs in front of my desk, where my eye lands on it daily and it nourishes my soul.

This isn't a mass-produced piece. It's an original, and I don't think there are prints of it. Only I and people in my home get to enjoy this work of art. Does that make it less worthy? It's worth a great deal to me—it brings me joy every day. Is that not art's highest calling?

Original acrylic by Amulya Malladi

This is a vase made by my great-aunt I never knew. I think its workmanship is amazing—the perfection of its shape, its smooth texture, the colors of the glaze. It's a simple piece, and the creator gifted it to a family member with no expectation it might enjoy wider acclaim than that. Does that detract from its merit as art? Yet here I am two generations later admiring it every day.

My mom has painted several watercolors for me, copies of artworks I have admired or that she thinks I would like. They take her many months to complete, and she works hard on the meticulous details. All that effort and time...just so it can be enjoyed by a single person. Yet my mom lights up when she presents me with the finished paintings, and even more so when she sees my reaction. And she loves seeing them featured prominently in our home every time she visits. They make me think of her every day, and her love for me. Would I judge this art as pointless?

Why are we so quick to do that with our own? Why do so many creative souls impose a barometer of worth on our work that has nothing to do with the work itself and is beyond our control or creation—like reviews or sales or acclaim? To have a vision in your head, to develop that vision, to set it down in words and bring it to life on a page...what an accomplishment that is! How rare and special to bring something wholly original and your own into existence. Why must the work achieve more than that to be considered worthwhile? Who is the judge of its validity if not us, its creator? Why isn't the *making* of art—the astonishing process of creating something from nothing—considered success in and of itself?

I always think of the pinnacle of my former career as an actor—which included a number of higher-profile film and TV jobs—as the curtain call of a show I did many years ago at a regional theater. I don't even remember for sure which theater or play it was, but I do remember looking out to see a man on his feet, clapping with everything in him, tears running down his face.

I remember feeling that *this* was why I acted. That night that man had an *experience* as a result of what he saw on that stage. I don't know what it was, or whether it "changed his life."

But for that moment, something I was part of creating connected profoundly and intimately with another human being. It brings tears to my eyes still to remember it.

To paraphrase Kurt Vonnegut, If that isn't creative success, I don't know what is.

Yes, in a perfect world of course we want everyone to read our stories and to love them. We want to support ourselves and our families with our work.

But that's not the measure of its worth, and it has less than nothing to do with the creation of that work and what that brings to you and your life as an artist.

What if your career always stays more modest than you might have hoped? Will it still be worth doing? Would you feel satisfied with simply the privilege of pursuing what you love? Could that satisfaction and joy it brings to your life be its own end, whether three people appreciate your work or three million do?

Knowing that answer can be the difference between a fulfilling, satisfying writing career that you can sustain, and one that leaves you feeling disheartened and dissatisfied, never measuring up to some uncontrollable external standard.

Josh and Paige give their answer every single day they show up at their restaurant, with every customer they greet by name and with a smile, and by the way their faces light up when they watch someone dig into their food and swoon over it.

I find mine every time I sit down to work on an author's story or a presentation or my books; every time I see an author bring her manuscript to the fullest expression of her vision for it.

What's yours?

Chapter Eleven

Why You Can't Rush Your Process

Not long ago I hit a startling career milestone: my thirtieth anniversary of entering the publishing field as an editor.

It gently blows my mind to look back over the journey that got me to this point, and not just because I don't feel three decades beyond that recent college graduate moving to the Big Apple and brandishing an English literature degree I never set out to get. But when my college counselor said I had to declare a major I picked the topic I had the most credits in, having taken a lot of English classes because they were fun for me.

I backed into editing as a career too: I started working as a freelance copy editor to support myself as an actor (because being an actor, not unlike being a writer, generally requires a career to support the habit). But within a few years I knew I'd happened into a career I loved. That degree wasn't such a fluke after all; there was a reason I had so many English credits racked up. Editing, it turned out, was my passion all along, but I had to take the time to find that truth. I had to live a bit until I found my way. I quit acting and focused on my copyediting work.

Then that, too, evolved with time; I spent years developing my knowledge and skill in my field and eventually moved into the developmental editing I do now, which feels like my truest calling.

What I love most about my job—and there's a lot, so it's hard to pin down only one—is helping authors find constructive, productive, creative ways to make sure the story on the page matches the vision in their heads, and does so as effectively as possible. To me editing and revision have always been the true craft of the craft—but they take time.

Writing—making something from nothing—is a heady, creative rush. I joke that first-drafting is the giddy thrill of courtship; revision is the long, hard work of marriage. Editing and revision aren't quite as glamorous as writing—sometimes they can be a slog. But it's usually where a story comes to life, where the true magic happens—as a result of damned hard sustained work on the author's part.

In our instant-gratification, shiny-new-thing world, writers are bombarded with information about furthering their careers: cranking out stories, getting them into agents' hands, finding a publisher or publishing yourself, building readership, developing a platform and a marketing plan, etc. It's easy to slip into panicked FOMO when a chorus of voices is telling you to churn, churn, churn to build a following, feed the machine, stay relevant. Add in our own eagerness to see our work in print, in readers' hands, and we may feel pressured to rush our process.

But you have to make sure that the foundation of all of it—what you're writing—is rock-solid before you try to build anything on top of it.

My last novel under my pen name, *The Way We Weren't*, started life as the first manuscript I ever tried to write—a decade and a half before its release. I made a tongue-in-cheek promotional video about its publication journey, offering my tips for how to write a novel in fifteen years: Take on a very ambitious story on your first time at bat writing full-length fiction; flounder to find the soul of the story.

Revise. Rewrite. Repeat. Fail to get an agent and put the manuscript in a drawer. Fish it out after you write a second manuscript; realize you still can't quite nail this story.[16]

Revise. Rewrite. Repeat.

A lot.

But when I say it took me fifteen years to write this story, I don't mean that I worked constantly on it all that time.

- In between revised drafts, I wrote and published five other novels, honing my writing skills by writing hundreds of thousands of words, learning what made a story work, developing my voice and my confidence and ability as a writer.
- I continued my work as an editor on other authors' novels, steadily honing my craft knowledge and skill by deeply analyzing thousands of stories, by teaching those skills to other authors in workshops and webinars, by writing a book of my own about the subject.
- I gained life experiences I had to have before I could write about a happy long-term marriage that implodes when a crisis puts a couple on opposite sides of a foundational issue in their relationship: I fell in love, got married, learned more about relationships than I could ever have known before I had a long-term, deeply intimate, intensely committed one of my own.
- I garnered fifteen more years of emotional intelligence and depth to understand and be able to develop the story's themes: how easy it can be to get lost in regret and resentment and lose sight of the people you love and what connects you. How being happy and content with your life is a choice you make, day after day after day.
- I learned how to take breaks when I needed to on a story I had become so overfamiliar with—and how to continue to come back to it again and again and again with fresh eyes and continue to try to excavate to the heart of it.

- I learned to believe in myself and my ability to tell a story I very much wanted to tell, despite years of falling short of that goal.
- I learned how to kill so many darlings.
- I learned how to fail…and not give up. To persist.

When I say that the book took fifteen years to come to full fruition, what I really mean is that *I* did. I needed to live fifteen more years of life and all the experiences it brought me, on a craft level and on a mental and emotional level, to be able to write it.

None of those years nor all that effort was wasted. In many ways this was the book that taught me how to write a novel, and taught me what it takes to have a successful writing career.

But even more important, it's the story that helped me understand what success was to me.

Let's face it: Taking fifteen years to fully hone a story just isn't that efficient, especially in a publishing market that often touts the book-or-more-a-year pace that some authors feel they must achieve. If my main goal were to attain that increasingly common view of what it takes to be a working author, then I failed spectacularly.

But that's *not* my main goal. As agonizing as it sometimes was to struggle to develop this story, it was one I felt a strong pull to tell. And I allowed myself the freedom and space to do that, despite that it didn't necessarily serve the business model that's often held up to authors as what creates a successful writing career.

The fact that I couldn't seem to leave this one in a drawer and move on to the next more marketable or expedient project taught me what matters to *me* as a writer. It was the work itself—the writing, the story, the craft—that I loved. While I obviously would have loved for it to have been a major bestseller (it was not), the pride and gratification I felt in finally getting it on the page the way I wanted to after all those years and all that effort felt like reward enough. I already had the experiences in writing it that made it meaningful to me. Everything else was gravy.

Your writing and the stories you want to tell mean every bit as much to you. So honor them by taking the time you need to make them everything you imagine them being. Some stories spring onto the page nearly reader-ready; others take more work. Every manuscript is different, even for the same author. Don't judge yourself if you realize a story doesn't come together after you've finished your first draft—or your second, or your seventh. Each one takes what it takes.

Remember the core reason you do this, your "why": because you love writing, love story (whether fiction or nonfiction or poetry), or because you want to affect readers, or shed light on our reality, or change the world. These aren't small goals. They may take time.

Trust the process—and if you can, *enjoy* the process. As hard as writing and editing and revision can be, the process is also gloriously creative. You can uncover depths you haven't fully mined, in both your story and yourself; find better, clearer, more elegant ways to convey your vision on the page. That makes the worlds and characters and stories you weave even *more* of what you set out to accomplish in the first place. But you might not discover those layers if you don't let your stories germinate and grow.

All those external goals will still be there when you're ready. Agents aren't going to stop seeking out manuscripts that speak to them, publishers won't stop publishing great stories, readers will always pick up a good book.

Taking the time your process demands allows you to give it to them—not when *you* may be ready, but when the story is.

Trust Your Creativity— Even When You Aren't Creating

A wonderful local program called Neighbor Woods encourages Austinites to register to receive free saplings from the organization in the interest of sustainability and helping combat climate change. Last spring they brought me four lovely baby trees, among them a pomegranate.

The pomegranate embraced life in my yard. A slow-growing tree, nonetheless it seemed to immediately spread its roots and its branches; it filled out, greened up, and I excitedly awaited my first harvest of its fruit.

And then a few months later its leaves began fading, then yellowing. They thinned out. My tree was failing.

I watered more frequently, and fertilized it. I did the things I thought I knew how to do to encourage growth.

Finally, when I did some research to diagnose the problem, I learned that pomegranates are deciduous. They naturally yellow and drop leaves preparing for the winter and then leaf out beautifully again in the spring.

I mistook a natural fallow cycle for ailing that needed attention. And with the best of intentions I gave my tree all the things it didn't need: too much water, unnecessary fertilizer. I jeopardized its health by trying to force it to grow during a normal cycle of rest and retreat.

Sometimes as writers, we can feel a little like my pomegranate.

The good times, when the Muse is dancing across our keyboard, and our careers and creativity are flourishing like my tree, can be exhilarating.

The bad times can be…less so. When new ideas don't seem to be coming as fast as they were or you have trouble focusing, when your productivity has stalled, when you find it harder to get to your WIP and create—or even to make yourself want to—you may start flogging yourself for the slack.

You may worry you've lost your mojo.

It's easy to panic when your creative force seems to desert you, but like so many things in life, creativity is cyclical. Things that require great energy and effort to grow also need time to incubate.

You can't keep dipping from a well that needs time to replenish.

As with my pomegranate, when our creativity is in a dormant stage we can inadvertently do more damage in trying to force it out of its natural resting cycle. We may push ourselves to meet our daily word count, grimly sit down at the desk every day, drive ourselves to get words on the page no matter whether or not we have anything to say at the moment. So many of us feel guilty every moment we are not actively working on our craft.

But lying fallow is part of the process.

Creativity is about creating, but writing is only one element of it. So much of our creative work is built on observing, processing, thinking, understanding...paying attention. Authors can feed our creative energies even when we aren't writing by analyzing the books we read, movies and television shows we watch, the music we listen to; by reading and learning about psychology and sociology and history and anthropology and current events. We deepen and expand our creative resources by watching other people and their dynamics, by noticing our own feelings, reactions, thoughts...and what provokes them. That's how we learn how to put those experiences on the page to affect our own readers.

Sometimes not only is that enough, but it's the essential work of being an artist, a writer. You can't create unless you fill the well. You can't leaf out again until you go dormant now and then and gather your nutrients and energy.

As with me and the pomegranate, when our creativity seems to falter, we must realize that what we're experiencing and feeling isn't death—of my tree, or of our creative spark—but recharging. We have to trust that our life force and our creative spirit will never desert us. They may just need to lie fallow for a bit.

Once I calmed myself down about my tree and realized it was simply in a natural life cycle, I was able to relax and enjoy the beautiful yellow of its leaves when they caught the sunlight in a way that the opaque green leaves did not, and lit it up like a golden nimbus in my backyard. I can notice it looking like a bare stick in the lawn each fall and winter without panic, knowing it's gathering its resources to flourish again in the spring.

We can give ourselves permission to do the same—to spend time baking or decluttering or catching up on sidelined chores while our little buds gather their energy to bloom. To walk in nature, have conversations, laugh, binge-watch movies and shows and books. All without guilt or worry that our creativity and drive have deserted us.

The measure of ourselves as artists doesn't lie in how much creative work we churn out. It's about the entire process—work periods and fallow periods, times when we bear fruit and times when we go to ground to shore up our energies for the next growth spurt. Give yourself whatever time you may need to go dormant for a while...trusting that when the time comes, your creative energy will always return.

When You Fear the Muse Has Gone

I'm writing this amid a period of great turbulence in our world, as disheartening a time as many of us have ever known. Fear and polarization are driving wedges between people; attacks on civil and human rights have been on the rise; a pandemic changed our lives in an instant; political unrest seems to be sweeping through nations; wars rage in multiple parts of the globe, and many of us live in a perpetual state of anxiety.

I'm not going to recap the many offenses of this decade. You all know them as painfully vividly as I do. And I'm not going to review all the good things that also came out of the bad—I hope you know many of those things too from your own lives: the goodness people show, the resilience and adaptability, the progress we continue to make despite the challenges, the way hardship can still bring us together.

What I want to do instead is to congratulate you.

In a period in history as fraught with reasons not to write as any I've seen in my lifetime, an era that in so many ways makes it harder to focus on the creative spirit, a time that invites us all to curl into a ball and give up—on everything—you haven't. Even if you aren't writing, you haven't given up—and I know that because you're reading this. Because you care enough about your creative impulse to keep a hand in the game, so to speak.

Maybe there are times you try writing and just can't connect to your story when life is so much more fraught and fantastical than anything you can come up with. Maybe you do manage to write, and then judge it as terrible, put the manuscript down, step away. Maybe you've felt battered by the ups and downs of a writing career—or the world, or life—and wondered if you have it in you to keep going. Maybe sometimes, in your blackest moments, you've felt hopeless or like a failure, thought about giving up.

But you're here.

So much writing advice tells you to write every day without fail, or on a regular schedule that's inviolate. We're told that writing is a wonderful and terrible passion and privilege and we must honor it by doing it no matter what—that we must, as the quote goes, sit down, open our veins, and bleed. That we must never, ever give up, even when we're absolutely tapped out and writing is a miserable chore, because by God, WE HAVE A CALLING.

Frankly all that sounds pretty brutal and oppressive to me—and it couldn't make me want to create *less*.

Maybe even just keeping things together feels like all you can handle at the moment. Maybe whatever you're dealing with in your life or psyche or our ever-volatile new world order is sucking every shred of creative mojo from you. Maybe all you manage to do in this time of unrest is sit on the sofa and read, or listen to the *Hamilton* soundtrack over and over and over, or binge-watch every single bit of programming Netflix shovels in front of you.

And you know what? You're still a writer. You're taking in other people's stories, filling the well, learning the craft. That's a crucial part of growing as a writer.

And if some days you feel like you may never go back to writing...that's okay too. If that's what you're feeling right now, then honor that. Maybe that will change and maybe it won't, but either way it makes you no less worthy a person, no less a creative soul. I haven't written a drop of fiction since that last novel published. My goals and priorities shifted, and writing fiction just isn't where my heart lies anymore. But I'm having a ball with my editing work; creating and giving presentations and workshops and keynote speeches for writers' groups and organizations; writing articles on writing craft and life for my blog and writers' sites and publications—and this book.

I've baked enough cookies and sweet treats to open a commercial kitchen, and tickled myself silly delivering "cookie bombs" to friends' and family's doorsteps. Taken up pickleball with my husband. Learned hip-hop dance and krav maga. Started a regular strength-training program I can't believe, five years later, I'm still faithfully dedicated to. Those have been my creative outlets, and honestly they've done more to salve my psyche than any amount of gritting my teeth and pounding out novels. I'm *living*, whether or not I'm writing.

During the pandemic I read author and editor Kathryn Magendie's courageous, honest, self-affirming post about her creative well running dry in the Writer Unboxed blog,[17] and it spoke to my soul. Some of the comments fell along the lines of the oft-repeated exhortations I mention above—"Don't give up! Keep writing!" But I was blown away by Magendie's honesty and the way she honored her *self*—not her writing or her career, but her *person*—by listening to the impulse that kept her away from her keyboard and let her experience something like this:

> **Oh, the freedom just to walk around as My-Self and not as Novelist. I tasted and explored and did stupid as hell crap and did smart as not-hell crap; I lived the life I normally gave to my characters. I busted out all over and**

created chaos and memories and that will enrich my writing if I'd sit down and actually do any.

Doesn't that sound life-affirming and marvelous? Doesn't the person who experienced those things sound like someone who will have so much rich life experience to funnel into her creative pursuits, if and when she decides to pursue them? Doesn't it sound unfettered and open and joyful? Stepping away from writing isn't a betrayal of yourself and your art. It's the exact opposite—it honors both. When you're out of juice you have to recharge.

So here's to you, my friends. Whether you're writing right now or not, whether you're proud of your creative output or not, you're coping and surviving. You love and cry and laugh, worry and celebrate and rage...and you *live*. You're simply living your life.

And that's enough. It's always enough.

Part Three

ROADBLOCKS

Chapter Twelve

When the Demons Come for You (And They Will)

When you love what you do, when you have a genuine passion for it as so many creatives do, it feels like a privilege to get to do it. I always joke that my worst day at work is still a pretty good day.

But here's the flip side: When you love what you do and you have genuine passion for it, and suddenly you are not only struggling to do it but wondering whether what you're doing is effective or good, it can pull the rug out from under your whole identity.

Writing is a career where there can be so many outside forces between you and your goals: work or home commitments that may keep us from our writing time; the agents or publishers who stand at the gates of career "success"; the booksellers or reviewers we need to help us reach readers.

But often the most formidable foe of our writing lies within ourselves.

I like to refer to these internal antagonists as the demons, those destructive little buggers who live within many of us and periodically marshal their forces for a concerted attack on our productivity, confidence, and self-image—insidious internal voices that instill us with self-doubt.

Everyone's demons are different, but what they have in common is that they like to party, and sometimes they come out of their cave to play. And by play I mean tromp all over your confidence, your motivation, your self-image, your productivity, and your state of mind.

And they want you to stop everything you're doing and party *with* them, so they do their best to make it hard for you to focus on anything but their shenanigans.

I used to think I was alone in all too frequently entertaining a cadre of marauding demons…until at a writers' event I led some years ago, where each evening we held group discussions about a variety of writing-related topics, one night more than forty attendees showed up eager to talk about their demons—a subject brought up literally by popular demand.

It turns out most of us seem to suffer from some sort of demons that can derail our confidence and creativity.

What Are These Demons?

Personal demons aren't confined to our creative efforts. They may assail us in the workplace as we doubt our ability or efficacy, or at home, as we worry we're failing as a parent or partner, or in the mirror, as we compare ourselves to the artificial standards held up by models and celebrities and social media.

But they seem to be especially rampant among creatives.

- Recently an author whose debut novel has won a dozen awards posted about self-doubt and feelings of comparison with other authors' careers as he works on his second novel.

- Another author I worked with, whose last book remained in the rarefied air at the top of the Amazon charts for many weeks after its release, garnering thousands of reviews and a 4.5 rating, castigated herself during the editing process on her follow-up novel for the amount of revisions the story entailed—wondering why she didn't "know better" by now.
- An author who has had more than half a dozen well-received and popular published novels lost his publisher and worried that no other pub house would ever want to publish him.

These are demons I've witnessed among highly accomplished authors considered successful by most metrics. For authors who haven't yet achieved certain career milestones the demons can grow even louder and more aggressive: "What makes you think you can write?" "You'll never finish/get an agent/get published." "You don't have what it takes."

And worse. Horrible personal judgments and attacks we'd never dream of saying to someone we cared about—or even to a stranger. Yet we batter ourselves from the inside with such negative, hurtful, destructive messages—we who should always be our own greatest champion, the one person we can count on for support no matter what.

My army of demons may look different from yours, but they tend to sort themselves into some standard regiments: Comparison. Competition. Procrastination. Perfectionism. Impostor syndrome. Fear of failure. Fear of success. You may have a few different corps in your psyche, but most of them operate from the same tactical playbook: a sudden invasion that overwhelms your equanimity and confidence. They tend to have two things in common: At their root they all feature some version of "not good enough," and they keep us from fully stretching our wings to see what we can do and reveling in our own achievements.

Their frequent target is our creativity—and even when it isn't, that's often one of the first casualties of the skirmish.

How the Demons Operate

In any business as subjective as art, a certain measure of periodic self-doubt is normal. In fact it's healthy to question what you think you know and to have a mindset that there is always more you can learn. Stumbles, struggles, and even failure are part of that process.

But often when we're in company with the demons they can infect us with a poisonous, erroneous mindset I call "globalization and eternalization": Everything sucks and it will always suck. Meaning that it's easy to forget that these low moments are a common part of the creative process—and, in fact, of life—and instead to believe that things have somehow taken a turn for the catastrophic and there's just no changing it, now or ever.

This, as you might imagine, does not make the creative process that writers may already be struggling with any easier. And it does not make us any more likely to succeed.

But the work must be done. We have personal and professional goals. We may have responsibilities like contracts and deadlines. We may fear losing ground with what we've already accomplished.

I have danced with the demons many times. We've had rendezvous and roundelays aplenty when I have felt myself falling into old unhealthy mental patterns, and each time it undercuts my confidence and presents challenges with my work.

"Leave me alone," I try to tell the demons at these times. "I have things to do."

"I don't think so," say the demons, chortling and cavorting and yanking me by the hands.

And then there we are, in a standoff.

Wrangling the Demons While the Party Is Going On

Here's the challenge at times like this: *Rationally* we may know we have all the tools we need to handle not only the demons, but our work. *Rationally* we know that we have done it before and evidence likely shows we've done a decent job more times than not. *Rationally* we know that that is enough.

But it's so hard to be rational when the demons are filling you full of smack because they think it makes you way more fun to party with.

Another fun thing this party often entails is attacking ourselves for it happening at all. A better person, a more confident, competent, fill-in-the-blank person would never let those goofballs run wild in the first place. It's beating ourselves up for beating ourselves up, and the demons love this because now they know they've got us where they want us: doubting ourselves and doing a lot of their work for them.

And now the party is in full swing.

In the middle of all this, when your defenses are already down, how do you put a stop to the demon festivities before the little bastards burn the house down?

STEP ONE: REMOVE THE AUDIENCE

The first step is to turn the volume down on this shindig to give ourselves some space to think. In the middle of an acute attack, the most important thing to do is to stop it immediately. The longer you let those automatic erroneous messages play on in your head, the more they gain steam and the more destruction they can do.

We need to stop that, and that usually means, just as with a truculent toddler throwing a tantrum, simply leaving the room.

Don't wrangle the demons or try to reason them away. It's almost impossible to do that in the middle of the chaos anyway. Just ignore or distance yourself from those voices in whatever way you can. Do not entertain their messages for one second.

For me that means finding things that distract me from the demon bash in my head. That might be an evening out with girlfriends. A walk with my dogs in nature. Doing some absorbing activity or task that I enjoy, like cooking or painting. Watching a favorite TV show with my husband.

Call a positive, supportive friend or loved one who always makes you laugh. Go see a movie. Get lost in a hard run or workout. Take a bath and bury yourself in a great book. Do whatever you can do to quiet that noise in your head.

Ignoring the demons doesn't make them go away. They're still partying back at the house when I get back. The reason they came out in the first place was that they weren't feeling very attended to, so now attention must be paid.

But I can't do that effectively until I can calm myself down enough to be a centered, calm, mature leader, the adult in the room.

Even if you can't step away from your creative efforts completely for whatever reason, find ways to take some of the pressure off. For me that usually means I need to *do* a little bit less, ask a bit less of myself.

One of my demons, perhaps the clan leader of the demons, is perfectionism, and he loves to tell me that if I'm not doing it all and doing it perfectly, I'm failing.

So the best way to prove him wrong is just to stop: stop taking on projects, no matter how fun they may sound, and stop trying to be an infallible or completely comprehensive editor or teacher.

Recently I turned down an opportunity I very much want to do, but I reminded myself I don't have to do it right at this moment. There will be other times. *Phew.* Already that makes things a little quieter in here and I can think.

STEP TWO: IDENTIFY THE ATTACKER

You can't engage them if you can't see them or pretend they aren't there (as is my usual wont).

And you can't deal with them until you understand what you're dealing with—identifying which particular demon (or demons, if they're partying in a group) has popped its head into your psyche at the moment.

Chances are excellent that your demons are often the same select few: Mine tend to be impostor syndrome, perfectionism, and comparison. Think about the commonalities in your recurring bouts of self-doubt and see if you can put a name to yours.

I'll be fully honest here (and probably reveal way more about my own psyche than you wanted to know), but I kind of mentally talk to mine: "I see you, Perfectionism Demon (or Comparison Demon, or Fred, however you like to think of yours). You're not so stealthy."

For me this serves a few purposes beyond just identifying them:

- **It lets me begin to separate from these thoughts.** They are not "me" and they aren't the truth. They're these external little demon-thoughts that periodically come out of their cave.
- **It starts to neuter their impact.** Talking to them like my dogs when they think they're getting away with something reminds me that the demons are just id-driven creatures with impulse-control issues, and I'm the rational adult.
- **It lets me start to reestablish healthy boundaries of who's in charge**, like when my dogs think I don't see them begging at the kitchen counter until I shoot them a hairy eyeball and they slink back to where they're supposed to be.

STEP THREE: ACCEPT THEM

This is a hard one, because everything within most of us says that if you're attacked, defend. But I've found—and cognitive psychology supports—that the harder I fight against these pervasive thoughts and feelings that undercut my confidence, the more ground they gain. I can deny all I want to that I'm not feeling like a fraud, say, but in the middle of a bout of impostor syndrome I'm not fooling any of the demons, and certainly not myself.

I may not *want* to feel that way, but I do, and accepting that is always, always an instant relief. I may be feeling inadequate or fearful or fill-in-the-blank, but at least I'm not wasting energy or denying reality by pretending I'm not.

I think we worry that if we lean into these feelings, we're opening the door to them. And we are—but trying to shut it is useless. The demons are already in the house. Slamming the door and locking it now just traps them in there with you.

STEP FOUR: ACCEPT THEM EVEN MORE

But accepting them has another component too—one that's even harder: Stop seeing them as the enemy.

Despite the fact that they come pillaging through your equilibrium and they may *feel* like attacking forces, they're not.

They think they're trying to help you. They're just too immature to understand how to do that.

Our personal demons don't spring up out of nowhere. They are born somewhere in our past (usually childhood, like everything terrifying) as responses to something that scared us, or hurt us, or shamed us, etc.

In our limited childhood understanding at the time, when we tried to make sense of the world with each new data point of experience, we formed a belief about that experience that may not have been based on rational thought. We put the pieces together wrong. (I mean, kids patented the "If I close my eyes I'm invisible" fallacious corollary.)

For example, if you were a star student but flunked out of the elementary school spelling bee on a relatively easy word like "analyze" (as may or may not have happened to me. But it did), you may have decided you must not be as smart as everyone thinks you are...or that a single mistake undermines every other success you might have had.

Hear that slap on the butt and two sharp cries? That's the sound of little baby demon twins being born, Impostor Syndrome Demon and Perfectionism Demon.

But they came into the world not to torment you, but to *protect* you.

"This hurt us!" they say in their reedy little demon voices. (Just let me keep anthropomorphizing and infantilizing them, okay? It helps me.) "In order for us never to feel this hurt again, we must never let anyone see how stupid we must be! We must never, ever make a mistake again!"

Poor silly little demons, misinterpreting the situation completely. You didn't know any better either, so it made sense to you at the time.

But the thing is, *you* grew up—the demons didn't. As a rational adult you understand that of course people make mistakes, and doing so isn't a measure of your intelligence or talent or skill or worth. It's how we learn.

But your demons stayed little hurt children inside you. So even now, when something hits on that same scary place that made you feel so bad last time—a danger, a failure, or sometimes even a success that threatens to reveal what they worry is the actual truth about you (and them)—out they swarm with their childish defense mechanisms to try to save you (and them) from feeling that hurt.

Your demons are coping devices—just ones that never evolved with your adult understanding of the world.

(Sound familiar...? Like your characters' "wound" and the misconceptions about life they form as a result that serve as obstacles in the way of their goals? Look what those demons are teaching you about writing and storytelling! Thanks, demons!)

Remembering that lets me stop treating them as hostile forces and futilely trying to beat them back. It reminds me that they are simply frightened children—the frightened-child part of me, in fact—who need comforting. They need to be reassured that there's a rational adult in the room—also me—who has everything under control and will protect them.

It lets me be kind to them—by which of course I mean kind to myself. And it even lets me love them a little for trying so hard, in their silly-immature-demon way, to protect me.

But it also lets me put my proverbial big-girl panties back on and take control—to corral those demons running all over my psyche like toddlers hopped up on Pixy Stix and gummy bears and patiently, rationally, nonjudgmentally soothe them till they relax.

I have to remember that they are part of me and they're out here partying because they were not feeling heard or were feeling threatened in the cave. Making enemies of them just keeps us in that standoff, so before they burn the house down we need to have a parley and I need to see what's going on with them and what it is they need. And by them I mean me.

"Okay, demons," I begin. "What is it."

The demons would like me to know that our upcoming webinar, let's say, had better be perfect, and we need to be high-energy and one hundred percent engaging, and it has to be the BEST ONE ANY AUTHOR EVER SAW or we will lose any good reputation we have for our work, as well as our entire career, and make a complete fool of ourselves.

I see that they are very scared of this. So I reassure them.

"No, demons," I gently explain. "All we have to do is offer something useful to at least some of the people who will be there. And we do that a lot—pretty much every time, in fact; remember all that great feedback we've had for previous presentations?"

They look skeptical, so I continue:

"Remember that we know this material pretty well based on all the experience we've had working on stories, and it's solid and well organized. That's enough. And it's okay if we're not feeling especially high-energy today—we can just show up where we are, and that's enough too."

The demons rustle, but I see that they're calming down. They aren't quite ready to settle completely and go back to their cave yet, but that's okay. I can do this presentation with them in the room as long as I just focus on the work itself and what I enjoy about doing it. Pretty soon I'll forget they're there.

They may be waiting when I'm through with it, of course, but that's okay too. We've all calmed down enough now that we can take it a little easier on ourselves so we can do what we need to do *well enough* to feel *good enough* about it. That's all we can ask of ourselves.

Eventually, when I'm ready, I can go back in for cleanup—with the demons' help, because it's also good for them to learn to take care of their own messes. And it's good for me to do it with them side by side, because after all, we're on the same team.

And don't be afraid to reach out to your support network and share some of these feelings and fears when the party is going on. While my demons often want me to believe that admitting all of this to anyone will only let everyone else see the terrible truth about us, Rational Adult Tiffany always feels a whole lot better sharing something genuine and real with people—an implicit message to those demons (and myself) that we're okay. We're human. And there's nothing wrong with us that needs hiding.

Coexisting with the Demons

The difficult truth is, your demons will likely never be vanquished or banished. They are part of you—yours forever.

As we get more and more adept at handling their little sorties, they may play quietly in their cave for more extended periods of time. Perhaps we'll look in on them now and then, say hello, see if they need anything, but when they're perfectly content in there, doing whatever it is demons do when they're not busy marauding through the psyche, we're unlikely to miss them, strong in our confidence and focus and feeling good.

But they must miss us, because periodically they swarm back out and the games begin again.

Our job as creatives, as rational adults, as human beings, is to overcome those negative messages our demons whisper in our ears at those times to free ourselves to achieve our full potential—not just as writers, but in all walks of our lives.

The trick is to learn to understand the demons, how to manage them, and ultimately how to coexist with them. That means finding the patterns, so you can better predict what's likely to bring the demons out to party.

Once you've quieted an active storm with the above tactics and are feeling solid and strong again, trace back what was happening in your life or your work at the time the demons attacked. I've learned that when things are going extremely well for my career, my impostor syndrome demons come swarming out of their cave to shoot me down. When I find myself stuck—for instance in creating a new workshop or course, writing an article for publication, or even in an edit—often it's the perfectionism or comparison demons gleefully holding me back.

Knowing the triggers allows you to get a handle on the demons before they run rampant over your psyche. Then you can reframe how you think of them, and how you approach them.

Remember the demons' messages are intended to keep you from feeling pain, but they've never matured past their childish misinterpretations of what caused it, and their delusions come from irrational fear.

Luckily you have become an adult. You can reassure those demons that all is well and you have things under control, just as you would with a child scared of monsters. This not only defuses their power, but it lets you even learn to love the demons a little, to be grateful to them for trying, in their limited understanding, to keep you safe.

And then hit them with a big dose of reality.

When I have impostor syndrome, for instance, I remind myself of my time and experience and track record in my career. I'm not putting anything over on anyone—I legitimately have this knowledge and am simply looking to share it.

When your demons tell you that maybe you don't have the chops to succeed, remind yourself of evidence to the contrary. Or that growth is a normal part of mastering any skill. Or that this is as mercurial a business as any on earth and rejection isn't necessarily a reflection of your or your work's merits. Reaffirm that success doesn't come from external definitions, but only from your own. That you aren't in competition with anyone else. And that you're a "real writer" because you write.

The most important thing to remember—over and over again—is that these automatic messages are false, simply maladaptations to emotional pain that have been allowed free rein for so long, they've convinced you that they are the truth about you.

They are not.

Take yourself seriously—as a person, as a writer, as an artist. You are all these things, and you have nothing to prove to anyone, even your demons.

Even yourself.

Chapter Thirteen

Impostor Syndrome

Did those words send a little worm of self-doubt turning in your belly? Did they bring up an uncomfortable rush of emotions, or slide a knife of uncertainty about your writing between your ribs?

At some time in our lives most of us, especially creatives, are likely to experience something like impostor syndrome—that feeling that we don't deserve or aren't qualified for whatever endeavor we're attempting or even succeeding at.

When I wrote and released my first book for authors, *Intuitive Editing*, it was the culmination of more than twenty-five years of experience working as an editor in the publishing industry. It became an Amazon bestseller in several categories almost right away, reviews were better than I dared to imagine, and it's continued to sell steadily in the years since. I still regularly receive emails and feedback from authors saying how much the book has helped them with their writing and revising. It's everything I could have hoped for from what was, for me, a passion project to share with writers what I'd learned over the course of my career about an often opaque process.

And yet not long after its release, I found myself beginning the insidious slide into self-doubt. As I began speaking and presenting much more—partly as a result of the book's success—I started wondering why I was bothering, what I thought I had to add to this crowded space of teaching craft, and just who I thought I was to set myself up as an expert.

This is after spending *my entire career* in this field working with major publishers on thousands of books, many by *NY Times, Wall Street Journal, Washington Post,* and *USA Today* bestsellers.

Impostor syndrome is not logical.

The Dunning-Kruger Effect (Or Author Despair Syndrome)

Think about what it felt like when you first started writing. Most of us were drawn to this field because of our deep love of story and a strong creative impulse, and our earliest writings were probably easy, fun, joyful expressions of our creativity. How awesome to make up people and stories and worlds in our head and be able to put them on the page. The ultimate game of make-believe, where readers get to play along.

But then maybe you send that piece of writing to someone, or you join a critique group, or you start submitting it, and suddenly you start getting feedback that your little baby isn't as perfect and delightful as you thought.

People start pointing out the shortcomings in it. Maybe your plot doesn't hold together, your characters aren't believable, there's nothing at stake. Maybe your story is all interiority and no action. Maybe it's clumsy in places, heavy-handed. Maybe you left out essential elements you didn't even know you needed, like suspense and tension or a cohesive throughline. Maybe you said the same thing over and over in fifteen ways, or strung together a series of entertaining little vignettes that don't add up to a story.

Suddenly this exact same piece of work that you felt so good about at first, that gave you so much confidence, now feels foundationally flawed. Inadequate. Your confidence sinks. You suck. You should quit writing. Whatever made you think you could do this? Everyone will see through you to the no-talent you actually are.

This is the Dunning-Kruger effect, a psychological phenomenon in which a person tends to *over*estimate their knowledge early in learning something new, and *under*estimate it as they gain more knowledge and skill.

Or as I like to think of it, Author Despair Syndrome (ADS).

Imagine a simple graph where the y-axis is confidence and the x-axis is knowledge. According to the Dunning-Kruger scale, initially people overestimate their knowledge of a topic and thus have higher confidence.

As their knowledge grows they understand the complexity of the subject much more deeply and realize how much they *don't* know. Their confidence decreases even as their knowledge increases.

It usually looks like this:

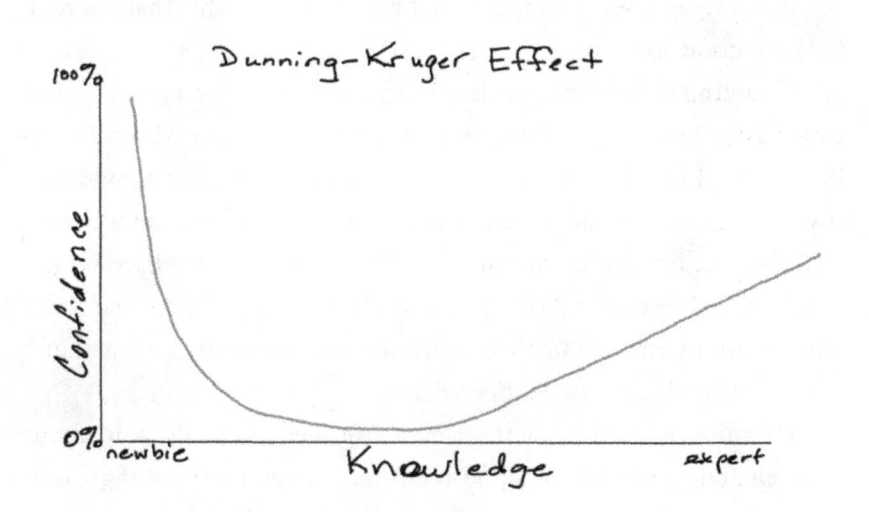

(Highly scientific image created by author)

The reality, though, is that at this point you know much more about writing than you did when you first sat down to pound out a yarn. You are undoubtedly a much better writer now than you were when you started, or five years ago, or five months ago, or even five days ago. The more you learn, the better you get. And yet the more you realize how much there is still to learn. You've moved along the x-axis of knowledge but dropped on the y-axis of confidence.

Otherwise known as impostor syndrome.

Learning about the Dunning-Kruger concept is unexpectedly comforting to me. It suggests that those times when we may begin to despair about our talent or skill or accomplishments are indicators of just how far we've progressed in those very areas.

It's easy for a fledgling writer to think they're going to be the next Hemingway when they have little conception of exactly how complex the skills they're trying to master really are. We've all seen versions of this in comically cocky query letter examples, or mentally rolled our eyes hearing newer writers espousing how they've written a modern masterpiece.

But it's when we genuinely start to get good at this that we may *feel* least good about it.

Knowing about the Dunning-Kruger effect can be a great way to counter Author Despair Syndrome. As the great editor Maxwell Perkins said, "If you get discouraged it is not a bad sign, but a good one. If you think you are not doing it well, you are thinking the way real novelists do. I never knew one who did not feel greatly discouraged at times, and some get desperate, and I have always found that to be a good symptom." I find that quote so spot-on and resonant that I closed my book *Intuitive Editing* with it.

Dunning-Kruger explains *why* those feelings of despair about yourself and your work are good symptoms. They are signs of growth and expansion in your knowledge and skill, exactly the opposite of the way we usually take them, which is as an indication of how much we suck.

They're actually showing you just how much you *don't*. In fact, you know so much now that you're able to see the shortcomings in your own work. And that's the best place from which to productively address them and make your work even better: the intersection of reality and humility.

And in the process, guess what? You're increasing your knowledge even more. So don't be surprised if your confidence dips again as a result: You know even more now about how much there is to know.

But maybe these dips in confidence, rather than big red flags to your psyche indicating that you are inadequate, are instead green all-clear flags signaling that you're on the right track—full speed ahead.

Notice that in the (highly scientific) rendering of the Dunning-Kruger scale, there's an uptick after what we shall call the Trough of Inadequacy. At some point after your confidence is initially shaken, you begin to regain it as your knowledge and skill in your subject deepen—notice that hopeful little upward curve on the right side of the graph. No matter how many times our faith in ourselves falters as we learn how much there still is to learn, we won't live in that Trough of Inadequacy forever.

Your confidence may never get back to the stratospheric levels of your naïve little baby author days…but it doesn't have to. Dunning-Kruger reminds us that the reason we have doubts about our abilities at all is because we're so much better and more experienced than we once were. We don't have to be infallible or expert to be legitimate.

Here's what I finally realized, as I battled those insidious little doubt demons telling me I had no business teaching what I knew to others: Impostor syndrome is not tied to whether you've "earned" the right to pursue whatever it is this malignant little misbelief wants to make you doubt.

That's how it misdirects you: It focuses on your achievements and holds them up against the entire historical spectrum of human accomplishment to batter you with just how insignificant your ability or knowledge or experience really is in order to distract you from the real truth of creative work: You don't have to earn your right to share what you know and think and have learned. You don't have to prove anything to anyone.

You—and your writing—don't have to be the be-all, end-all of creative achievement. Your story doesn't have to be the greatest thing ever written. It doesn't even have to be the greatest thing *you* have ever written. It just needs to be as good as you can make it at whatever stage of learning and development and skill you're in at the time. You don't have to be perfect to be good enough.

I had unwittingly subscribed to that false narrative—that I had to hold myself up against every other editor, every other writing teacher, every other book or class on craft, and earn my place in the pecking order. That I had to create the perfect, most comprehensive, universally helpful classes and workshops that every author who saw them found to be the best they'd ever seen, or I was a fraud.

I do not.

I'm not in competition with anyone—in any field. I have ideas I want to share, and I feel they're of value to others in my arena. They may not resonate with every single person, but they don't have to; chances are good that they'll resonate with *some* people. They don't have to completely and deeply address every single element of the topic, just offer some helpful insight into the subject. And they don't need to shake anyone's world—just offer useful information that I've gleaned over a long career working in the field I'm teaching in.

That's all—that's it, the simple little secret impostor syndrome doesn't want you to know. Like the monster under the bed, it's scary only until you take a look under there and see that it's just empty shadows, ephemeral as air, without substance.

The answer to impostor syndrome, as with any inner demon, is simply to refuse to accept its distorted perspective as fact. It's the bully who's all bluster till you face him down, when he folds like origami. Impostor syndrome wants to convince you that you aren't good enough, even when all evidence indicates that you are. It wants you to believe that if you aren't perfect and infallible you are a phony, even though that's an impossible standard.

Defang that monster under the bed by shining the flashlight right on it with a laser beam of reality. If impostor syndrome roars that you're a fraud as a writer, what's the evidence to the contrary? How long have you been writing? Have you written other stories or pieces you're proud of, or that others have told you they've enjoyed? Do you study and practice your craft, take it seriously, work to grow as a writer? Have you gotten positive feedback on your writing? Signed with an agent, been offered a publishing contract, sold some books? Clearly you are *not* a fraud—you are a writer, working at his craft, who has had successes with it in the past.

If impostor syndrome tries to make you believe you're a phony because you aren't as far along as you want to be or as others are, where are you accepting unrealistic standards? Are you mistakenly allowing that monster to convince you that you have to be perfect or "the best"? To make you believe that you have to be agented, or published, or traditionally published, or a bestseller, or any other artificial arbiter of "good enough" to be legit? Clearly you are not a phony, because that ridiculous monster is imposing standards that simply don't exist in determining whether you are in fact a writer. You're a writer because you write—full stop.

Making this realization a part of my psyche meant looking into *all* the places where I'd allowed impostor syndrome to dupe me into self-doubt, and one of those was with my own fiction writing.

For many years I kept my Phoebe Fox identity rigidly separate from my work as an editor. I told myself it was because while I love writing, editing is my priority and my soul (which is true), and that

I never wanted the authors I work with to feel they weren't my main focus.

But I finally admitted the rest of my reasons too, the darker ones I hid even from myself: I doubted myself as a writer. I worried that my books weren't as good as those I'm privileged to work on, or even that I might sacrifice some standing as an editor if I admitted I also have been in the trenches with every other author seeking representation or publication or sales or reviews. I was afraid I hadn't earned my place as an author the way I was generally confident I'd done as an editor.

I realized that defanging my monster under the bed meant bringing all aspects of myself out of the shadows and fully into the light. With my last novel (*The Way We Weren't*) I fully "outed" myself as Phoebe Fox, blending that identity with my identity as an editor and adding those books to my website.

When that book was released I felt excited and nervous and hopeful and anxious—all the things almost every author goes through in her career. I hoped readers liked it. I hoped it sold well.

But I didn't worry I'd reveal myself to be a fraud as a writer. Not anymore. My fiction was good enough to net me an agent, good enough to win a publishing contract with first a small press and then a major Big Five publishing house. Good enough to garner some positive reviews and reader reactions.

None of my books were bestsellers. They weren't the greatest stories anyone ever wrote. I doubt they changed anyone's life. But those metrics aren't what make me a writer. I'm a writer because I write. I stuck my flashlight under the bed and found out my monster was only in my head all along.

Now go write your stories, authors. You are already everything you need to be.

Chapter Fourteen

Perfectionism and the Fear of Failure

When my last novel was published, I sent out a newsletter post to my fiction subscribers sharing a bit about the writing of the book.

At seven a.m. on book-launch day my phone rang—my mom. (Hang on—this isn't going where you think it is.)

"Oh, honey, I wanted to call you as soon as I could. I don't know how to tell you this, but I didn't want you to hear it from anyone else."

(At this point I am understandably a bit panicked. Mom continues....)

"You have a duplicated word in today's newsletter." She goes on to explain where I did indeed double-type a word and hampered a sentence. "I'm so sorry—I knew you'd be mortified if someone pointed it out and you didn't know."

But here's the thing...I *wasn't* mortified. In fact I found the whole thing pretty funny—and was also strangely touched by my mom's well-meaning effort to save me from something that *she* felt would be embarrassing: a shortcoming in my professional efforts.

Now, I am an obsessive perfectionist from a long line of perfectionists, and I wrangle with those damn demons every day. But it broke my heart a bit to hear those family demons from my mom, to the point where a minor error like that might have indeed mortified her.

What "Failure" Actually Means

Are you squirming a bit in recognition here, authors? I have to confess that I've heard from writers many similar sentiments to the one I heard from my mom about their mistakes and oversights. Sometimes it's about typos or grammatical errors, more often about what they perceive as their "failures" and shortcomings in drafts and revisions during our work together.

Lately I've had an unusual number of conversations with authors along these lines: They've lost faith in themselves or their creative work, for whatever reason—they have yet to garner an agent, or to get published, or to be a bestseller, or even to finish a draft—and they're wondering if the universe is trying to tell them something. Whether it would be best to simply quit trying.

I suspect this collective loss of faith has something to do with our global frame of mind right now, amid the continuing reverberations of the worst pandemic we've known in our lifetimes, widespread geo- and sociopolitical unrest, the increasingly dangerous effects of climate change, extraordinary polarization, and more.

But I also believe it's part of the creative mindset, that area of our psyches so close to our tenderest, most naked selves.

When you learned to walk did you denigrate yourself and give up when it took time to get the hang of it? Or when you learned to tie your shoes or ride a bike or balance a checkbook? (Kids, these were little ledgers where we recorded our expenditures manually.)

In areas outside our vulnerable creative efforts, we generally understand that learning any new skill takes time, practice, and diligent effort as you master the needed abilities—more so the more difficult or complex the challenge you have set for yourself. If you set out to learn to play the violin, you no doubt accept that there will likely be a lot of frustration and failure before you can make music instead of caterwauling.

Writing is one of the most complex and nuanced undertakings I know, combining countless elements of craft, language ability, logistics, a deep understanding of human psychology, imagination, and more in a complicated balancing act, a marionette with infinite strings. Besides that intricacy, like any creative pursuit it's also one of the most subjective fields I know: Even if you master your craft, your work may not appeal to a particular "gatekeeper" guarding the portal to where you want to go.

Failure Is an Option

There's a wonderful quote often attributed to Thomas Edison: "I never once failed at making a light bulb. I just found out ninety-nine ways not to make one."

The actual quote is less meme-able: When asked if he was disappointed, after so many experiments with electricity, not to have gotten any results, Edison said, "Results! Why, man, I have gotten a lot of results! I know several thousand things that won't work."

I love the intention behind Edison's sentiment. It's so commonsensical and obvious, yet so often we regard our unsuccessful attempts on the road to finding successful ones as "failures." Yet this is the very definition of the scientific method, where you fail and fail and fail until you succeed. It's the failures that pave the way to your success.

Failure is not only an option—it has to be—but a requirement. It's a necessary step on the path. You will—and you should—fail more than you succeed, or else you're playing it too safe, not stretching yourself so you can grow beyond your current abilities.

Not long ago a young friend of mine decided—at age thirteen—to take up photography, after finding an old Kodak camera at a garage sale. He started taking pictures of *everything*, from rooms in his house to his family to nature images to endless photos of the neighborhood dogs. And a lot of them were…well, let's just say we were seeing a lot of pedestrian images like this, of my Great Pyrenees:

But one day he was snapping photos of our other dog and he got this, which I think looks like a feature photo for a magazine profile spread called "The Stars at Home":

Photos by Evan Wolfe

That doesn't mean that every single photo he took after this one was this well shot. This one is what my techie husband would call a data point, a milepost of progress my friend is making on his path toward learning the skills of photography and honing his talent at it. He's still taking so many pictures he's running through piles of batteries, and most of them are still unremarkable.

But little by little, more and more of them *are* remarkable.

They won't all be—that's just not the nature of creative work. Even with the professional photographers I've engaged for headshots over the years, many of the images aren't all that usable. Often it's because of me. They may not capture the exact moment I look my best, or that precise expression or demeanor that shows what I was hoping to convey.

And sometimes it's for technical reasons: They're a little out of focus, or the composition feels a bit off, the lighting not quite right. That's not a judgment on the photographer's skills—they're professionals who've been at their craft for years. It's that they're working in a subjective medium with endless variables, from the light to the shutter speed to the exposure to the living, breathing, changing, moving, mercurial subject matter.

Sound familiar?

As an author, with every story you create whole worlds; fashion cohesive, fully dimensional living beings from nothing more than the ether of your imagination; invent intricate courses of action for them to take, in the course of which they are fundamentally changed in some complex emotional/psychological way. There are countless subjective variables you must get just right, and falling short in any one of them has the potential to keep your story from succeeding—meaning getting your vision onto the page as effectively and impactfully as you can make it.

And then you must go back in and figure out what went wrong… and try something else to correct it. And if that doesn't work you must do it again. And again. And again. You may have to find ninety-nine ways *not* to tell this story before you light on the way that works.

That's what we in the business call "editing and revision." Also known as "the process." And it's not only normal, it's what writing *is*. It's what any creative pursuit is—or any pursuit at all.

Though society may teach us—and we may even believe—that there is some external definition of success and failure, that's an illusion. Like Edison, *we* define it. If we can come to accept failure without judgment as a natural part of the process, that's how we learn from it. We're able to objectively assess what went wrong and why, and then, in the words of Mark Watney in *The Martian*, we can "science the shit out of it" and figure out how to make it go right.

If failure is an option, then it does not lose its sting but it may lose its power to tamp down the very parts of us that can continue to try to achieve success. We can remind ourselves not to shut our creativity down by getting all in our head with judgment about ourselves or our abilities when something isn't working. That's just another data point for us to work with in discovering what will.

Our next efforts could still "fail," of course. We may still not have lit on the right structure for the book, or it may not flow as cohesively as it needs to. We may not have adequately developed our characters or plots, or established clear or strong enough stakes. We may not have gotten our vision on the page as effectively as we wanted to.

But that doesn't mean we've failed.

It just means we've learned one more data point of what *didn't* work for our intentions…and can try again to succeed at finding what *does*.

A Rational Antidote for Emotional Thinking

Can you imagine ever having this exchange with your child—or your spouse, best friend, or even a total stranger?

> "I'm afraid that I'll never be good enough, that I'm a failure."
> "You may be right. You should probably quit."

If you're like me—like most of us, I expect—you have a visceral recoil reaction to this precipitous, heartless stomping out of someone's internal flame.

And yet how often do we do this to ourselves as writers? We may fail once or twice—or even hundreds of times, with abandoned story drafts, negative feedback and reviews, rejection letters piling up into a towering monument to failure—and decide it means we don't have what it takes. Maybe we contemplate quitting altogether.

I'm not saying grit your teeth and persist in something that has lost its shine for you if your priorities or desires have shifted and writing is no longer giving you joy. But if your contemplation of throwing in the towel is a result of discouragement, frustration, loss of belief in yourself—which are all entirely natural cycles of the human psyche, never more so than in the areas closest to our hearts where our deepest passions lie—then allow me to share a method I've developed for dealing with these dark moments of the soul in a rational, effective, useful way that I adapted from the psychological field of cognitive behavioral therapy (CBT), digging down to the root of one's personal misbeliefs, to borrow a writing concept.

(Stick with me. This is more fun than it sounds.)

I walked a writer friend through this process recently when she was having a crisis of confidence, and here's what it looked like:

Despairing Writer: I need to just quit writing.
Me: Why do you think so?
DW: I haven't even been able to get an agent. I must suck as a writer.
Me: What if you do suck as a writer? What would that mean?
DW: It would mean I was a failure.
Me: What if you are a failure? What would that mean?
DW: It would mean I should stop writing.

Me: What would it mean if you stopped?
DW, laughing: I'd be miserable. I'm not going to stop.

I've talked about knowing your why, and in this (admittedly abridged) version of our "CBT-ing" her loss of faith in herself, my friend very quickly realized hers: She isn't writing to get an agent, or even to get published. She's writing because she loves it. Writing makes her happy, fulfills her, lets her relish the joy of creating that drives her. And all that before she ever gets an agent or a publisher or a broad readership or reviews.

She already has her brass ring. She's already achieving her most important goals and fulfillment in her writing career—and that, even she was forced to admit, means she's not a failure.

When these crises of confidence happen to you, it can be helpful to examine your premises. Not only was my friend misdefining her terms—"failure" not applying after all—but in rationally exploring her argument we very quickly poked a lot of holes in it.

"What's your evidence that you suck as a writer?" I asked her. "Has anyone said that to you about your writing?" No. Was there any time she had evidence of the opposite—that her writing has merit? Yes: She's won awards for her fiction; successfully worked as a journalist and magazine editor for many years; frequently hears compliments from coworkers, crit readers, and others about her writing; has had interest and encouragement from agents in the past. Again, she had no real basis in fact for her blanket statement of failure.

When the perfectionism and failure demons take you over, it's so easy to succumb to the little bastards. They're insidious, gaslighting you with hyperbole and lies. We're not rational in these moments.

But we can be. Take a deep breath and a step back and examine your premises through the cool lens of logic. Know your why. Remember that mastering the art and craft of writing—like any difficult, complex skill—is a process and takes time.

And keep the faith in yourself. If you're in a place where that feels too hard right now, I will keep it for you. I believe in you.

I want to tell you what I didn't tell my mom that morning she called me about my typo, and wish I had:

- Perfection doesn't exist, and the quest for it strips away our ability to enjoy our efforts to create the best we're capable of, handicaps our growth as artists and as people.
- When perfection is our standard, any mistake becomes more than simple human error as we stretch and grow our abilities; it becomes a value judgment on who we are, a public flag announcing our inadequacy, and a private flog to beat ourselves with it.
- It robs us of self-esteem, of our confidence, of righteous pride in our work and our worth, our learning and our growth.
- Perfection is a hungry demon whose belly will never be filled as he holds the bar higher, ever higher, always raising it just out of our reach and demanding that we keep jumping high enough to prove ourselves.

But here's the lesson I remind myself of day after day after day: You have nothing to prove. Not to that damned demon. Not to anyone—even yourself.

Perfectionism often lies in the insidious unconscious belief that we have to earn our place in the world, every single day, and we're only as good as our last achievement or accomplishment.

And every day, all the time, in every instance when this pervasive little demon (who may be with us always and with whom we must learn to coexist) comes out of his little demon cave to stomp on our psyche, we can remind him that we are not our achievements or the work we produce. We do not have to earn our ticket to ride. We *are* our ticket.

And mistakes, shortcomings, oversights, and even failures aren't indicative of our worth. In fact they're all part of our glorious growth—which isn't possible without them.

When that demon pops his little red head out of the cave, just remind him—and yourself—how marvelous it is that we continue to expand and evolve in our work…and gently send him back inside.

Chapter Fifteen

Comparison and Competition

You know better than to do it, even while you sit there doing it for hours on end: scrolling through social media feeds and marveling at the shiny lives and impressive accomplishments featured in post after post.

You want to be happy for other authors' success. You do. And of course you are. Mostly. But who can deny feeling a twinge at seeing someone else achieving what you desperately long to achieve?

A writer you know finally got an agent...a book deal...a glowing review in a major publication you'd *kill* to be in. An author you follow trumpets selling their hundred thousandth book...or giving a keynote at that high-profile conference that won't even invite you onto a panel...or the massive crowd at their book signing when you had *three* people show up for your last one!

Ugh, and there's Alex Writersuck, crowing about yet another stupid award his book won...fake-blushing over his 4.8 rating on Goodreads...writing some smug-ass article for that writer's magazine where he mentions his own book like *seven separate times*. And you *read* that book—it was terrible! In fact *Alex* is terrible, always lording it over other authors like he invented the Gutenberg press, throwing all that money into publicity campaigns and acting like he thinks he's the Bradley Cooper of the writing world.

And then seriously, are you *not* supposed to resent that?

This is envy, coveting what someone else has for yourself, or jealousy, begrudging their success and perhaps believing that you're more deserving of it than they are. It may be small comfort to wordsmiths to understand the difference and pinpoint which nuance of the green-eyed monster they're feeling when the end result is the same: that cold, slick stiletto in your belly of watching someone else get what you want.

These excruciating feelings arise from a couple of demon brethren who often keep company together, comparison and competition. Comparison is the act of holding yourself up against others to determine where you fall in the pecking order, a self-imposed stack-ranking where you gauge yourself in relation to other people. Competition is the belief that to attain a value you must beat out others who also want that thing.

These thoughts can decimate our self-confidence, destroy our faith in our writing, and make us cynical and guarded, dismissive or distrustful of other authors. That alienates us from the heart of our writing—the work itself—and keeps us focused on external barometers of success. It can shut us off from our writing community, the people who are most likely to support and help you in your journey.

Add in the follow-up act, which is beating ourselves up for feeling that way, and pretty soon these demons can do such a number on you, your work seems pointless, your chances of success nil, and you feel like a petty asshole.

I don't know you personally, but I don't believe you *are* a petty asshole, even if you succumb to the pitfalls of the competitive, comparative mindset as an author. But I do know it's probably hurting you, not helping you.

Why You're Not an Asshole

Let's start by relieving you of the burden of self-judgment you may be flogging yourself with for these perfectly understandable, common emotions: You're human and these are human feelings.

You're also conditioned by a world where from the moment we're born we're ranked by body weight and length, slotted into percentiles all through childhood, taught to evaluate ourselves in context of others all our lives through contests and grading curves and sports, swipeable dating sites and stack-ranked work reviews and actuarial tables.

In its most destructive form, that mindset can lead to things like our current dysfunctional political environment, where winning can seem far more about beating your opponent than running on a platform to genuinely help the community you want to govern. It's what leads to religious wars—brutal contests of whose god is "best"—and pretty much all wars for that matter, attempts to seize or destroy whoever has what others think should be theirs.

Competition and comparison hurt you as a writer when they take the focus off of the actual work you're doing and how you can continue to improve your skills, and put it on getting whatever flag you have your sights sets on—product rather than process. They make your opinion of yourself and your work dependent on other people: If they're up, it means you must be down.

But writing and publishing aren't a competition against other writers. No one else's success detracts from yours or your chances of it. No editor or agent is sitting in their office going through the slush pile and carefully weighing one manuscript against another to decide which magical Chosen One they want to represent or publish. They want any and all stories that fit their tastes and needs. Readers will buy or borrow a book that looks good to them even if there are ten other books in their cart, even if they have hundreds of others on their shelves already.

When you download a song, or pick a piece of art, or for that matter choose a friend, are you weighing them against every other option out there and deciding whether they're the best one, or simply connecting with what resonates with you? And does that mean it's the *only* song or artwork or friend you want or will ever have?

Writing and publishing are not a zero-sum game. It's not a pie with limited slices. It's the pie *factory*, a Willy Wonka wonderland of unlimited options—and you're a baker. You couldn't possibly make enough pie to satiate the universal appetites for pie; nor could you satisfy every individual pie preference. You have to focus on making *your* pie, to the best of *your* ability, and seek out those who have a taste for exactly that kind of slice.

But let's be real for a hot second: Few of us will ever become so enlightened that seeing others get what we want engenders nothing in us but equanimity and rejoicing in their success. We're human—it's going to sting a little.

Yet like all demons, these two bros are in fact trying to help you, in their dumb little demon way, if you can learn to use these uncomfortable feelings productively, rather than letting them corrode your confidence.

How Comparison and Competition Help You

Comparing ourselves to others is a useful skill for human evolution, in both the big-picture and the individual sense.

On a societal level, it helps us avoid stagnation and continually expand our perspectives and our understanding, which allows us to thrive in the world. A culture or clan isolated from all others develops in a vacuum, failing to reap the benefits of other societies that may have developed new ideas, advances, technologies that can improve a people's health, economy, lifestyle, and well-being.

An author who develops in a vacuum has no barometer to hold their work up against, no insight or perspective on how to develop their storytelling and writing skills. They may fail to grow and improve because they aren't learning from authors who may be farther along the path in their skill and knowledge and ability.

It's when those healthy comparisons lead us to recognize areas of weakness in ourselves that they start to feel pretty unpleasant. Instead of using others' strengths as fuel to foster our own, we may attack ourselves for being inadequate and lose confidence, diminishing or abandoning our own efforts. Or we may denigrate or dismiss others' achievements or ability in order to make ourselves feel better—denying ourselves the opportunity to learn from them.

But these demons are trying to tell you something, if you can learn to listen past their screechy fears. They're helping you identify where you stand to improve in your own writing or career. And just as with handling any other of your personal cadre of demons, instead of wasting energy on self-castigation or resentment in a futile attempt to fight those uncomfortable feelings, try leaning deeper into them.

What exactly do these other authors do so well that it makes you feel inadequate about your own work? How do they do it? This is how you identify specific areas of weakness in your own storytelling or writing abilities and can start to address them.

It's one of so many reasons analyzing other authors' work is so instructive and useful. It lets you see how they're making their pie you find so irritatingly tasty and learn to incorporate some of those ingredients or techniques into your own pies so you make better pies. It doesn't mean copying anyone else's recipe, but picking and choosing from it what might make *your* recipe even better.

I'm going to admit to a dirty little secret: I sometimes get territorial and resentful of other publishing pros in "my space" of offering editing services and writing advice to authors. Is it possible that I occasionally might read some article or post by an industry expert and mentally heckle all the places I think they're wrong? Do I ever watch someone teach and just want to fling them aside like a wannabe alpha ape and take their place on that stage? Does it—just every little now and then—feel like drinking acid into my soul to see glowing testimonials about an editor on some author's social media posts or in gushing praise in their book's acknowledgments because it isn't ME?

Um...*maybe*...

I do not feel great about these reactions, friends. But I do know how to deal with them.

First is tolerating the discomfort: I have to face my feelings, as squirmy as that may make me, acknowledge and accept that they're there. Then I can handle them more rationally: Do I want to edit all the authors in the world? *YES, I DO*, the demons scream. *No, you don't*, my rational adult side whispers. I'm already commonly booked out six months or more in advance, with a teaching and speaking schedule that's often at the limit of what I'm able to accommodate. It's ludicrous to imagine I can possibly meet the vast demand for editors and educators.

Not only that, these experts do different things, have different approaches, work in different genres, have different experience and knowledge and skill, and are better fits for different authors. Do I think I can be all things to all writers? That's unrealistic and embarrassingly grandiose—and I can admit that with humility and humor, which takes out the sting of seeing these shortcomings in myself. I can remind myself (and I do!) that these are normal feelings everyone experiences from time to time and it doesn't make me a bad person. It helps me grow in self-awareness and be healthier.

And then I can see what these people are doing well to determine whether I might benefit from tweaking any of my own approaches or skills. I learn a lot from industry pros at the top of their game, like Jane Friedman, Donald Maass, Joanna Penn, Rachael Herron, Steven James, Michael Hauge, Joni B. Cole, Maddie Dawson, Lorin Oberweger, and so many others. Humility without self-judgment is what opens the door to my being able to do so: I don't know everything and I'm not good at everything—and that's okay. Recognizing that is the first step to learning more and improving my skills.

This kind of healthy comparison is also what leads to healthy competition, the kind that sparks you to work harder, reach deeper, stretch yourself rather than tear anyone else down or let their success define yours.

Realistically of course I know there is no competition for best presenter or best editor or best anything. We're all in that pie factory, and I don't expect anyone to only and always want to eat my pie. There are a lot of delicious pies out there, and most of us want to sample that variety (including me).

But seeing someone do extraordinarily well something that I'm striving to master ups my game. It makes me better, driven and inspired by seeing someone truly excellent and wanting to reach for those same heights.

Not long ago I sat in on a session at a writers' conference led by Ann Garvin, a successful author and a friend, as well as a renowned and accomplished teacher. And, folks, she *brought* it. From word one Ann had the sizable crowd eating out of her hilarious hand. Her material was excellent—well organized, well paced, insightful, and useful. It was a home run of a workshop.

I'd already had my first presentation of the weekend, which had gone just fine, and was gearing up for my second one later that afternoon. I had to follow *that* tour de force.

But rather than feeling deflated by Ann's star turn, I felt inspired by her; she set a high bar I wanted to clear as well. Her energy and humor energized my own. Her teaching style made me stretch a little further to convey my material in a clear, effective, and entertaining way. Her accessible, easy delivery reminded me to center myself in that same approach. I wound up feeling I'd had one of my best presentations as well—not in spite of Ann's rollicking success with hers, but partly *because* of it.

There was plenty of room for both of us to succeed, and in fact doing so benefited the authors in attendance and the entire conference: win-win-win. This is *good* competition, the kind that makes you better.

Competition Caveats

Like all wayward souls, your demons need clear boundaries, so in courting comparison and competitiveness to help you grow as a writer, keep a few guidelines in mind.

COMPARE APPLES TO APPLES

Studying with Pulitzer prize winners if you're just starting your writing career can indeed help you learn skills, but expecting yourself to be on that level or holding your work up against theirs is only going to be discouraging.

If you want to get better at a sport, you're not going to start by playing in the big leagues with the pros. They're so good they're just going to leave you in the dust, disheartened. But don't play Little League either. Sure, you'll win, but you're trouncing a bunch of kids just beginning to learn. Being the best in the group teaches you nothing.

Play with people who are close to where you are in skill level, but just a little bit farther along the path. We grow by surrounding ourselves with people who can push, teach, and inspire us to be better at whatever level we're at.

FORGE YOUR OWN PATH

I have two very different dogs. Alex (Alexander the Great Pyrenees) is, true to his breed, as laid-back a dog as has lived. He pretty much has one setting: giant lapdog. He's never so happy as when he's taking it easy and being loved by any human being on the planet, and he moves at a single speed: poky.

Our shepherd mix, Gavin, is wired a little differently. He loves only a handful of people, and he has limited use for anyone else. He can chill out for a period of time, but after a while he needs stimulation: a bone to chew, people to bark at, something to scavenge (and in his case that's anything—the dog practically has pica).

Gavin thrives on obedience training; he's eager to please and to learn new things. Alex will not be dictated to, and sits calmly in passive resistance until we come to our senses and just give him the treat.

We love them both desperately.

Neither dog is good or bad (although ask us during certain frustrating behaviors and we may offer another answer). They're just different, and we dog-parent them accordingly, Gavin learning lots of commands and getting brisk walks and athletic sessions of fetch, while Alex gets plenty of petting and brushing and nice, slow meanders through the neighborhood.

Hopefully most of us would take a similar approach with our pets, our children, our loved ones and friends: Accept them for who they are without judgment, and try to give each of them what lets them thrive as individuals. So why do we so often do the opposite with ourselves?

When you do associate with other writers who are more successful or better than you, let it be inspiration. Learn from them. But also realize that their path is not yours. What works for them may not work for you. What they have done to become successful may or may not be what you want to do. Their particular gifts may not be yours. We're all different, like Alex and Gavin, and that's not just okay—it's the natural order of things.

COMPARE THE WORK, NOT THE RESULTS

You will hear a lot of writing advice as an author: tips and tricks, how-tos, surefire systems, hacks, all designed—sometimes even guaranteed, if you follow their instructions—to get you whatever reward their creators promise: fast and easy drafts, publication, big bucks, a huge platform.

These aren't lies. In most cases the people sharing these insights with authors have indeed used these systems to succeed with their own writing careers. The problem is that they're often presented as the One True Path, satisfaction guaranteed for everyone as long as you do what they did.

But you already know, as a writer creating your unique career and as a lifelong human being yourself, the fallacy of logic this is based on: that everyone is the same. That's not true in any sense except that we share a genus and species and certain basic universal needs and desires. And it makes a lot of underlying assumptions about other people's abilities, resources, goals, values.

Even if an author could meticulously follow step by step what worked for another author, you may not have the exact same abilities and talents or resources or connections. Their techniques may not yield the same results for you. Or it might not be sustainable or satisfying for you—so Very Successful Author's foolproof, magical One True Path to creating a writing career may not get you where you want to go.

Don't judge yourself against someone else's *results*; gauge your progress against other people's *work*.

ACCEPT REALITY

Is there injustice in the world? Do some stories and authors get lucky breaks: the right query at the right time, the full marketing push of their publisher, major review coverage? Do some authors grease the wheels with contacts or connections or opportunities not available to every writer? Do some maddingly mediocre books get published and even become bestsellers?

Sure, they do. That's life. As much as we might like to live in a golden utopia where we all contentedly grow in our own patch of dirt under the same happy sun, the truth is that there *are* varying levels of skill and even talent; there are disparities in opportunity and access; and sometimes you *are* vying for a singular goal for which there can be only one winner—and the best person doesn't always win. As my college debate professor taught me like a brick to the face of my enduring naivete, no one ever said life was fair.

The myriad factors that play into success in this field are mostly out of an author's control—and them's just the breaks, friends. Control the things you can—your art, your work, your goals, how you run your career—and let go of the things you can't, which is pretty much everything else.

Sometimes—kind of painfully often in this business—we don't get the golden chalice. But if it was not you, it was never going to be you, even without your "competition." And if it were it would have been by default, absent better options. And are those really the terms on which you want to succeed?

KNOW WHEN COMPARISON AND COMPETITION DON'T BENEFIT YOU

As I drafted this book, this chapter kept sucking until I stopped thinking about trying to make it as good as advice on the same topic by other educators and thinkers I respect. It wasn't until I decided to just write it my way, from my frame of reference, and not worry whether I was hitting all the right notes as well as other people that it finally came out in a way I'm happy with, a way that felt true to *me*.

Holding yourself up against others can hamstring your writing when it smothers your creative freedom and voice. Learn to use these twin demons when they help you, but recognize when they work against you.

EMBRACE YOUR SUPPORT NETWORK

Other writers are not your competition but your community. They will support you, help you and your writing, create a network of connections that are likely to be instrumental to your writing career. Their success can help facilitate your own with the benefit of their knowledge or experience or contacts. A rising tide lifts all boats.

You build a ladder together. You may push someone up to reach one rung, and they reach back to help you up.

Sure, not everyone will. It's not a quid pro quo. But embrace your writing community with an open heart and a willing hand—and give more than you get. I have built a career out of trying to do exactly that, and it has redounded to my benefit tenfold.

PUT YOURSELF AT THE CENTER OF YOUR CAREER
So often we're busy measuring our lives and our success by the *lacks*: what we haven't accomplished yet, our goals that we feel we've fallen short of compared to everyone else. But what if we flip that around, look not at the empty space in our glass, but how much we've managed to fill it?

Scrolling through my own social media feed recently, I got a panoramic view of what I've done in the last few years: publishing several books, starting a blog that's grown my subscribers substantially, launching a successful teaching and speaking prong of my business that has exponentially expanded it.

I always think I lead a fairly ordinary life, but in the past few years I've done bungee fitness, ax throwing, self-defense classes, and hip-hop dancing. I met my goal of deadlifting my body weight; officiated three weddings; learned to cut my own hair and cobble my own shoes. I've traveled to New York and LA and Alaska and the Colorado mountains and Key West.

All of it scrolling past created an enviable retrospective—except there was nothing to envy because I had actually *lived* all those experiences.

Take time now and then to notice and appreciate what you've done, how far you've come. Realize that as impressive as your public-facing life may look to other people, you know the interstices: the mundane, the difficult, the disastrous. Remind yourself that's what other people's posts—and lives—are too.

Read some of your past writing and see what loveliness and truth you've managed to put on the page, now that you're not in the midst of judging it. Don't denigrate your older work if it's less polished than you write now. Look how far you've come! Look at how you've grown. Look at your persistence and dedication. Take a moment to respect and enjoy how you continue to learn and practice your craft, how you continue to hone your skills.

Other people can be a useful metric and goad for our progress, but *yours* is the most important yardstick for you.

Sometimes when I look through old pictures, I joke with my husband that if I'd known what I looked like back then I would have been walking around in pasties and a thong, instead of worrying about my appearance. He always offers the same reply: that in ten years I will look at pictures of myself now and have the same thought.

What current experiences, achievements, and enjoyments are you having that you won't fully appreciate until you revisit them ten years from now? What if we flipped the script and let ourselves enjoy them fully in the moment, as we're living them? What if we gave ourselves more credit, more kindness, more grace?

What if we celebrated every win, however big or small, as admirable and a key piece of what makes life worthwhile—not just other people's, but our own?

Chapter Sixteen

*If You Feel Like Sh*t, Sit with It*

Over lunch with a friend recently, I told her I was working with the idea of tolerating discomfort in my life. She literally shuddered. "I don't even like to think about that," she said.

I couldn't blame her—frankly I don't like discomfort one bit. Historically I'll do pretty much anything to avoid it: do more, shut down, give up, or most commonly, berate myself and then try to fix whatever is making me—or anyone else—uncomfortable. (My husband does not find this latter one of my more endearing traits.)

But I've also found historically that these behaviors don't always (or even often) seem to work as well as I think they should. If I'm having a bad writing day, for instance, coming down on myself for it and then trying to continue to work harder just digs me deeper into the pit, stresses me out more, and hamstrings the tender creative part of me that may need encouragement or gentleness or rest.

Or if I try to avoid discomfort and step away from my writing, then I tend to beat myself up for that too, which also does not create an environment conducive to creativity.

Discomfort, by its nature, is...well, uncomfortable. It's unpleasant. Sometimes it may feel flat-out painful and intolerable. And isn't our aversion to pain simply basic self-preservation? If you put your hand on a hot stove, the instinct to snatch it away protects you from melting your skin off.

But discomfort isn't the same as pain. It may be more a signal of something outside our comfort zone that might be an area where we need to stretch or grow.

The truth is that discomfort *is* tolerable. And often it's necessary—we all know what results from that which does not kill us.

"What makes us stronger" isn't always a result of our surmounting whatever issue is making us uncomfortable, though. Sometimes it's simply where we have to accept the human truth of living in a flawed world where much is random, much is outside our control, and things don't always go the way we want them to. Constantly fighting against it is often what causes a lot of unnecessary anxiety and demons: "I'm not doing enough." "It's not good enough." "*I'm* not good enough."

I'm having some discomfort right now as I write this. It's not coming out exactly the way I wanted it to, and I have a stacked to-do list pressing me to wrap it up and get it edited so I can move on to other commitments. Both these issues are frustrating and uncomfortable.

But there are also some realities to consider:

- I have a publishing deadline for this book, which means I have to deliver the completed manuscript by a fixed date. That means getting it done is a higher priority than getting it perfect. Perfectionism is one of my demons that usually results from my unwillingness to tolerate the discomfort of not getting something exactly right—an impossibility in an imperfect world.
- I keep a very full schedule, and at the moment I'm working on several other projects I've committed to: another publisher's

deadline for an edit; a couple of articles for writer's outlets; creating a new course and a keynote speech for two upcoming presentations. "I'm not doing enough" is another of the band of demons who live in the cave of my psyche, a result of my fighting the uncomfortable reality of time being finite when my ideas and goals may feel infinite.

- Some writing days are better than others; some days my mind is clearer and more focused in general, or more focused on a certain topic than another, and it's not productive to dedicate my efforts where my mind doesn't want to go. Sometimes the message you think you're conveying isn't what winds up coming across on the page, and you have to decide whether to fight that and push it where you think it should go or let the writing become what it wants to be instead. This hits squarely on my control demons (there are a *lot* of them in that cave), unwilling to accept the fact that creativity isn't a machine and doesn't operate flawlessly upon command. It's subjective, and it's variable and inconsistent.

Any of this hitting a chord? Here are some of the areas where authors may regularly feel discomfort:

- **Writing**: "It's bad, I'm stuck, I don't know where to go, I don't know what's wrong," or any of the countless ways writing can be difficult and frustrating and mercurial.
- **Querying/submitting**: "It's overwhelming." "I'm not good enough." "Why aren't they replying?" "Why are they rejecting me?" "Every other submission is much better than mine."
- **Critique/editing**: "I suck." "This story is garbage." "That person/editor doesn't know jack." "I will never master this craft."
- **Revising**: "It's too much." "I don't know where to start/how to fix the issues." "I'm making it worse." "I can't do it."

- **Publishing**: "My editor wants to change my story." "I hate the title they chose." "This cover is all wrong." "They aren't putting much marketing behind my book." "They hate my proposal/pages for my next book." "They aren't renewing my contract because they've lost faith in me/I'm not good enough/I'm a failure," and all the many aspects of publishing that are out of our control.
- **Marketing**: "I should be doing more." "I don't know how to talk about my book." "I'm terrible at social media." "Why did these people unsubscribe?" "I don't know how to do it." "Nothing is working." "I hate marketing."
- **Reviews**: "Why does this person hate it?" "This one-star review is tanking my rating." "They reviewed the shipping, not my book." "No one is reviewing me." "They completely missed the point of the story." "Maybe I actually suck?"
- **Life**: "I don't have enough time to write." "I'm not doing what I should be doing." "I shouldn't take time away from my family for writing." "I shouldn't neglect my writing because of other obligations."

If any of these quotes hit home, notice how each one results not from the problem itself, but from our thoughts about the problem. So much of our discomfort arises from our reaction to what is causing it, our resistance to the reality of it, our efforts to fight against it.

There's a parable I love about the second arrow. Here's the gist: A person is walking through the forest when a hunter's stray arrow pierces them. Damn skippy it causes a mess of discomfort—it hurts like a son of a bitch.

But if we react by wailing and moaning at the pain, by railing against the injustice of having been struck or the carelessness or poor aim of the hunter or how it has destroyed our plans and ruined our lives, or by berating ourselves for being so stupid as to be out walking during hunting season, that's the second arrow, a pain we cause ourselves beyond the pain of the original event, and one that may keep us from doing what needs to be done in the moment: pulling out the arrow and dealing with whatever problems it has caused us.

We can't keep ourselves from being struck by the errant arrows of life. But we can learn to accept that they happen, and free ourselves to take action where possible, and accept reality where it isn't.

We need to operate despite discomfort.

With my recent writing challenges, I did a combination of both that helped me move past the issues I've been having and reconnect with my creativity. First I let myself experience the discomfort of my ideas not feeling as if they were coming together the way I wanted them to, and that it felt frustrating and discouraging. I reminded myself that this is the process, quite often—and that in my editing work I often convey that truth to authors: "This feeling is normal, and it's no reflection on you, your talent or skill, or the worth of your writing." I accepted these realities I can't change.

Then I examined what was causing the discomfort and realized that part of it was coming from my worrying more about how my writing was coming across, rather than more organically figuring out what I want to say. I was writing from the outside in, rather than the other way around—focused more on product than process. That's a familiar demon from my cave, and I know how to deal with him. I let the discomfort serve as a yellow flag for an issue I needed to examine and I (hopefully) grew a little from it.

Compassion researcher Kristin Neff has a sort of mantra that sums this approach up for me: "This is a moment of suffering. Suffering is part of life. May I be kind to myself in this moment. May I give myself the compassion I need."

It reminds me, as the Serenity Prayer goes, to have grace with myself to accept what can't be changed, the courage to face and change what can, and the wisdom to know the difference.

Chapter Seventeen

Overcoming Procrastination

For all my writing about the challenges that may beset authors and waylay their creativity, it wasn't until I was nearing the finish line of this book that I realized I hadn't included procrastination as one of them—even as I drafted an entire section called Roadblocks.

But there's a reason for that, I realized as I started digging deeper into this common writer affliction (and it's not, for all you smarty-pants readers, that I'd been putting it off). It's because procrastination is a symptom and not a cause. We don't fail to write because we're suffering from procrastination—we procrastinate because something is discouraging us from moving forward in our writing.

Why We Procrastinate

The underlying reasons that make us put off doing something most writers would swear they passionately want to do are as varied and unique as every individual author, but they tend to fall into a few common categories:

THE DEMONS

You knew I would start with these little boogers, didn't you? They're not the root of *all* our evils, but Occam's razor says that when something's gone hinky, check the most obvious explanation first, and these mischievous little scamps are so often the source of our internal shenanigans.

Procrastination is one of the many clumsy weapons in our demons' arsenal for trying to convince us not to do the thing we want to do (or think we should be doing) so that we don't risk feeling something unpleasant that we don't want to feel. It's not the task itself we're avoiding—it's the attendant emotions.

Those are usually based in fear: that we aren't good enough (hey, there, perfectionism demon); that past successes were a fluke or we're a fraud (I see you, impostor syndrome); that we'll never be able to compete with other, better writers (comparison demon, what up, my man).

We may feel discouraged by lack of progress in our writing or in our writing careers, or by rejection, or by past or future failures, real or imagined.

If considering any of your demons hits an uncomfortable nerve as you dig down to what underlies your procrastination, you've probably diagnosed the problem—and that's the first step toward addressing it. Then you can pull out the tools you've developed for dealing with your particular demons:

- Be kind to yourself—always the first step. You're not bad or lazy for procrastinating; everyone does it. Berating yourself will only make things worse. Take a breath, take a break, and unclench.
- Acknowledge that the demons are there—you can't fight an invisible enemy—and identify which specific one(s) are manning the roadblocks to letting you get to work.
- Rationally counter the irrational thoughts the demons are

filling you with. You can find specifics on how to do that in every chapter in this section.
- Invite the demons to play. Those little guys take everything so *seriously*. If they're dead set on blocking the path you want to travel, see if you can convince them to cut loose and go off-roading with you. Lay some rubber on the shoulder and skid into the mud; bounce crazily over the rocks—hell, do a full *Thelma and Louise* over a cliff and see what it's like to fly. Have fun with whatever ridiculous stunts you want to try, knowing that there's always a safety net because no one ever has to see whatever weird writing results from it, and at least it gets you moving again.

YOU'RE DISTRACTED

You know you're doing it even while you're doing it: looking up this "one little fact" for your story and finding yourself lost in an internet rabbit hole; or checking email or social media "real quick"; or answering a call or text that you know good and well isn't urgent; or finding yourself online shopping for items you suddenly realize you have to order *this very minute*.

Here's the hard but simple truth about distractions: If you know you're a crack addict, don't keep hanging out at the crack den. Minimize temptation around your weaknesses.

That means if social media is your crack, block those sites during your writing time. If every time your phone makes a peep you jump like a trained rat (which is pretty much what you are—studies show we're trained to react to those notification sounds as surely as Pavlov's dogs were conditioned to drool at the sound of a bell), turn the damn thing off, or leave it in another room—or better yet, both. If you need help with willpower to keep yourself from compulsively web surfing or checking email, there are plenty of programs that will brick your computer from doing anything except word processing. Need to look up a word or an arcane detail about something in your story? Drop an "X" in the manuscript and keep going—you can research it later.

And be proactive about distractions: If you're worried something might become one, don't even get involved in it. All of us already have plenty of pulls on our attention that challenge our focus without seeking out more. Despite being a lifelong word nerd, I have yet to play a single game of Wordle because I hear too much about how addictive it is and I honestly don't have the time to spare for another distraction, even one that is self-limiting like Wordle. I intentionally have no TikTok account and I do not scroll through the videos, because I've seen too many friends spend chunks of time doing exactly that—time I do not wish to spare from higher-priority things I want to be doing.

That doesn't mean you have to live like a Luddite (or Woody Harrelson, eschewing even a cell phone). Just limit your writing distractions to time outside of your actual writing time. You can even use them as a reward: "If I hit my five hundred words today, then I can get online and buy that thing/check my email/scroll through Instagram/dive into that Wikihole," etc.

YOU'RE BORED, UNINSPIRED, OR STUCK

I don't know about you, but to me it feels pretty normal to not want to do something that's no fun to do.

Yes, writing can be hard, and revising even harder, but remember that essentially what we're doing is indulging our creativity and our imaginations. If you're avoiding writing because you're not enjoying that on some level—even when it's challenging, even when it's maddening—consider that something is wrong...and fix it.

Maybe your characters aren't fully developed, so they feel flat and dull, even to you. Maybe the stakes aren't high enough or you haven't established what they are or you've lost sight of them, so the story feels too quiet or trivial or pointless. Maybe you've created an episodic plot where there's no compelling throughline to entice you back into the story, and no momentum to carry you through. These are diagnosable and fixable problems. Figure out what's sucking the life from your story and your desire to write it, or keeping you stalled out or in neutral, and address it.

Maybe your story is dead-ended, or took a wrong turn, or has petered out or no longer speaks to you right now. Moving forward in your writing can be filled with these kinds of stops and starts. Back up, review the route, and figure out the way to get back on track. Or if you're feeling so stuck you just can't see your way out of the ditch, try setting aside this scene or even the story for a bit and work on something else to kick-start your motivation. Sometimes you have to not just change lanes, but get on a different highway to get moving again.

Once you can identify the specific issue in your manuscript that's bogging you down and making it feel like a slog, you'll clear the path forward.

YOU'RE UNMOTIVATED OR OVERWHELMED

These may seem like opposite problems, but they're just two ends of a continuum.

Not having clear goals, expectations, or deadlines can make it hard to tackle the project you're working on (or avoiding working on). Most of us need some kind of accountability to light a spark under our behinds.

Create that for yourself by imposing deadlines (with consequences!), or instigating rewards for various milestones, or finding an accountability buddy, like a writing partner or crit group. Make a public announcement about what you're working on or when you'll finish—nothing like setting expectations with others to inspire you to meet them.

On the other end of the spectrum can be too *much* pressure—a dauntingly large task ahead of you, a looming deadline, terrifyingly high expectations—that makes you rebel and shut down.

If the task in front of you feels discouragingly immense, try breaking it down into bites. Don't concentrate on reaching the top of the mountain, but on the single step right in front of you. One step at a time, you'll get there.

If the relentlessly ticking clock of a tight deadline is making you feel panicked or resentful or immobilized, reconnect with what motivates you internally, rather than feeling as if you're racing against an external finish line. Instead of flogging yourself with the stick of "should" or "must," find the carrot of "want." How will it feel if you meet your daily word count and stay on schedule, finish the manuscript, turn it in on time? What values does it buy you for your writing career: your agent's or editor's goodwill, your reputation for reliability, the release date you wanted, the freedom to move on to that other story that's been tickling your creative cockles, etc.?

If outsize expectations are freezing you up, address those feelings of fear or doubt and remind yourself to work inside out, not outside in—in other words, to focus on what motivates or rewards you about the process, which is within your control, rather than the product or how it's received, which is not.

Ask yourself, "What is important to me about this? Why did I want to do it in the first place?" If I'm creating a course for writers, for instance, and I start to feel hamstrung by the fact that it's due on a certain date and I haven't finished creating it yet, I remind myself to go back to my core impulses and drives. Why did I pitch this subject to this conference or writers' group? Usually it's because I've seen authors struggle with a particular problem and I want to clarify and simplify the issue, pick it apart so I can figure out why it challenges writers and formulate techniques so they can identify and address what may be hampering their writing. Reminding myself what nourishes or inspires me about what I'm doing restarts my engine.

When All Else Fails...

...accept the inevitable. There are times when none of these coping devices seem to work, and at that point you may have to simply grit your teeth and push through. It's often the least constructive and productive way to deal with procrastination, and it rarely results in our best work, but it gets the job done.

Find whatever tools or tricks help you plunge in and start writing: Create a routine and stick to it, even if all you do during your allotted writing time is free-write or journal or write the word "procrastinate" over and over. Set yourself up for success by working where and when you work best: If that's huddled over your computer in a coffeeshop in the afternoons when the kids are in school, do that. If it's early mornings or late nights before work or when your family is asleep, do that. Set a schedule you can keep, just as you would for any other commitment, and train yourself that you don't miss it except for bona fide disasters.

Commit that during your writing time, you *write*. Set a timer if it helps, as in the Pomodoro method, and don't get up from your writing until it goes off. Create some ridiculously low barrier to entry, like telling yourself you have to write only twenty-five words, or for two minutes, or a single paragraph. Sometimes just forcing yourself into action, no matter how much you may want to resist it, is enough to break past the roadblock of procrastination, and chances are once you've gotten started you'll keep going.

No matter how daunting or unnerving or uninspiring a task may feel, we inflict twice as much suffering on ourselves by building it up, stewing on it, dreading it, and putting it off. Remind yourself of the big picture: While our creativity may be limitless, our time on Earth is finite. Once you're mindful of the amount of time you have left to do all the things you want to do, you realize you need to do them.

We have this one marvelous, singular life (as far as we know) to explore the far reaches of our imagination, tell our stories and bring them to life, share our vision and our *selves* and leave our mark in this world. The more we procrastinate what we're working on, the greater the chance we won't get to everything we dream of doing. Let that be the spark that reignites your engine when you stall out along the journey.

Chapter Eighteen

"Writer's Block"—or Getting Unstuck from the Wall of WTF

Not long ago I was working on an article about POV in story... and it was not going well.

Point of view is one dense and slippery little sucker, and the topic just seemed overwhelming. How could I possibly condense anything useful about it into a twelve-hundred-word article? Every time I broke it down into a more manageable subtopic, out popped another Hydra head somewhere else.

I took three cracks at writing it, all of them meandering and unusable. I realized I clearly know nothing about point of view or anything at all about writing, in fact. I wondered why on earth I had represented myself as someone who did.

I was spiraling. I'd hit the Wall of WTF.

What Is the Wall of WTF?

I'm guessing I don't have to expand on what I mean for most authors to get it. The wall can take any number of common forms:

- "WTF, this makes no sense/is superficial/isn't new or fresh/[insert self-criticism here]."
- "WTF, I'm off-track."
- "WTF am I forgetting or leaving out?"
- "WTF, how will I ever finish?"
- "WTF am I even talking about?"
- "WTF does it matter anyway?"

The Wall of WTF is more commonly referred to as writer's block, a term I don't like because of its implications that it's some unavoidable affliction that visits paralysis upon authors and renders them helpless.

Our feelings that we can no longer write are an outer manifestation of some inner unrest or misconception that needs addressing. All these WTFs are the result of the self-doubt demons coming out to play. And every creative—every human—has their own personal cast of those.

Like the most demanding and irritating of home buyers, they like to let themselves into the house as it's being constructed and start trashing it before it's anywhere near finished: The closets aren't big enough. The hallways aren't wide enough. How will their living room furniture fit with the fireplace in that corner? It all looked so much better in the blueprints....

Like little hoodlums, they might start defacing the joint or knocking out support beams or stealing the copper pipes—they might even crack the foundation. Something like that can derail the whole construction if you don't get hold of those little vandals before they do damage.

Spiraling deeper into self-doubt and paralysis just digs a trench under your feet that makes the wall loom even higher. Instead, reach for the right tools and equipment to help you scale your own personal Wall of WTF.

Accept the Wall

Getting past the Wall of WTF starts with recognizing you've run headfirst into it and understanding that it's just a stage—a normal one in the process of creation.

That's the first line of attack. Take a deep breath and remind yourself that *this is normal*.

The drafting process is messy just as the construction process is messy. There's dust and dirt and scraps that result from the process and clutter up the site. There may be miscalculations that may not reveal themselves right away, but which have to be dealt with or they may affect the entire edifice. There are changes that may be made as the building goes from 2D to 3D and you see what it's like to move around in it.

This is how a house gets built. This is how anything creative gets built. It's normal for there to be chaos and mess before there is structure and order.

Step Away from the Wall

It feels like you should power through the "stuck" in those moments, but that usually just results in digging the hole deeper. Put the shovel down for a minute. You need some distance before you can start figuring out what's wrong and how to fix it or you might get buried under the chaos.

You have to stop the automatic thoughts paving the wall from continuing to feed on themselves. No matter how great the temptation to plow your way out of it, once you're in the spiral you can't. You have to get some space—some mental peace and some objective distance. When you're out of ammunition, you get out of the foxhole.

Go for a hike out in nature, breathing the air, focusing on your steps on the uneven ground, drinking in the cool green of the trees, the steady constancy of the rock formations, the dappled sunlight filtering through the canopy. Watch *The Great British Baking Show* or other comfort TV. Play with your pets, make a meal and eat with loved ones, take a nap. Whatever lets you step away from that intimidating wall.

Do *not* let yourself keep puzzling out whatever you're stuck on. Do *not* berate yourself—at all. Beating ourselves up for "letting ourselves down" only exacerbates the block. Would you treat a friend having writing problems that way?

Only once you've given yourself some space and some grace is it time to scope out the situation.

Assess and Address the Wall

You've recognized the problem: You butted right up into a wall where you wanted no wall to be and it's hindering the construction of your story. But you still have to determine the wall's composition and scope to figure out the best way to deal with it.

The most common causes of the Wall of WTF tend to lie in one of several main areas:

STORY ISSUES

The root cause may stem from problems with the story itself: You've lost sight of what's driving your characters forward, stakes aren't clear or have dropped, the plot has detoured into a dead end that stalls out story momentum, etc. Those are concrete craft problems that can be tackled directly with writing and editing techniques.

SITUATIONAL ISSUES

Writing—like any artistic expression—isn't an endeavor based solely on skill, knowledge, and technique. It's deeply influenced by the creator's own inner—and outer—state: their surroundings, circumstances, environment, situation, physical state, their state of mind.

Are you preoccupied by other things going on in your life: worries and concerns, responsibilities, pressures? Are there distractions preventing you from focusing fully: noise, poor lighting, the Internet or your cell phone or social media? Are you in an emotional state that needs attention before you can free your mental focus: upset, grieving, angry, excited, etc.? Are you tired, or uncomfortable, or overcaffeinated, or hungry? Have you been working too long and just need a break, time to rest and reset?

Do an internal check and see if you can pinpoint what situational factors may be waylaying your creativity, and once you've diagnosed potential issues, address them if possible. Your Wall of WTF may crumble once you've dealt with overtly pressing discomforts and concerns.

Of course, would that it were so easy to handle some of the more acute concerns of life. They don't always resolve neatly enough to free you to write unfettered. That's one of the reasons behind the writing rituals many authors have: lighting a candle when they sit down to write, meditating or a mantra before each writing session, retreating to a writing location that feels removed or sacrosanct from the tribulations of our lives. Find a method that allows you to close the door on all the many distractions every human navigates for however long you have chosen to dedicate to your regular writing: five minutes, an hour, more—whatever you've found works for you. Your concerns will still be there when you emerge, but unless something is metaphorically (or literally) on fire, it can wait. Practice letting yourself let go of those troubles for that little while to fully focus on your craft.

PSYCHOLOGICAL ISSUES

The openness and sensitivity required to truly, deeply pursue any art can sometimes come with a backlash: being especially vulnerable to misapprehensions, illusions, assumptions, and a whole host of complicated cognitive distortions that can derail our confidence and creativity.

We may compare ourselves to others ("Will it be good enough?" "Will I measure up?"); expect our writing and stories to be perfect; be haunted by the specter of failure; fear we are or will be revealed as a fraud; or a whole host of other doubts, fears, and insecurities—our demons.

INTENTION ISSUES

Sometimes when stories feel as if they're going off the rails, it's because the author has lost sight of their purpose and intention in writing it.

When I work with writers on their manuscripts, the first thing I do is ask them what story they want to tell. What made them want to write this story in the first place? What's the central nut of it that animates and inspires them? What main story intention did they want to share or convey or explore?

This serves as a guide for me as I'm working on editing their manuscript to help me help them actualize their vision on the page. But I also ask it to help clarify writers' own thinking on the heart of their story, because it's so easy to get lost in the forest of every other element that goes into creating an effective one. Defining and staying in touch with that central story intention can serve as a beacon, a light to guide you on your journey and get you to your destination.

It can help to write this intention down for each story you write, and keep it somewhere you can easily refer to it for those stuck moments. Don't trust that you'll remember it; concretely articulate it and commit it to writing.

Don't worry about making it sound good or marketable. This isn't your logline or pitch, and it may never even make it overtly onto the page. This is for you—your guiding light, your North Star. Say it any way you want to, as long as it encompasses that animating spark of inspiration that got you excited about the story in the first place and keeps you coming back to it. Say it in a way that reminds you what the most important kernel of your story is, the throughline that vitalizes it and makes it matter to you.

When you get lost in your WIP, when you lose steam, when you feel overwhelmed or discouraged, go back to that mission statement, that driving purpose that moved you to write the story. Read it, think about it, let it percolate and reinvigorate you.

And then go back clear-eyed and do what you set out to do in the first place.

As with the multiple factors that may cause any kind of crash, in diagnosing what ran you into your own Wall of WTF you may find that several of these areas are the culprits. Perhaps you're tired from a poor night's sleep after a fight with your partner that's still upsetting you, and constantly checking your phone to see if they've returned your text…while also wrestling with issues of character motivation in your story…and wondering all the while if you have the chops to write it at all.

Once you've identified whatever you determine the issues to be, start solving them one at a time.

With my own struggles with my POV article, the problem didn't lie with the subject (the "story") itself. I had a specific topic to tackle, a solid understanding of it, and a clear outline based on concepts I've worked through with thousands of manuscripts.

It wasn't situational either; I was rested and focused, working in my quiet office that I've deliberately designed to be conducive to the way I work best, and as I habitually do while I'm working, I had my internet browser closed and my phone in another room with the notifications turned off.

That left psychology and intention—and this was where I'd gone off the rails.

Psychology

In digging into what was freezing me up in the article, I realized that I was worrying about whether I was hitting every question and concern every author might have. Whether I was going into enough detail for the more experienced or trained authors while not losing newer authors. Whether I was covering every eventuality in enough depth.

The reason I kept locking up was because I wasn't writing what I know and wanted to write, but instead was trying to predict what others might want and what I should be writing, or how I should be writing it. I was so worried about the ultimate *effect* of what I'm working on that I lost touch with my own perspective and what I wanted to say, the impulse that motivated me to want to write about the topic in the first place. I kept approaching my writing from the outside in, rather than from the inside out, and as a result the writing felt dull and flat, and I wasn't having any fun doing it.

And my central tenet for my career (and frankly most of my life) is to *find the fun*. Not only does that create the intrinsic rewards of anything you do, but it frees you to do it from the most genuine and original place within you.

Intention

So I asked myself why this article mattered to me—why sharing any of my thoughts on craft does; why do I write at all? And the answer is always the same: I love sharing useful tools I've gleaned from my years as an editor to help authors bring their vision to the page. I love breaking down and simplifying what can often feel like confusing or opaque or overwhelming topics.

Reminding myself of what drives me shifted focus from the effect of my article to my intentions: How could I convey this topic in a way that made it clear and easily understandable? And that put me right back in touch with my purpose and my rational mind (not the irrational one overcome with doubts): This was information I have and wanted to share.

And I didn't have to offer the ultimate compendium of POV—just share some insight in the hopes that it might be useful to other authors. Nor did it matter what else has been written about point of view, or how well or comprehensively. My take is my take, and others may resonate with it and find it helpful too. As I heard a motivational speaker say once, I don't have to help everyone; I'd just like to help someone. It takes the pressure off.

Once I stopped worrying about how any of it would come across or be received and just focused on what I wanted to say about this particular topic, getting it down on the page was much more effective—and much more fun.

There Is Always a Way Past the Wall

No matter how high or wide your Wall of WTF, there are ways around, over, under, or through it if you persist—if you keep tackling the wall until you find it.

Remind yourself to have faith: in yourself, in your creativity, in your imagination and skill and vision and your ability to convey it. And even though there may sometimes be things you also *don't* yet know, or areas where you may struggle, have faith in your ability to learn them, to figure it out, even if it takes time.

Remind yourself to have faith that your story, your words, have value. Not all of it may resonate with every reader. Not all of it may be fresh and new to them. Not all of it is even fresh and new period; in story as in so many areas of creativity, there's nothing fully new under the sun. Every tale is as old as time; what makes that story an author's own is how they may interpret and shape and package all those universal constants that run through every story ever told into their own unique vision. Your singular perspective that may resonate with a certain reader at a certain moment and allow them to more deeply understand their world, their struggles.

You don't have to tell a story that changes someone's life in major ways. You don't have to write a story that appeals to everyone, hits every bestseller list, or gets nothing but five-star reviews.

The noblest purpose of story is to connect; whether that's with one person or one million people doesn't matter. Your job is simply to find a way to tell a story that is meaningful to you in as effective a way as you can, and find the people with whom it also connects in a meaningful way. That's all. And you are capable of doing that—as an artist, and as a human being who shares many of the wants and longings and drives and fears and experiences and needs of other human beings.

The most important faith to have in yourself at this stage is that no matter how difficult or dark the slog may seem when you're face-first against the Wall of WTF, eventually you're going to get to the other side. That you have—or can attain—the tools and the skill to do it.

And then, just as you have to get right back on when you tumble off a horse, sit down at the keyboard and come back to the work.

Don't Let the Wall Stop You

Legion are the stories that get stuck behind the Wall of WTF and never make it out. It may be because a writer has let the demons run rampant and failed to corral them. It may be because they hit a snarl in a story and give up too quickly, telling themselves it's not good enough, or not marketable, or not worth it. It may be because they've lost faith in their ability to make it through this stage, or they've forgotten that it happens to everyone and is a normal and regular part of the creative process.

But perhaps most often it's because battering against the wall over and over hammers away at a writer's confidence and determination.

At their persistence and spark and fire. And at some point, when all these WTF walls begin to spring up, it can feel easier to stop trying to surmount them and give up.

There's a difference between good quitting and bad quitting. When reevaluating your goals and priorities and where it's worth dedicating your energy and time leads you to let go of some things that are no longer serving you, that's good, positive, healthy quitting in order to redirect your efforts somewhere more fulfilling.

But bad quitting is when you walk away from something you still acutely want because it got harder than you expected, or took longer, or you believed the screaming demons who convinced you you'd never achieve it.

Some stories spring onto the page nearly reader-ready; others take more work. Every manuscript is different, even for the same author. Don't judge yourself if you realize a story doesn't come together after you've finished your first draft—or your second, or your twentieth. Each one takes what it takes.

Remember the reason you do this: because you love writing, love story (whether fiction or nonfiction), because it adds meaning and insight to your life. Maybe because you want to affect readers, or shed light on our reality, or change the world. These aren't small goals, friends. They may take time.

Trust the process—and if you can, *enjoy* the process. As hard as it can be, these struggles can yield some of the richest parts of your stories, uncovering depths you may not have fully excavated down to in earlier, easier drafts. You may find better, clearer, more thorough ways to convey your vision, saying more closely what you wanted to say, making it *more* of what you set out to accomplish in the first place.

Taking the time your process demands allows you to create the most powerful, effective, impactful writing you can—not when *you* may be ready, but when the story is.

I often say that the biggest secret of building and maintaining strong personal relationships is just showing up. I may not always say the perfect thing in a tough time, may not buy the perfect gift for an occasion, may not be able to be there day in and day out with distant friends and family.

But I show up in the lives of the people I care about, whether that's just through dropping a text or email to let someone know I'm thinking of them, sending a little gift for no reason, setting up a get-together or call, or flying into town for an important event. With the relationships that matter most to me, I make sure that I'm present in whatever way I'm able to be, over and over and over.

That also applies to your writing. So much of success is simply showing up at your computer, in the chair, with the manuscript you're working on. You may not always have a home-run writing session. You may not always have time to spend hours and hours working through thorny plot points or drafting or editing.

You may butt right up against a Wall of WTF and get stuck there for a while, like a Roomba in a corner. But successful writers show up, whatever that looks like, day after day—one minute, five minutes, five hours; it doesn't matter.

A lifetime of those little incremental show-ups for people creates the most meaningful relationships.

A lifetime of showing up for your writing creates stories—ones that you finish—and a writing career.

Part Four

FEEDBACK

Chapter Nineteen

Assessing Writing Feedback: Criticism, Commentary, and Critique

Imagine living in a world without mirrors. Even if you consider yourself the least vain and lowest-maintenance of people, how would you check that weird mole you felt on your back, or whether that sudden cold sensitivity in your mouth means you're getting a cavity, or realize you almost left the house with your fly down? Sometimes it's essential to have a reflection so that we can make accurate assessments.

We like to think of writing as an isolated effort, a one-person show, an auteur art form—and in many ways it is. Part of the challenge of this pursuit is that the main engine is ourselves. We are largely the ones who have to get motivated, come up with an idea, get it on the page, do the work of revision and polishing, get it out there, and get people to read it.

But art doesn't exist in a vacuum. Because it's a medium that fully comes to life as a collaboration between artist and audience, it's crucial that creators take that "end user" into account, which is a fancy way of saying that we often need outside input on our writing to help us ascertain how our stories are coming across on the page, as opposed to how they live in our heads. That's a disconnect we can often be blind to because we're filling in the blanks with the benefit of our extensive knowledge of the story that our reader doesn't have unless we make sure we convey it.

And you know what that means, friends: feedback. That may take the form of editors, coaches, beta readers, critique partners. We rely on people to give us their impressions of our work, to hold up a mirror to what we have created so we can assess whether it's coming across the way we intended, just as we check our status and condition in actual mirrors.

And yet that input can sometimes come in a form that isn't useful—or worst-case, is destructive to an author. I've heard too many horror stories from authors who nearly gave up on a story or on their writing altogether thanks to poorly offered (even if well-intentioned) critique.

The problem, of course, is that people aren't as straightforwardly objective as mirrors, which cast back a simple reflected image of reality. Humans, on the other hand, may color it with opinion, instruction, and their own subjective perspectives, some of which may be useful to an author, and some of which can cloud the reflection or even distort it like a funhouse mirror.

It's up to the author to discern which is which so that you can determine how best to use your readers' impressions, and one helpful way to start sifting through feedback is to identify what category it falls into: criticism, commentary, or critique.

Criticism

Most of us know it when we hear it, because criticism generally yields a visceral recoil in the recipient. Rather than simply reflecting back to you what they see on the page, the critic is more likely to convey their judgment of it. "This character isn't interesting." "This doesn't make any sense." "That's a terrible name for a hero." "It's boring."

Criticism runs rampant in venues like online reviews, where readers may be only too happy to pass judgment on the worth of a story and point out all the ways they believe it to suck. Rather than being focused on the work itself, criticism is centered on the person giving it—not the effectiveness of the story, but their opinion of it.

To be clear, all feedback is opinion. *All* of it—including that of professionals, like editors and agents. In those cases it's opinion backed by (ideally) years of experience in the industry and expertise in craft, but still—opinion.

But there's a difference between filtering your opinion through your personal preferences and biases as opposed to assessing the work on its merits through the lens of your own understanding. The latter is unavoidable for humans. The former is an unconsciously (or sometimes consciously) arrogant assumption that the giver of the criticism is the arbiter of acceptable standards.

However, if you can get past the almost universally negative reaction most of us have to criticism, this type of feedback can still be useful in helping you pinpoint areas of your story that may benefit from more polish or clarification.

The vague and annoying "This doesn't make any sense," for instance, is still an indicator of something that didn't come across clearly to your reader. You can ask for more detail, or if you're tired of hearing them talk, simply use their opinion as a beacon to guide you to an area of story that might need more clarification.

"It was boring" tells you that something wasn't holding their interest. That could be a personal issue or preference, like it isn't their genre or type of story, or they weren't fully focused on it, or they suffer from ADHD. But again, if you're willing to ask questions about what specifically didn't engage their interest, it may help you pinpoint a potential reader concern.

But remember also that if you're receiving feedback in the form of criticism, it may simply have more to do with your critic needing to assert their perspective than it does the story itself. Learn to discern between the two to determine what is valid for your story and what you can safely disregard.

Commentary

Like criticism, commentary tends to be more about the person giving it than the work itself. Commentary occurs when the commentator wants to convey their feelings or thoughts or preferences or personal associations about something in your story.

It can take several forms, the most common being feedback where they tell you a better way to tell your story, or how they would do it. It may also be taking issue with something in your manuscript because the commentator had a similar experience and that wasn't at *all* how they reacted or felt or what actually happened and they want to tell you their real-life version and explain to you the more accurate way you could present it.

Sometimes it takes the form of commentators who want to educate you on writing. I was in a critique group once with a member who would show up for each meeting with a tall stack of printed notes on the areas of writing craft he felt that week's author had insufficiently developed and lessons on how they could do it "right."

There's still information to be gleaned from this type of feedback, though you may have to sift away more chaff to get to it. If you're kind and have lots of time, hear the person out; people who give this type of feedback often feel unheard or unimportant and want to assert themselves, and you can give them the gift of your attention.

Or you can gently head off their exposition or instruction with a statement like, "I would love to hear more about that over coffee sometime, but right now I'd like to ask you a few specific questions about your impressions." And then once again guide them toward the kind of feedback that's useful and actionable based on what they've said.

For instance, if they had a similar experience and take issue with the way you presented it, focus them back on your story and ask what about the event they're referring to didn't ring true, specifically. Listen carefully to their answer for whether it brings up a valid plausibility concern, or they're simply filtering it through the narrow lens of their own personal experience.

If they want to school you on writing craft, offer a similar redirect back to the work itself and ask where exactly they felt the story didn't succeed for them and what specifically about it felt ineffective. This generally refocuses them on their actual impressions rather than their advice. (With hard-core blowhards you may need to redirect several times—some folks love to hold court and "educate" you. If they persist, you may not be able to get the actionable feedback you need from them, and you can find a polite way to cut the conversation short and cut your losses.)

Critique

This is the gold standard of feedback—what you can expect from skilled editors and coaches and the most effective critique partners. Critique focuses not on the merit of the work or the personal opinions of the critiquer, but offers as objective an analysis as is possible in the subjective world of humans based on how effectively the story the author wants to tell is coming across on the page.

Critique points out specific places in the manuscript where the critiquer felt distant from the characters or story, or confused, or uninvested. Skilled critiquers will also clarify why they felt this way:

"I didn't understand what the character had to gain or lose in this scene," for instance, or "The character didn't seem to care enough about what was at stake, so I found it difficult to as well." Both those statements tell you there's a problem with stakes and character—they aren't clear, developed, or important enough—and that's actionable feedback you can use to address the issue.

Critique may include suggestions, but unlike commentary it's not prescriptive but rather illustrative. In the above example, for instance, the critiquer might offer some specific thoughts to help illustrate their point, like, "It might help if readers were reminded that the bank is foreclosing on the farm tomorrow if the protagonist doesn't come up with the past-due payment," or "I would have liked to understand more clearly why the farm is so important to him and his family or what it means to them if they lose it."

This kind of feedback leaves the creative decisions to the author, but shines a flashlight on the area so the author can clearly see the possible paths forward and choose one that resonates for their story.

While you can't guarantee the input you receive will be constructive, useful, and specific, you can give yourself the best chance of it by choosing the right critiquers, and guiding them toward the kind of critique you need.

Other writers are wonderful sources of insight, because they can often offer feedback that's framed in the "writer language" of craft. But it helps to choose authors who write or read in your genre, and who match or exceed your own level of skill and experience as writers.

Feedback from nonwriters can also be valuable as long as they're experienced readers, preferably in your genre, and not someone too close to you who may be hesitant to be frank about their impressions.

Let your readers know up front that you're not looking for prescriptive feedback of what's "wrong" with your story or how to fix it. You simply would love to know their impressions of and reactions to the story.

One of the most useful ways to yield useful, actionable critique is to provide your readers with a questionnaire to guide them in offering it. Asking specific questions helps readers know exactly what you're looking for in the way of feedback, and it helps you pinpoint how effective the key areas of your story are, how well it holds together, how your intentions are coming across on the page. For example:

- Rather than "What did you think/how did you like it," ask "What parts of the story most engaged you, and where did you feel less invested? Can you pinpoint why?"
- Rather than "Did you like the characters?" ask "Did the characters feel real to you, and if not, in what way? Did you care what happened to them?"
- Instead of "Did it hold your interest throughout," ask "Were there any places you lost interest, or felt confused? In what way?"

In soliciting useful feedback, you're looking to pinpoint what may not be working as well in the manuscript as you hoped or intended—not for your readers to instruct you on what you did wrong or how to fix it.

But What About the Pros?

That said, trained and experienced professionals like agents and editors will sometimes offer more prescriptive input: not just how the story comes across to us on the page, but why certain areas may not be as effective as they could be, and sometimes suggestions for ways you might address the issue.

It pains me to say this, but some of the horror stories I've heard—no small number of them, in fact—involve these industry professionals. They may be harsh in their tone or assessment; might try to tell an author what she should or must do with her story; might co-opt her vision with the person's own preferences, biases, or market needs. None of that is helpful to you as a writer.

A good editor/agent should offer feedback that, as with beta readers and crit partners, reflects her reactions—"Readers may not understand why she would leave her husband here after such a minor disagreement," for example—as what they are: personal impressions and opinions, not absolute fact, as in, "It makes no sense why she leaves here."

That may seem like a hairbreadth distinction or simply a nicety of phrasing, but it's more than that. The former fulfills the proper function of any objective feedback, which is to hold up that mirror to the author so she can more clearly see what she has on the page, rather than what she's filling in mentally because she knows the story so well.

Our job as professionals is to tell you how what is on the page may come across to readers, based on our hopefully broad experience not only with many other manuscripts, but in your genre and in the current market. Good agents and editors weigh and need intimate knowledge of all those areas.

Trained professionals also ideally have a broad and very deep knowledge of writing craft, so they can share with an author *why* something may not be working—the kind of actionable, practical input that lets them figure out how to address the issue. For instance, in the above example an editor might observe that the character's motivations feel unclear and the stakes feel a bit low, because readers aren't yet specifically seeing why saving her marriage is important to the character.

Industry pros may even offer occasional suggestions for *how* an author might address areas that could benefit from strengthening—but it should be a suggestion only: "Perhaps you could let us see a scene where her goal of becoming an artist is a bit more concrete, and how her husband doesn't support it. For instance, maybe she's throwing a new piece of pottery and he casually walks in and criticizes it, or she gives him one of her pieces for their anniversary and he tucks it into a drawer, or something similar that illustrates their dynamic more clearly?"

Suggestions like that should be used simply as a "for instance," to illustrate the point and perhaps spark ideas. The author might love one of the specific suggestions and run with it, or they might use the ideas as a springboard to come up with their own version that accomplishes the same end: Showing this fuzzy dynamic more concretely, but in a way that feels more organic to the author's vision.

But even with (in fact especially with) professional feedback, the tone should always be positive, constructive, and respectful of your work, your vision, and you as a writer.

Indie publishing has marvelously democratized the industry. But it also means a lot of people are hanging out their shingle who perhaps don't have the qualifications or temperament to do so, from small presses to agents to developmental editors to book coaches.

I can't stress this enough: Vet the professional you are paying or contracting with to assess your work. Not just by checking their experience, track record, references, etc.—although that's also crucial—but get a sample of their work. See how they approach your writing.

Just as editors can tell from a few pages what areas of a story may benefit from strengthening or clarifying, authors can tell from a few pages of sample edit whether an editor is offering practical, actionable, positive critique. (You can download an extensive free guide on finding and vetting professionals on the Resources page of my website, FoxPrintEditorial.com.)

Receiving any kind of feedback on our stories short of "This is perfect; don't change a thing!" always stings. But learning to distinguish between what's about your story and what is a foible of the person giving feedback can be helpful—as well as what's actionable and useful and what is simply opinion. (And you know what body part those are likened to....)

How to Effectively Give Critique

If you're asking for critique from other writers, chances are good you'll be asked to offer it as well. And hopefully you will be generous about doing so. Building the supportive writing community every author needs means giving back as much as—maybe more than—you ask for. Remembering that good critique is one person offering you their impressions of and reactions to your work may help you give it in that same vein.

Think about how you might review a movie to a friend: Most of us don't start by breaking down what the director or actors did wrong or should have done differently. We report on our *feelings* about the story: We felt moved or exhilarated or entertained…or we didn't; we were riveted all the way through, or we lost interest halfway in; we were satisfied with the ending or we weren't, etc.

As a critiquer (or a "critter," as author Laura Drake humorously calls them) you're being asked for your *impressions of* and *reactions to* the work, not assessments of its worth or effectiveness or prescriptions as to how to fix it: simply what was effective for you, where you were confused or something felt unclear or you wanted or needed to know more. You're being consulted as a test audience, not an expert adviser, showing an author how successfully she has conveyed her vision on the page.

- **Offer your impressions—not a manifesto.**
  You're not being asked to sit down with your red pencil and point out areas where the author failed, or what they did wrong, or how they should fix it. You're simply reflecting what came across to you on the page for the author and letting them know how it struck you. You're a focus group reporting on your impressions about the product—it's not your place to tweak the formula.

- **Take a positive and constructive approach—critique is not criticism.**
Remember the Golden Rule of feedback: Critique unto others as you would have them critique unto you. Think about how you might answer a friend asking, "Do you like my haircut?" or "Is this outfit flattering on me?" He may want your honest opinion, and you may give it, but most of us would never offer it in a hurtful or negative way. The intent is to help, encourage, and support our writing friends—not bat them down like Whac-A-Mole. Before you offer any piece of critique, imagine how it might feel to hear the exact same observation from someone about your own work. You can be honest and still be kind and constructive.

- **Say what you liked, as well as what didn't work as well for you.**
Yes, your author friends are looking for help identifying possible areas of weakness in their story that they may be blind to, but don't forget to also point out some of the things that were especially effective or that you enjoyed. It can do wonders for an author's reception of the critique and for their confidence. A simple smiley face or "LOL" or "tears" noted in the margin carries a lot of weight for authors and makes it easier to hear the feedback on what wasn't as effective. Medicine goes down a little easier with the proverbial spoonful of sugar, and knowing what's working well is as valuable for an author in honing her work as knowing what might not be.

- **Be specific.**
The beauty of asking other writers for critique (as opposed to lay readers, who can also offer valuable input) is that they can often help an author pinpoint specific areas that may

need strengthening. Instead of "I didn't relate to her," offer something clearer and more actionable like, "Her motivations felt unclear in act one." Instead of "It felt a little slow to engage me" you could clarify: "The momentum picked up in act two, when I understood what he was striving for." Just remember, you are not the ultimate arbiter. These are your *opinions* of what's working and what could use shoring up, not statements of fact or a how-to manual.

- **Don't make blanket statements or provide instructions.**
  Remember, *all critique is opinion*, and you're not being asked for prescriptive feedback. Instead of "The plot is unclear here," simply state *your* reaction: "I wasn't clear on how he planned to defuse the bomb" or "I got a bit lost trying to figure out what was specifically happening in this scene." One tool I often use is to ask questions instead of make categorical statements. Rather than, "This character is being a jerk," try something like, "Did you mean for him to seem unkind here?" or "How does she react to the sharp way he talks to her in this scene?" or "Why is he being so short with her?"

- **How you say something is as important as or more important than what you say.**
  This should be self-evident for anyone who has ever had a relationship of any sort. Just as you're more likely to get a positive reaction if you tell your partner, "Do you mind taking out the garbage?" than if you say, "You *never* help me around the house!" there's a big difference between "This didn't make any sense" and "I didn't understand why she would snap at her son when he was just asking her to tuck him in."

  Don't rush through your comments about another author's work. Yes, it takes a little more time to offer positive, constructively phrased, thoughtful, specific feedback, but isn't that what you'd want for your own work when you need input? If you don't have time to do the job properly for someone, better to let them know that than try to shorthand a critique that's likely to result in a loss of confidence or hurt feelings.

Critique is a tool of editing, so that the author can use that feedback in determining how to approach revisions. That means the proper function of critique—even from an editor or agent—is simply to aid the author in seeing his work through the eyes of an objective reader. But the job of addressing whatever may need attention as a result is strictly up to the author.

Let's look at how to deal with the plank in the face that receiving any kind of feedback so often feels like, how to determine what feedback resonates for you and your vision, and how best to utilize it.

Chapter Twenty

How to Handle Feedback—and What to Do with It

No matter how much you may want or know you need it, and no matter how prepared you may think you are for it, even the most helpful critique of your manuscript will probably hit you like a faceful of bricks. Artists tend to be deeply sensitive about our creative work, which stems from the most naked parts of ourselves. Knowing that helps when we get our knees knocked out by feedback…but not much.

What *will* help is knowing how to receive it in a healthy, constructive way, and how to process and utilize it in making your story stronger.

Take It in and Then Step Away

First, make sure you're in a good state of mind when a critique comes in. Give yourself ample time to absorb it, rather than rushing through it. Pour yourself a nice glass of wine or a good cup of coffee and then approach the feedback with a level head and an open and receptive attitude.

Remember the parable of the student who came to the spiritual teacher full of ideas and seeking guidance. The master poured him a cup of tea, continuing to fill it until the cup overflowed. "Stop!" the student cried. "The cup is already full—it can hold no more!"

"Yes," the teacher said. "Before you can learn you must empty your cup."

Come to the feedback as much as possible with an empty cup, setting aside your preconceptions about what your story lacks or needs, or even what it's about. Be open to whatever impressions your critiquers may have to offer.

Read the feedback in its entirety, meaning not just any separate editorial notes you may have gotten, but also any comments embedded in the manuscript itself. Read all of it, all the way through—and resist the temptation to start addressing it. Do nothing for now except read or listen.

The comments are likely to smart—a lot—because deep down we all *really* want to hear, "It was perfect; don't change a thing."

You won't.

But we're not generally in the most receptive or creative place immediately after taking in someone's thoughts about how our baby isn't beautiful, so it's essential that you put the input on a back burner for a day or two and just let it simmer. After you've read or heard it, leave it alone for a while; step away from it completely.

Meanwhile, be very kind to yourself. Take a bubble bath. Hug your pets. Maybe go for a long nature walk. Stab a voodoo doll in the shape of the critiquer if you need to.

Then read it all again.

> *A few other crucial tips to keep in mind when receiving feedback:*
>
> **Whatever you do, don't argue.** What's the point? Remember all critique is opinion, and you won't be there to explain your intentions to your ultimate readers. Either your intentions came across on the page to your critiquers or they didn't.
>
> **Try not to take negative feedback personally.** Remember critique is simply a tool for you to use or not use, as you determine. You don't get mad at a hammer if you needed a drill; you just put the hammer down.
>
> **Remember to thank your critiquers.** I even tend to write thank-you notes and/or send small gifts to my beta readers. Whether you like or agree with their feedback or not, be gracious and appreciative—they took time out of their lives to try to help you (even if they may have done it clumsily).

Assess the Input

I said this in the last chapter too, but it bears repeating: All feedback is the thoughts and reactions of a single person, not a definitive statement on the worth of your story or you as a writer.

An individual's input is only a tool, one that may or may not be useful for the job at hand. It's a reflection of how what's on the page strikes them as a reader, and as such it helps you as the creator to know where you may want to clarify or develop your vision and intentions.

Some feedback may be harder to swallow. I often dismiss critiquers' input initially, even from editors I trust, by defensively thinking, *They don't know what they're talking about.*

Usually by the next day I might allow that maybe they have a point about one or two things. By a few days later I almost always see that most of it is right on target, and then I'm ready to start addressing those areas.

But often there are one or two pieces of input that stubbornly stick in my craw, and I defend those points fiercely. Sometimes I realize eventually that I'm clinging to darlings that don't serve the manuscript or article I'm working on. And sometimes I stand by my vision, but perhaps find better ways to convey it. Don't dismiss any observation out of hand, even if every fiber of your being initially screams that it's wrong. Let it simmer, give it some serious thought, and once the initial flare of resistance or hurt feelings subsides, try to consider the input with a truly unbiased mind.

If you're hearing the same types of feedback repeatedly from several readers, look closely. All feedback is subjective, but if multiple readers call out the same issues, it's likely this area needs addressing.

After the initial sting subsides, you'll usually find that the feedback starts to coalesce in your mind into categories and usable insights into your manuscript's effectiveness, and that's when you can go back in and figure out how to best utilize it.

Now it's time to dig a little deeper into the feedback you received, decide what's right for your story, and determine how to put those changes into action.

All feedback is valuable— but not all of it is "right"

Regardless of whether your reader reflected their own reactions to the story, as in good critique, or erred on the side of criticism, commentary, or being unhelpfully prescriptive ("You should..."), their feedback is potentially helpful.

Generally you'll find that some of the observations feel like confirmation of what you already may have suspected wasn't working as well as it could; some draws your attention to areas you were blind to; and some elicits a whole-body "oh, hell, no" reaction from you. But give all three the same consideration in determining what your manuscript may need, as all of it is valuable in reflecting back to you what's on the page.

The comments that resonate with you right away are often easiest to address. These are areas where you already likely suspected the story might need strengthening, and a great place to start assessing the critique's feedback and translating it into actionable items to incorporate into revisions.

If the critique indicates that the characters aren't engaging or believable, for instance, start asking questions to pinpoint specifically why. Did your reader not care about what happens to them or not feel deeply invested? Why not—did he not understand what your characters want or what drives them or why? Did he feel they were unlikable, unsympathetic, opaque, unrelatable? (You can download an extensive sample of the kinds of questions you might ask yourself about every area of story in my Self-editing Checklist on the Resources page of my website, FoxPrintEditorial.com.)

This specific feedback about their reactions will lead you to diagnose the core problem: Perhaps you haven't clearly defined the character's arc, or their goal, what drives them, or what's at stake.

Once you've identified the concrete issues that may need addressing, ask yourself whether each is an element that requires more development from you as the author, or is it a lack of your intentions coming across clearly on the page? In other words, is it a problem of conception or execution? The former often indicates overarching issues (intrinsic throughout the story); the latter can be more scene-specific (something you can address by adding, deleting, or tweaking a line or two here and there).

If the problem is an intrinsic issue, then it's time to go back to "writer brain" and do more development in that area—flesh out and more fully develop your characters, or their arcs or the story arc, or develop the plot more clearly, or clarify or strengthen stakes—whatever the root issue is—as you did in drafting the story originally.

If you feel the story is fully developed in a certain area but not coming across clearly on the page, you can go through and identify specific places where you thought you conveyed that information. Then ask yourself whether you may need to clarify, elaborate, or let readers in more deeply.

If your critique noted specific places that created their impressions, that's helpful in pinpointing exact problem areas, but if not, for more on how to diagnose and address it yourself, my book *Intuitive Editing* breaks this process down in each area of craft into "How to Find It" and "How to Fix It" sections.

Do this same process for each area of feedback that resonates for you, and keep asking yourself questions to circle in on what may be missing or need clarification or development or trimming to more effectively convey your intentions.

LOOK BEYOND PERSONAL PREFERENCES OR MISGUIDED INSTRUCTIONS

Feedback that reflects the critiquer's personal opinions or biases, or that's prescriptive or based around "how they would do it," can still guide you to areas where your story could be strengthened.

I once had a crit partner—an older man who wrote lean literary fiction about taciturn Texas men—tell me that he found the glimpses into characters' inner lives in one of my stories a little overdone and distracting. My initial instinct was to dismiss this feedback. I wrote women's fiction, and character development and insight are the soul of the genre; plus he was a man, and one writing very different types of stories.

Instead I sat with his input and considered why he'd felt that way. Whether he was "right" or not, something pulled him out of my story at certain points—the antithesis of what any writer wants—so I took a closer look at those areas and how much internality I had in them.

And despite my genre's different conventions, he was right in certain places where too much inner life was stalling a scene's pace or lowering urgency and stakes on the action.

Even the "wrong" kind of critique can be valuable. If the feedback you receive makes the mistake of telling you what the critiquer thinks is wrong with your story or how to fix it, see if you can look beyond the reader's advice and winnow out the core of what prompted it.

For instance, if a crit partner advises you to cut scenes in act two to increase pace, that might indicate to you that their interest flagged in the middle of the story. The problem may be pace, but it could equally likely be momentum, stakes, character motivation, or suspense and tension elements, among many others. Don't worry about what they think you should do; analyze what they might have *felt* that prompted the suggestion.

Critique that rubs you the wrong way is often the hardest to process. An initial defensive or even emotional reaction in you can often indicate a darling. Maybe it needs killing—but maybe it's simply an indication that a certain element simply isn't as effective or developed as it needs to be.

Author Bianca Marais (host of *The Shit No One Tells You about Writing* podcast) related in one episode receiving editorial feedback on what became her debut novel (*Hum If You Don't Know the Words*) that given the story's prominent elements of racism, additional themes about homophobia and antisemitism felt like too much.

Bianca felt strongly about including those elements, as they're key to the South African sociopolitical environment she was writing about. But the feedback told her that they might not be coming across effectively. So instead she developed them more clearly and deeply, addressing the core problem beneath the editors' suggestions without killing her darling.

Knowing when to kill and when to stand your ground and unknot or develop a problem area is some of the hardest work of revision. Allow yourself to consider the feedback and ways to rework that element of the story. You may be surprised to find the story could be better served without it, or you may decide the critique is off base for your vision. But sometimes this kind of feedback can shine a spotlight on something that simply isn't coming together the way you hoped, and push you to find a better way of effecting your intentions on the page.

Make a Game Plan for Revisions

It can help to organize the feedback you receive, especially if it's from several sources. If you're working with a professional editor, a good editorial letter should already have done this, breaking down the input into distinct areas that could use strengthening or development.

I like to suggest breaking feedback into three main categories:

- macroedit areas—the foundation of the story itself: character, stakes, and plot
- microedit areas—the story's support scaffolding: suspense, tension, momentum, pace, point of view, showing and telling, voice, etc.
- line edits—feedback specific to the prose itself

This system can help organize your thoughts as you assess the feedback per the above suggestions and formulate a game plan for incorporating it into revisions.

I recommend working from the ground up, meaning address the macroedit areas first—character, stakes, and plot—as this is the foundation on which the story sits. If that's not solid, the rest of the structure can't stand. Then you can examine microedit issues, which scaffold the story, and save line edits for last, since you might find yourself doing unnecessary revision if there are more foundational elements that need addressing that change the manuscript substantially.

But you might prefer to start with the small stuff—like the line-edit issues that are easiest to address—to give you a jump-start on incorporating feedback. Each author's approach depends on the specific story's needs and your personal style and preferences. As with everything in creative pursuits, there's no "right" answer or one-size-fits-all technique; it depends on each individual story, and you as a writer.

Remember that all feedback is opinion—even that of a professional. Ideally professionals who have spent years reviewing hundreds or even thousands of manuscripts, who have worked within the publishing industry and understand its standards and expectations and marketing realities, are offering you their opinions based on that. That doesn't mean their feedback is always "right"—or right for your story—but take into consideration the benefit of their experience and expertise.

But just as with any other reader, these are still subjective impressions and can be based on more than simply whether someone thinks the story is good. Readers may be influenced by their personal preferences, market trends, the author's platform or reputation, a publisher's or agent's current list of authors/titles, even their mood. Which means no critique or criticism is a referendum on the objective worth of you, your story, or your writing.

And if someone tells you in any fashion that your story—or you as a writer—has little or no worth, walk away from them and never look back; never give it a second thought. That kind of feedback is utterly unproductive, and frankly it's flat wrong. In all my years working as an editor with everyone from major bestsellers to first-time authors, I can truthfully say I have yet to see a manuscript without worth, that doesn't have something the author and I can work with and build on. Nor have I ever seen an author who should hang it up and stop writing...because you are human, and as such you have a story to tell—multitudes of them—and you, and they, are fascinating.

And because this is the process: Writing is rewriting. It's how we improve. Good critique helps you dig out that gold; it doesn't blow up the mine.

But how do you know how much feedback you need, and when—and how much is too much? What happens when you get so much feedback that instead of helping you improve your story, it starts confusing it, or homogenizing it, or even shutting you down as a creator?

Knowing When "Help" Is Helpful

In 2012, during the Abu Dhabi Grand Prix, driver Kimi Räikkönen famously (or infamously) barked over the radio to his engineer, who'd been conveying a steady stream of advice to the Formula 1 driver, "Leave me alone—I know what I'm doing."

The terse rebuke was broadcast on international television (and lives perpetually on in endless internet memes).

Anyone who's ever felt overwhelmed by too much input will relate to Räikkönen's outburst. In the midst of driving a high-pressure race, he had a relentless voice in his ear constantly directing him on what to do.

His engineer wasn't wrong to be coaching Kimi—the man was an expert and a key part of Räikkönen's team. He was doing his job and probably doing it well, and his knowledge, objective perspective, and counsel are part of what allowed Räikkönen to do *his* job well.

But Räikkönen was the one in the driver's seat. He knew the car, he knew the track, he knew his specific job. And at a certain point he had to just *drive*.

In recent years publishing has seen an unbelievable expansion of services and professionals available to writers that were once reserved fairly exclusively to big-name authors with big-name publishers.

In many ways this is a huge advantage for authors, who now have direct access to expertise that can vastly improve their skill, craft, and professionalism: guidance to improve their craft as writers; help with motivation to write; assistance with their story and structure; objective input on how well it's coming across on the page. All that help can be invaluable.

But ultimately *you* are the one who has to write the story.

THE RISKS OF TOO MUCH FEEDBACK

Years ago I was part of a critique group where we offered one another intensive feedback chapter by chapter as we drafted.

But despite the skill and excellent insights of my crit partners, I soon realized that our sessions were counterproductive for me. Hearing detailed feedback as I was still drafting and finding the story flipped me into analytical "editor brain," rather than creative "writer brain," and made me start questioning everything I'd done and how I wanted to move forward. Too often it stalled out my drafting.

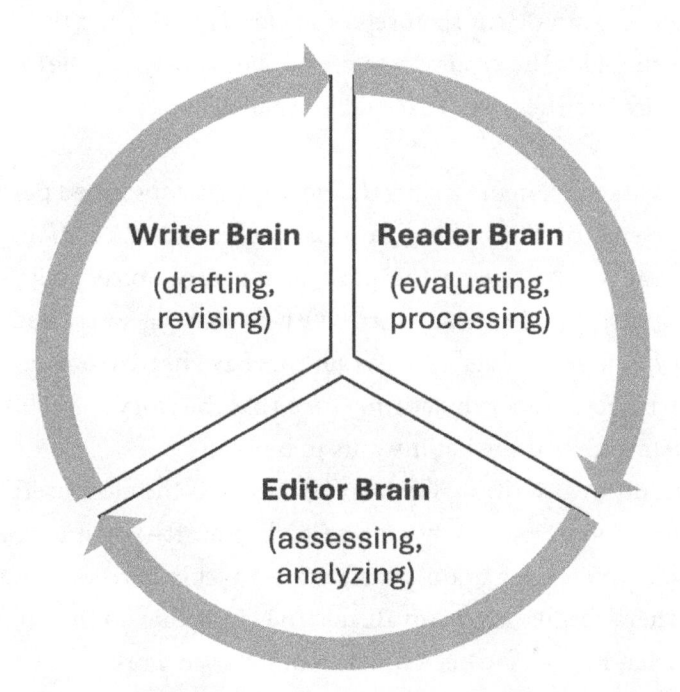

Writer Brain (drafting, revising)

Reader Brain (evaluating, processing)

Editor Brain (assessing, analyzing)

The Three Stages of Writing

As soon as you get in your head about your story, you're judging it—and that's a surefire way to shut your creativity down. And trying to consider or incorporate too much input while you're still finding what the story wants to be organically can dilute it. Too many cooks spoil the broth.

Despite the many advantages outside input can offer you—whether a coach, a crit partner, an editor, or beta readers—leaning on it too soon or too heavily comes with risks:

- Authors can "get in their own head" and shut down, or lose sight of their own story.
- Authors can get too dependent on outside input and feel they can't create without it.
- Authors can subscribe to the erroneous idea that they can't complete or sell a story without hiring an expert.
- Authors can orient themselves so closely with what they've been told is the *right* way to create their story that they rob it of life and the spark that makes it their own.

I've worked on manuscripts that technically subscribed perfectly to every tenet of storytelling or a particular school of thought or dogma, and yet lie flat on the page, stripped of voice, stripped of originality, stripped of excitement. Others may be so stuffed with "key storytelling elements" or ideas authors have heard from an editor or coach or beta reader or writing guru that the story is muddied or overwhelmed, unsure what it wants to be.

With my own writing, I quickly learned that the most useful way for me to receive feedback was on a finished draft—when I *needed* to transition into "editor brain" to effectively tackle revisions, and my crit partners' feedback was invaluable in helping me do that, helping me see what I may have been blind to in my own work.

Even as an editor, when working with in-house editors at publishing houses who often send me their feedback as I'm working on edits of an author's manuscript, I don't usually look at their thoughts until at least after my first cold read of the story. Later I incorporate the in-house editor's feedback, but getting their observations in my head as I'm orienting myself to the story may color my impressions of it, when I need to come at it with my own fresh perspective.

Too many voices in your ear dilute yours. Too many opinions neuter your story. Too many instructions can get you in your head and freeze up your creative impulse.

A race-car driver may lean on all the training and input and expertise of their team, but every car is different, every track is different, every race is different, every *driver* is different. In the moment, as the race is happening, he or she is the one behind the wheel.

You can't drive by committee, and you can't write by committee either.

DRIVING YOUR OWN CAR

Your job as a writer is to develop your writing and storytelling skills, which encompass most of the functions you may hire or solicit outside input for: understanding of story and structure, knowledge of craft, motivation to write, the ability to assess and revise what you've written.

You may need or want to bring in outside help with any or all of these functions at certain times—and when you do, make sure to get the best help you can get.

But remember what the core of this creative pursuit is: the writer telling her story. Input can be a wonderful resource, but *you* are the one in the driver's seat. And you are there for a reason: This is your story.

When you're running the race you need to get into the zone. Like Räikkönen's engineer, experts in skill and strategy may offer big-picture perspective at the right time. But *you* know how the vehicle is handling.

Even if you're still honing your skills—and we're all hopefully always honing our skills, regardless of how long or broad our experience—at a certain point writing, like auto racing, is simply one butt in one seat doing one job.

A fun coda on the Kimi Räikkönen story: When he retired, for his final race his crew painted on his car the words, "Dear Kimi, we will leave you alone now."

Get out of your head and write. Have the courage and faith and trust in yourself to know that you *do* know what you're doing—even if you seek out feedback when the time is right.

Needing Help Doesn't Mean You're a Bad Author

Needing outside input to get a sense of what you have on the page, or improve your writing, or even work through thorny storytelling elements doesn't mean your story or you aren't good enough.

I build follow-up time into every editorial contract I offer so that authors know if they need anything—to clarify a point, sound out an idea or bounce it off someone, rework an intention, or get a set of eyes on revisions as they're working—I'm here, their "beck and call girl," as I joke. The handmaiden to their creative process.

Some authors never use their allotted time. But some may want clarification of certain points in the editorial notes, or to discuss them more deeply. They may ask for brainstorming sessions, or emergency troubleshooting calls when they're feeling stuck. They may want help working out a game plan for revisions that may be especially vexing or complicated; a sounding board for rethinking their approach; or sometimes just a good old-fashioned pep talk when their confidence is flagging.

But here's what almost every one of these expanded edits has in common: At some point the author apologizes for needing the extra help and expresses discouragement with their own talent or skill because their manuscript needs so much editing and revision—especially if they've had a long, successful track record as a published author, as many of the writers I work with do.

To which I always offer a version of the same response: This isn't just a completely normal part of the process—it *is* the process.

I'm always a bit in awe of how authors take pages of editorial input, process it, determine what resonates for their vision, and incorporate that onto the page. It feels like alchemy: I hold up a mirror to an author's story and offer objective feedback on what I see…and then it comes back to me magically transformed, even richer, deeper, and more affecting than it already was.

It's as if I hand an author a bag of groceries and they bake the most astonishingly delicious, beautiful cake.

But here's a valuable writing (and life) lesson I learned from *The Great British Baking Show*: Even with a recipe, even with a dish you may have made perfectly hundreds of times before, even if you've been baking your entire life, sometimes the bread doesn't rise, the soufflé falls, or you accidentally used salt instead of sugar.

Writing, like baking, is an ephemeral art, affected by so many factors. With baking it's temperature, humidity, altitude, quality of and variation among ingredients, and so many more.

In writing there are equally as many factors that might influence an author's creativity: time, mood, life pressures, stress, worry, complexity of a certain story, writing in a new genre, self-doubt, even hormones—and far too many more to list.

If flour and yeast and eggs are temperamental and unpredictable, imagine how much more so a faceted, endlessly complex human being is.

Think of how easy it is to get derailed in even common everyday situations: You're out of coffee, giving you a headache that derails your productivity, which makes you miss an important deadline, which gets you yelled at by your boss, which decimates your self-esteem, which comes out in snapping at your spouse, which hurts his feelings, which sparks a fight, which leaves you feeling sad and alone on a day you desperately needed love and comfort.

Is it any wonder that authors may sometimes have trouble with writing?

It's worth saying again: *This is normal. You are normal.*

Athletes suffer from injuries or conditions that may hamper their usual performance. Most of us wouldn't decide that negates their talent or skill as an athlete or invalidates their accomplishments; it just means they may need more practice and coaching now and then to push through that impediment and get back to peak form.

Life—like good story—is *always* full of challenges and setbacks, suffering and pain, uncertainty and insecurity. And artists are often the sensitively calibrated barometers of all those tribulations.

Be gentle with the delicate equipment of your soul. Reach out without self-castigation for the help and support and solidarity and reassurance that are available to you. Do not judge yourself or your talent or your worth for that. This is human, and it's *normal*.

Sometimes you must ask others to hold the torch in the darkness when you need it to help show you the way.

And sometimes you will be the one holding the light for them.

Chapter Twenty-one

Rejection, Criticism, and Crickets

Twenty-two years ago, early in his acting career, actor and comedian Connor Ratliff was cast in a small role: a couple of lines in the show *Band of Brothers*, an HBO miniseries based on author Stephen E. Ambrose's book of the same name. It wasn't a major part, but the show was already hugely high-profile, created and directed by the heaviest of heavy hitters, Steven Spielberg and Tom Hanks. Ratliff's episode was to be directed by his idol, Tom Hanks himself. It was a dream job—and a potential game changer for his career.

Until, days before shooting, he heard from his agent that he was being called back in to meet directly with Hanks because he felt Ratliff had "dead eyes." Ratliff went back to audition again—for a part he thought he'd already won—and lost the job.

I'm guessing that most writers feel this story right in the gut. Creative careers are filled with rejection, criticism, and outright indifference to artistic products that often demanded enormous time, energy, and heart from artists in the creation of them.

Ratliff's story hits hard for so many of the reasons poor response to our writing often does: because the work meant so much to him, and he wanted it so badly. Because the rejection feels so painfully personal, especially in this case. Because he gave his all and thought he'd be rewarded accordingly—and in fact had every reason to believe he would be. Because he had his dream in his grasp, only to have it snatched from his fingers.

These are such common occurrences in the life of an author. Our work often receives much more rejection than acceptance in seeking representation or publication, if we even hear anything back at all from submissions. Feedback may be harsh or discouraging—even from people we expect to support us. Reviews might be indifferent or brutal or thin on the ground. Book releases may barely make a ripple.

Somehow creatives—those whose work depends on lowering the protective barriers between themselves and the world to plumb the full range of human experience and emotion—are expected to grow a thick skin and shake off negative feedback, to carry on full throttle even when our work seems to fall into a void.

It's easy to say, and it makes perfect sense—of course it does. Keeping the creative fires burning means learning to tend and feed them ourselves. But what do we do when it feels as if rejection or criticism or indifference is depriving that flame of oxygen?

What Do You Do When the Worst Happens?

Ratliff's *Band of Brothers* rejection crushed him, and for a long while it defined him, sidelining his career and creativity: Not long afterward he left acting altogether, spending the next thirteen years working as a dishwasher and preschool teacher and bookstore employee.

But eventually he returned to acting, performing improv comedy with the famed Upright Citizens Brigade, which eventually expanded to a respectable series of roles in projects like *The Marvelous Mrs. Maisel* and the *Mean Girls* movie remake.

And two decades after the rejection that had chased him away from his creative work, Ratliff used it in creating a podcast based on the incident, *Dead Eyes*—not to smear Hanks or as some kind of vendetta, but simply to make sense of this seemingly random event that had had such a profound impact on the rest of his life and career.

The result was one of the best podcasts I've listened to, especially for creatives: a thoughtful, in-depth exploration of the creative process and life, its demands and rewards, and—most trenchantly and poignantly—rejection, what it means, and how to face it.

The podcast seemed to become a high-water mark for Ratliff's career too—one that has included no small amount of success as an actor and comedian—receiving delirious reviews in high-profile publications including *Vanity Fair, Esquire,* and the *Guardian,* and making "best of" lists of podcasts in magazines like *TIME, The New Yorker,* and *Rolling Stone.*

And after two years and thirty episodes—featuring guests at every level and in nearly every walk of show business, including Jon Hamm, Seth Rogen, Judd Apatow, and Colin Hanks, all offering revealing insights into the crucibles of the creative life—Tom Hanks finally came on the program to talk to Ratliff about the incident directly.[18]

It's not an opportunity creatives often have: to discuss with someone who rejected our work their reasons for it, what it meant. Too often we're left to ponder—to obsess sometimes—over the cause: what we did wrong, where we fell short. Ratliff spent twenty years doing exactly that, but one of the things I found inspiring about his podcast was reliving with him the process of coming to terms on his own with that crushing rejection that took his feet out from under him for so long, and how he got himself back up long before he talked to Hanks.

That formative experience became a cornerstone of the way he approached his creative career the second time around, and the fuel for his reclaiming it.

"What I found when I looked back on the experience was that it had built a lot of character in terms of when I returned to show business, I knew not to take everything so personally," Ratliff says. "I knew that for everything that can go right, it can also go wrong just as quickly."

Rejection and Writing

Like acting, writing careers are filled with moments like Ratliff's "dead eyes" experience: You get the yes or the no and it feels like everything in your career hinges on that. Someone's rejection cuts your knees out from under you—and yet you don't know how to fix whatever it was they may have seen as a fatal shortcoming in your writing. Your confidence flags. You flounder and struggle.

Maybe you give up—on that story, or your writing, or yourself.

If your dream agent or editor or reader isn't connecting with your work, what are you doing wrong? How can you fix it? What, exactly, does that even *mean*?

Often the answer to all these questions is, "Nothing."

When Ratliff finally had the chance to talk to Hanks directly, his idol didn't even remember making the "dead eyes" comment at all. He remembered Ratliff, remembered the incident, but couldn't recall his reason for wanting to recast the role, and all he could offer Ratliff was conjectures: It may have been a height issue, a physical-pairing issue with other actors in the scene, a standard casting decision that might have been based on any number of arbitrary factors out of the actor's control. Hanks didn't know. He took full responsibility for having made the comment reported by Ratliff's agent's assistant—but in reality did he even say those painful words that so impacted Ratliff? In that complicated game of telephone, who can say?

"There's no bad guys here," Hanks says to Ratliff in the podcast—one of the most genuine, thoughtful, and revealing celebrity/show business interviews you may ever hear. "It's not like you offended me and so therefore I sought retribution by not giving you this job…. When we have narratives we break it up into 'I was a victim of *blank,*' or, 'I triumphed over bad guys.' And that's not the way the world works."

It's certainly not the way creative careers work. Rejection letters from industry pros are far more often than not simply form letters with empty but probably well-intentioned phrases meant to cushion what they know is always a blow for authors: "I just didn't connect with the story. "It's not right for us." "We don't know how to sell this, but another agent may feel differently." These palliatives are the equivalent of that old breakup standby, "It's not you; it's me."

Take that at face value. These generalized phrases of rejection could mean dozens, hundreds of things: The editor or agent is looking for a specific type of story at the moment and this wasn't it, or it doesn't fit her list, or he just signed someone else with this same concept or style, or she's having a bad day, or isn't in the mood for this kind of story today, or the hero has the name of their ex, or he's slogging through a towering slush pile before lunch and as he skimmed the query or pages all he could think about was how hungry he was, or the marketing department just put the kibosh on more stories about X, or maybe even that she doesn't represent this genre (if you haven't done your homework on submissions).

"I just didn't connect"—or any of dozens of other meaningless, vague form rejections you can read at the literary agent database QueryTracker.net with a membership that unlocks a forum where writers share rejections/responses they receive from agents, among myriad other wonderful resources if you're submitting—are niceties, canned phrases industry professionals developed over usually years of sifting through submissions, the vast majority of which won't catch their eye. They mean nothing specific about the quality or marketability of your manuscript except that this story on this day didn't quite catch the attention of this particular agent or editor for any of thousands of reasons you cannot possibly know.

Unless you get a personal, detailed letter from an agent or editor, or an R&R (revise and resubmit) where they took time to give you specific, actionable feedback, rejections like this mean absolutely nothing except this story isn't the one for this person. There's no telling why, any more than Hanks remembered why he decided Ratliff wasn't the right fit for the role in *Band of Brothers*. What you received is a form rejection necessitated by the volume of inquiries these professionals receive daily.

And *that's okay*. Do you connect with every single book you pick up? Would you want an agent or editor who didn't feel passionately excited about your book—who acquired or signed you with a nice, ringing "meh"?

It's *not* you. It's them. It really, really is.

I liken it to any other relationship. When you're dating, if someone doesn't want to see you again—or at all—do you assume it's you and try to mold yourself to whatever they might be looking for? Or do you realize that person isn't the one for you and keep seeking someone who digs you just as you are? Hopefully we eventually learn the healthier, more realistic option.

High Praise, Big Promises...and Crickets

Sometimes the opposite happens: Your work is praised to the skies, or an answer comes and it's a yes, or you've got stellar reviews and marketing and support lined up for a gonzo book release—and then nothing comes of it. As Connor Ratliff's experience attests, it's often less crushing never to be offered the cookie at all than to have the cookie held in front of you, fresh and warm, and then snatched away before you can take the first bite.

A reader of my blog wrote me about having this kind of experience. This author worked with a professional on one of their stories who was very helpful and very complimentary. The pro offered to help get the manuscript in front of some other industry professionals' eyes.

This is the kind of dream offer that doesn't come around very often: a champion who believes in your work and in *you* offering to connect you to the often-elusive gatekeepers. The kind of help and connection that can set an author apart from the slush pile. So of course the author was extremely excited.

And then...nothing. The offer never materialized, and eventually the author let it go, feeling disappointed and confused about what had changed.

We spend a lot of time in our writing careers talking and thinking about rejection, harsh feedback, or even the black hole where you submit your work and you hear absolutely nothing back. Those are common challenges of any writing career.

But what about when all the stars seem to align and you're poised to absolutely kill it, but instead your work just...dies?

You may immediately start to wonder what changed. What did you do wrong? Did you overstep? Did people, on further reflection, realize your work's not that great after all, you big impostor, you? Were they or the universe messing with you? Leading you on?

Generally in this business, as in most of life, I don't think most people are out to actively hurt anyone or mislead them. In his *Dead Eyes* interview, Hanks's concern and upset over his unremembered rejection of Ratliff is palpable in his voice as he relates hearing about the podcast from two of his children and the incident's impact on Ratliff: "I was aghast. I was...I actually got chilled. My heart rate skyrocketed and I said, I did—I did what? I did *what?*"

Agents, editors, and other pros aren't evil sadists plotting how best to destroy writers' psyches either. They're all generally in this line of work because they love story and writing and authors and books. Everybody pretty much dreams of finding the next [*insert bestselling author here*]. They're all pulling for you to be that person. Every submission they read, they're hoping as hard as you are that it's exactly what they're looking for.

And sometimes, if they find something that does have potential, that's the Holy Grail. Or at the very least they hope it could become so. Or maybe they simply want to help and encourage a particular author with great promise. And with every good intention, they offer their high praise and maybe make big promises.

But then perhaps they are overwhelmed by their crushing schedule. Maybe their situation changes in some way. Maybe they didn't get backing from the rest of their team or the other departments in their company—in modern publishing decisions are often made by committee. Maybe their mood shifted, or they overcommitted elsewhere, or they simply realize they overpromised what they can deliver.

It could even just be sheer forgetfulness. This happened to an author courtesy of *me* not long ago, when a writer friend told me about her current project and I mentioned an agent I knew of who might be a good fit to whom she could submit when she was ready.

Many months later, when my friend finished the manuscript, she came back to ask me again for the name and I'd completely blanked on who I was thinking of. Perhaps this feels like a broken promise to her, when really it's just forgetfulness. (But for the record I did own up and did not ghost her.)

But the crucial thing for you as the author to realize is that it's not you. Generally if someone liked your work enough to offer you encouragement or hope in the first place, you're doing everything right. It just wasn't in the cards at this moment with this person for this story, for a host of possible reasons you cannot know.

But whatever the reasons, in each case the legacy you're left with as the author is the same as if they'd rejected you outright: confusion, loss of confidence, dashed hopes, and profound letdown. What are you supposed to do with all that?

How to Cope with Rejection, Criticism, and Indifference

Hanks repeatedly uses the word "dispassion" in the *Dead Eyes* interview as a central tenet of how creatives must approach the business of their art. You have to find a way to do this passionate thing with a measure of dispassion—yet how do you navigate the impersonal career aspect of this most personal pursuit?

"How do you process disappointment when something doesn't go your way?" Ratliff asks at one point.

Hanks doesn't hesitate: "Oh, my lord. It's by going into it with absolutely no expectations whatsoever."

We are creators not because someone buys what we create, or gives us the yes, or says we've made the cut. We're creators because we create. That's the crux of what we do: the work itself.

Disappointment is a feature of every life, but in a career that involves putting ourselves and our work out there over and over and over again—with every story, every submission, every single reader of our work—authors are going to face it more than most. And in a business based on something as subjective as art, often it has little to do with the worth of your work or of you as a writer.

What *is* in our control is how we react to these setbacks. What we do with them. Ratliff eventually turned one of the worst moments of his creative life into a meaningful exploration of disappointment that became a wonderfully meaty creative outlet, a critically and listener-acclaimed creative product, and the platform for myriad other creative collaborations.

It's not the most fun reality of our business, but this sort of thing is likely to happen to you, and more than once. Creating a lasting writing career means finding productive ways to deal with these realities.

- **Understand why it sometimes happens and realize this is simply a normal and unavoidable part of this business.** That understanding alone can rob these events of a lot of their sting.
- **Because of that, adopt a set-it-and-forget-it strategy.** Years ago when my mother and brother taught me about investing,

they said to treat all the money I put into my investments as sunk costs. To think of it as money already completely gone, as a way of insulating myself against the market's constant rise and fall and keeping myself from ever touching the principal. The same philosophy is often touted for saving: Commit a certain amount to "paying yourself" and treat that money as gone forever.

I've always found this philosophy helpful with things like submitting to agents and publishers too: Send out your queries and then forget about them. If you hear back it's a delicious surprise, and if you don't, no big deal. You've already let go of the result and can move forward with other queries.

- **But follow up when you need to.** There is not one thing wrong with following up on any submission, or a promise, or an offer of help. Generally people make you those offers in earnest and they meant them, before life got in the way. So it's perfectly fine to kindly, politely send a gentle tickle.

  Keep boundaries in mind, however, as well as the many limitations on these professionals' time, and keep your requests brief and only occasional. The quickest way to get any kind of offer of help rescinded is to badger the person who made it. But offering a gentle reminder to a colossally busy person who may simply have accidentally let you slip through the cracks is often greatly appreciated.

- **Remember rejection is not the end of the world—or your writing career.** This business is full of opening and closing doors. It is one of its most prominent characteristics, regardless of how successful an author may become. You may be on top of the mountain one moment, but you assuredly will find yourself knocked off of it now and again and crawling your way back to the summit. That's just the way this industry goes, even for the most successful writers. If you miss one opportunity, another will come. The authors who succeed are the ones who simply stay in the game and look for those opportunities, and swing at every single one. Don't take any of it personally.

- **Put it into the work.** That's not to say by any means that your manuscript is a thing of perfection and you should stand by your words exactly as written no matter what, as if they're fossilized in amber. Writing and storytelling are a process, one that often takes a lot of revision and rewriting to get the story on the page as effectively as you're able to make it. And sometimes, just as with dating, you also need to do the work on your own to be the best version of yourself you're capable of at the moment—not to please anyone else, but simply to be your truest, most genuine, healthiest self. That's what will attract someone who's right for you.

  So do that work. Tell your story—to the best of your abilities. Write it, and then edit, revise, rewrite, and repeat until you have made it as close to the shining vision in your head as you're capable of making it. And then submit until you find an agent and editor and readers who feel as strongly about it as you do—your team, your champions…your people.

  Or, as Ratliff did, channel that rejection *into* your work. Let it influence and impact it, and maybe even send you in a new direction—one that may be even more satisfying and effective. You may find a new depth and dimension to your story you wouldn't have discovered otherwise, or move to a new project it inspires. Maybe you decide to stop submitting altogether and indie-publish on your own terms.

  Rejection isn't a roadblock for your writing—it's simply a stop sign or a detour. You can move past it and keep progressing forward.

- **Do for others.** A proven way out of dwelling on your own concerns is by helping other people with theirs. Reach out to others, help someone, give back, throw yourself into your

writing community. Multiple studies show that helping other people is a key source and indicator of happiness and good mental health. And in the process you're building your own support network and creating wonderful goodwill among people who will be there for you and perhaps help you find other open doors down the road.
- **Have a life.** Art is not life, and you are much more than your writing career. When your writing career is floundering is a great time to dedicate your focus to other areas that make your life meaningful, like loved ones or other interests and passions. Don't let one person's opinion or action undermine your happiness or your whole life.

The author who wrote me about being ghosted followed up with the person who'd made the offer of an introduction, and then when they still heard nothing back eventually let it go—because sometimes that's all you can do. But they also took it as an opportunity to spread their own wings a little more, trust themselves, and keep looking for the next opportunity—because often that's what you *need* to do... the hidden treasure of resiliency inside every setback and challenge, one that can make you stronger, better at your craft, and lead to even greater things.

"It's been such a gift because we never would have arrived at this place if I hadn't had my little show business nightmare," Ratliff tells Hanks at one point in the *Dead Eyes* interview. "It's been a real lesson in terms of even a negative experience can sometimes be the thing that is ultimately more rewarding than if I just had a lovely time filming for a day on *Band of Brothers*."

"Well, isn't that the serendipity that you must have faith in?" Hanks replies. "There is a type of seasoning of, Who knows what's going to happen? A pure, unadulterated chance that moves stuff along somehow. And it never stops happening in a career.... You don't have this magnificent story without some form of tragedy happening to you," he says of Ratliff's journey to a thriving career in their twenty-years-in-the-making conversation. "And that speaks to perseverance, about keeping going despite any number of bad news. It speaks to the serendipity of you never know what's going to come down the pike."

In a business like writing, we cannot know what's going to come down the pike—what seemingly soul-crushing, career-ending event might turn out to be the best thing that ever happened to us. We simply have to focus on our creativity itself, because it's so much of who we are.

And of course Tom Hanks, America's dad, offers us the wisest advice for how to do that:

"All you can do is to try to be fascinated by the work that you're doing," he tells Ratliff. "That's it…it's a journey of many steps and the only thing you can do is keep stepping, keep walking. That's the perseverance that's required."

Chapter Twenty-two

What Rejection Letters Do and Don't Mean

Let's just go ahead and acknowledge that rejection—in any and all of its many permutations—blows. It hurts every time—even when you didn't particularly care about the thing you're being rejected for. (Anyone who's ever been dumped by someone they weren't that into knows exactly what I'm talking about.)

No matter what, every rejection feels personal—even when it isn't. And when a tender creative soul starts to accrue enough of them, it can knock the knees right out from under you: daunt your hopes, damage your confidence, and decimate your spirit.

But rejection isn't an adjudication on the caliber of your writing, your story, or you as a writer—and it doesn't even always mean "rejection," per se.

Let's dissect the types of rejections you might receive, and see if we can take the stinger out of those vexing little bastards.

The Form Rejection

Most rejections you will receive are form letters—not because agents or publishers are assholes or don't care about you, but because most of them are inundated with submissions, and if they wrote a personal letter in response to each one they would have no time to do the bulk of their job, which is to sell, publish, or market their clients' books.

Rejection letters are a necessary evil, and most industry pros try to make them as gentle as possible. To cheer myself I made "rejection poetry" out of some of the truly lovely ones I accrued over the course of peddling my fiction:

> Thank you for your query,
> which I read with interest.
> Unfortunately, I am not the right agent for your work.
> Do not despair
> as another agent might feel
> quite differently.
> Thank you for considering me.
> I wish you the best
> with your writing.

> Thank you so much
> for writing me
> about
> your
> project.
> I read and consider each query carefully
> and, while yours is not (exactly)
> what I am looking for,
> I would certainly encourage you
> to keep trying.

I know your work
is important to you
and I am grateful
that you wrote to me.

Sometimes we must pass on books,
               (even very good books),
which are either out of our range or
               require an amount of attention we
               feel
unable
  to
    provide.
In addition, we cannot
               afford
to take on projects which we're not absolutely
confident
we will be able to sell.
But we do very much hope
               that you
                 will find
                   an agent
                     with the right
                       enthusiasm
                         for your work.

    I mean, these are some very kind ways to be rejected! They *almost* cushion the blow. (Almost.)
    Some letters are far less gentle—I once received back my original printed query letter (in the days of yore before email queries, kids) with simply a scribbled "No" in mean red ink at the top. (And

this was back when you also sent a self-addressed stamped envelope for the privilege.)

But an indelicate or thoughtless rejection doesn't mean or say anything about you or the worth of your work; it's merely a function of that agent and his or her approach. And at least it's an answer, as opposed to dropping into the black hole of no-reply.

As you can see from my rejections, the ones that are kind generally will say something positive with a delicately phrased "no, thanks." That's still a no, not a suggestion or an invitation to try harder, and it's still a form letter—don't try to read something into it about how you can improve your manuscript. A rejection letter is basically just the swipe-left of submissions.

But don't take them personally. It may or may not have anything to do with your story, your writing, or anything under your control. Most likely your story is simply not a fit for this agent or editor, and they don't have time to spend on anything that isn't.

The Hopeful Rejection ("No for Now")

If you do get any kind of personal feedback—and you'll know what's personal because it will be specific to you and your story—that's an excellent sign, even if it's a rejection. That means that in their unbelievably limited time, the agent or editor liked something about your query or submission well enough to carve out some of it to give you a personal response.

Take that as the encouraging sign it is. You are now not just another query on the slush pile.

If the agent/editor gave you a categorical "no" despite the personalized reply, this is still an open door to query again with a future project. They have already indicated they like you and your writing.

When you have a new manuscript to submit, remind them of your previous query and their positive, personal response (and *only* that—a previous form rejection will get you exactly nothing). If you have the email chain (and you should always save that type of email chain), write it on that thread with an updated subject line so they can see and remind themselves of your exchange.

But if the agent or editor gave you specific feedback without a definitive "no," it's an opportunity to resubmit if you take their input and revise accordingly—even if that's not explicitly spelled out.

Revise and Resubmit (R&R)

If an agent or editor gives you feedback and it resonates for your story, do it and reapproach them, no matter how much time has passed. There is no expiration date on an industry professional who liked your work enough to take time from their—I promise you—insanely busy schedule to give you specific, personalized feedback.

Take your time with these revisions. If you alter a few sentences or make cosmetic changes and return it to the agent or editor again within days or even couple of weeks, they're going to think you haven't done enough for them to take a second look. An agent isn't going to say no for a minor tweak, because that would be something they trust could be easily addressed once they sign you. If they say "no for now," it means they see potential but want to see if you have the ability to bring it out before they take the chance of signing you. And that usually means a more substantial edit. Thoughtful, meaningful edits take time. Even when I work with publishers on tight production deadlines, our first-pass turnarounds are rarely shorter than a month and usually longer.

When you do resubmit, remind the editor or agent who you are and of your previous exchange as specifically as you can—meaning when and where you met if you did, or when you submitted, and a brief summary that they offered you feedback and you have revised your manuscript with their input in mind, if they would be willing to take another look. Again, if it was via email, as it likely will be, send it on that same thread with an updated subject line.

But make sure you understand your story and your goals well enough to be able to assess the feedback you get and decide whether it's right for you. You won't up your chances by reworking your story to try to please every individual taste or perspective.

Some feedback may be excellent in helping you better effect your intentions on the page and make your book more salable. Some may simply be a personal preference or what that agent or editor happens to be looking for on their particular list, and may or may not be right for your story. This is the most subjective of businesses.

Ask yourself, if you have to change too much of your vision or goals to get an agent or editor to sign you, will you still be creating the work and the career *you* want to create?

What Rejection Letters Really Mean

When I was single—for a long time, not meeting my now-husband till I was nearly forty—I bemoaned to a friend that I felt discouraged not to have found someone I wanted to share a life with.

"But you just haven't met the right person yet," she said reasonably. "If you had, you'd be with them—and meanwhile every person who's *not* the guy gets you one step closer to the one who is."

It was almost comically simple, but it shorted out my brain for a moment, and recast the way I thought of dating afterward. I didn't have "failed" relationships; I was simply moving closer to a successful one. And with every single person who wasn't that one, I learned more and more about who I was and what I wanted, so that when I did finally meet someone I could see myself creating a life with, I was mature, confident, and wise enough to create a strong, successful, long-lasting relationship.

I didn't just hope for "the one." I held out for the *right* one.

Take a rejection as a data point of someone you're glad to have ruled out in your search for the right one, like dating—because that's what it takes.

Agents are in the business of sales and marketing. And while they do care immensely about the quality of the work they represent, you have no way of knowing whether a rejection means your work isn't quite to the level they feel is publishable yet or it's simply not something they think they can sell for a myriad of possible mercurial reasons largely out of your control.

You don't want an agent (or a partner, for that matter) if they don't want you. You want someone who is wild about your story and your writing. Your agent is representing your work and you on the marketplace. You want them to feel almost as much enthusiasm about it as you do. They are your representative, your PR person, your marketer, your champion.

A Few Final Rules of Thumb

DON'T:
- ...follow up and tell an agent or editor why they're wrong, or otherwise rant at or assail them in any way. This is the smallest of businesses, and everyone knows everyone. Your nastygram will make the email rounds among agents and publishers, and your name will be a big red flag of NOPE for anyone who sees or hears about it.
- ...explain what you think the person didn't understand about your story. They do not care—they just know you aren't what they're looking for right now. You're wasting your energy and their time, and making yourself look like someone difficult to work with.
- ...change everything about your story, or anything that makes it no longer the story you wanted to tell. If this agent or editor doesn't think they can market the kinds of stories you want to write, they aren't the right one for you.
- ...take it personally if it takes time to find the right agent or publisher. A lot of stars have to align to make that relationship a great fit, and literature abounds with stories

of successful authors who received dozens, even hundreds of rejections before finding success (including my own: I found my agent on query 113, and publication on the second submission round of my second manuscript).
- ...let rejection derail you. Even if you're receiving it because your work isn't quite ready yet, that's not a statement of your worth; it's simply a normal part of the process of sharpening your skills and honing a story. How will you know if you're "there" yet if you don't test-drive your manuscript with a few professionals? That's how a writer grows—there's no shame in that game. Toss that rejection letter or stash it out of sight and forget about it; then dust yourself off, get back in the driver's seat, and send out more—while you keep working on your next manuscript.

DO:
- ...thank the agent if you got a personal note or specific feedback.
- ...keep the email chain with any agent who sends a personal reply, feedback, or an R&R. Forever. Even if you sign with another agent, one day you may again be in the market for representation, and an actual thread with an agent who liked your work is a powerful introduction to a new query.
- ...share your rejection pain, frustration, and despair with trusted friends and colleagues. It really does lessen the blow, and can be a wonderful source of comfort and encouragement that can feed your fortitude to keep going. I tried to quit querying on rejection number one hundred, but one of my crit partners refused to let me.
- ...find ways to make light of it, as I did with my rejection poetry. It defangs the bite of rejection.
- ...persist. The only way to truly fail at finding representation or publication is to quit.

We might all wish rejection letters were as gentle and kind as this one from a Chinese economic journal, offered by writer and translator Estelle Gilson and shared in author James Clear's newsletter:

"We have read your manuscript with boundless delight. If we were to publish your paper, it would be impossible for us to publish any work of lower standard. And as it is unthinkable that in the next thousand years we shall see its equal, we are, to our regret, compelled to return your divine composition and to beg you a thousand times to overlook our short sight and timidity."[19]

Alas, they are not. But with the right mindset and resilience we can learn to see them as what they are: simply a single stepping-stone on the path toward our goals.

Chapter Twenty-three

Knowledge Burnout and Information Overload

Many years ago in my childhood, my mom dropped me off for an otherwise aimless summer day at the main branch of our central library for the first time. She thought she was doing a wonderful thing for her voracious-reader kid who couldn't get enough books, and sure enough I came out with a stack of them as high as they would allow me to check out. But when I got in the car my mood wasn't quite what my mother expected.

"What's wrong?" she asked at my crestfallen demeanor.

"I'll never be able to read all those books," I told her sadly, picturing the towering shelves.

Even as an eight-year-old I understood that there was more knowledge in the world than I would ever be able to consume, and I entered into my very first tiny little existential depression.

Now, many years later, we're living in a time of vast abundance of knowledge and information that seems like it should make our lives fuller and richer and help us grow. And of course it can.

But lately I'm seeing evidence of a whole lot of writers feeling like that little overwhelmed eight-year-old I used to be, daunted by trying to do the impossible and Hoover up all the information available as if we're ChatGPT uploading countless gigabytes of (largely unpaid-for, misappropriated[20]) IP into our brains.

Not long ago on a writers' forum I subscribe to, an author posted to ask other members how they manage to keep up with all the articles and blog posts about craft and business that they want to read. She said she barely had enough time to write and revise her own projects she's working on, and felt overwhelmed by also trying to find time for the informational and educational posts that also feel essential to growing her writing career.

An author posted a similar question[21] to Jane Friedman's Ask the Editor column, saying her in-box was filled with advice she can't possibly find time to read, and that she felt it was diverting her focus and time for actual writing.

I'm hearing a *lot* of author chatter about overwhelm and overload lately, and it's understandable.

The internet has brought constant news to our inboxes from every corner of the world. Social media has provided a steady stream of updates and info from friends, acquaintances, and people we follow.

Specific to our field, the explosion of indie and small-press publishing has resulted in a slew of experts flooding the market, and attendant expert forums offering information about every element of craft and business. There are countless books, webinars, conferences, retreats, classes, and articles, all geared toward helping you find the "right" way to write.

For those of us who are knowledge junkies and love our craft, it may feel like a Mecca. Anything you want to know about our field, bam, it's right there at the end of a search tag. You don't even have to trouble yourself touching the keys to create a search: One click of a button on a signup sheet and you can have your favorite writing outlets and blogs send posts right to your in-box, often on the daily.

Type a simple question into AI-powered search engines and they will spit back at you a vast array of information culled (or let's say appropriated without compensation[22]) from countless millions of books and articles.

Writers are trapped under an avalanche of information and we are not okay, y'all.

The Backlash of Information Overload

The desire to learn and hone our craft is an understandable one. We're in this field because we love it, and if we love it we want to get better and better at it to take us closer to whatever our goals for our writing careers may be.

And from the time we're born, it's inculcated in us that the way you get better at something is to be taught. We have to be taught how to latch onto our mom to get food; how to propel ourselves in space using our four limbs, and then later just two of them; how to stop peeing and pooping ourselves.

We're taught language and communication. We go to school and we're taught reading, writing, and arithmetic. If we want to learn any extracurriculars, like music or sports or debate, we're taught how to do that too. When we enter the workforce, we're taught how to do the jobs we were hired for.

So of course our instinct when we want to become better writers is to seek out teaching—the more the better.

But there's a backlash to that. Often it seems that the more you study, the more you may feel entangled by what initially felt natural to you. You may start questioning and second-guessing whether you're doing it "right" and freeze yourself up. You may try to faithfully follow the tenets you've been taught and strip the life and originality out of your writing.

Sometimes you may fall victim to what's often called analysis paralysis, where your efforts stall out entirely because you're so overwhelmed by input that you fear or don't know how to just move forward and *write*. So much of your time and energy is spent learning that you're not actually *doing*.

And yet still we keep lapping up more. It's like we have information and knowledge FOMO.

Overcoming Overwhelm

It's a strange thing: To paraphrase Jane Friedman in her excellent answer to the author who asked her how to combat information overload, I am one of the purveyors of that information, so it may seem disingenuous for me to suggest limiting your intake of it. But as an editor I've always said that if I'm doing my job right an author may need my services less and less, and I think that's true of teaching as well.

It's healthy to always be open to new information. To be willing to reconsider, rethink, and grow. I've been working in this field for my entire career and I still learn more about my craft almost every day.

But mostly I'm just *doing* it. And a lot of what I'm learning comes from that doing of it—hands-on, direct, and personalized.

Once you learn how to walk, or ride a bike, or play the flute, burying yourself in books and classes about how to do it isn't going to make you better. Periodically you may need more education to help you reach a new level of competence or overcome a specific challenge. But you've already got your foundation, and it's your job to build on it by *doing the thing*, over and over and over, learning from experience.

Face the FOMO. You can't possibly take in all the information that exists, much of it excellent, but much of it pedestrian and sometimes even downright bad or counterproductive.

Just as in your writing it can be easy to fall down a research rabbit hole and never actually write, don't let yourself fall down the perpetual-student mine shaft and never bring any of the gold to the surface.

You have to learn to discern: to be willing to let go of the idea of being able to take in endless information and use it effectively in your writing, and decide which and how much of these resources may be most helpful to you.

In the words of Ursula the sea witch, life's full of tough choices, innit? Here are some suggestions for how to make them:

- **Unsubscribe**. Having piles of posts accruing in your inbox just heightens the FOMO, feeling like an ever-growing to-do list you'll never make any headway on. Take away that pressure and guilt and stress and start unsubscribing from some of the newsletters and blogs you may have signed up for, even including mine (though I'll miss you desperately). Decide on a few you feel are most valuable for you or that most resonate, and bravely remove yourself from the rest. You can always come back if or when you decide you want to.
- **Pinpoint**. Drinking randomly from a fire hose of information about *anything* doesn't yield mastery. It makes you a dilettante, with a shallow but broad layer of knowledge, rather than an expert with a more focused but deep and thorough understanding. When you need specific info about a specific challenge or speed bump in your work, go find it. But keep in mind that often the best way to learn to master your stuck places is to work through them, steadily and directly.
- **Regulate**. As with any other field, set aside time you'll dedicate to continuing education—which takes a backseat to your actual *working* time. Stick ruthlessly to whatever that allotted time is. Don't fall down the mine shaft and let yourself be pulled away from your main goal and the number-one way of learning your craft: doing it.
- **Multitask**. My best information-intake time is often in the cracks of otherwise mindless activities where I can split

my focus: listening to podcasts and interviews while doing household chores or gardening or walking the dogs, for instance, or reading posts and articles while blow-drying my hair. This feels to me like found bonus time. Or take back the time from mindless social-media scrolling.
- **Let go.** But remember you don't have to fill every spare moment with knowledge intake. Just as your characters do, we need time to digest and process what we take in, and to decide how the information may affect our thoughts and actions. Give yourself space to let the information percolate. Remember the crucial importance and value of *rest*—for your work, and for your psyche.

Perhaps more important than all these suggestions, though, is one overarching one: Figure out what works for *you, your* writing, *your* story, *your* career, *your* life. All this available information and guidance is a buffet laid out for you. You're not expected to eat it all—and you shouldn't even try. Just select the morsels that look most delicious to you at each particular meal.

And don't fall into another common thought trap for writers: that any one system, theory, method, or "guru" is the One True Way.

F*ck the Cat

Let me say right out of the gate that this is not an attack on the Save the Cat theory of writing and storytelling. In fact I'm a fan of screenwriter Blake Snyder's system (and Jessica Brody's adaptation for novel writers). I'm a fan of Michael Hauge's Six-stage Plot Structure. I'm a fan of the Hero's Journey. The W plot structure. Three-act story structure.

All these theories of writing are wonderful tools for authors.

But that's all they are: tools. Where authors get wrapped around the axle is in maintaining a rigid devotion to these or any system of writing or storytelling theory.

WHY THE CAT CAN'T HELP YOU WRITE

An author I once worked with cited all the many excellent theories she had dedicatedly studied—including Save the Cat—and was working diligently to incorporate into her WIP, but she was still struggling in our work together to find the heart of her story.

She wasn't doing anything wrong and hadn't failed to understand the theories she was working with. She was just too rigidly trying to follow and incorporate all these systems, and as a result was freezing up her creative freedom, her voice, her style—and her story. She was lost in her left brain at the expense of her right brain, the font of creativity.

"Fuck the cat!" I burst out on one call. (Sorry for the down-and-dirty vernacular there, folks, but editing can be a very down-and-dirty business sometimes.)

She had to be reminded that she *knew* this stuff, that she knew her story, she knew her characters. That she had done the work and it was a part of her and of her creative process, and she could let it all go in digging deeper in our work together to bring the story more fully to life—organically, from the inside out, rather than trying to impose someone else's structure on it externally.

None of these writing-craft systems, or any storytelling theory, is a magic bullet or a one-size-fits-all formula. If they were, every writer who followed them would be a major bestseller. Obviously that's not the case, and it's not because you're not adhering to them well enough.

Imagine learning to dance. You study countless steps and moves, you practice them for endless hours, but when the time comes to perform the dance, if you're consciously trying to think of your training and choreography you're going to trip over your own feet. It's like having your instructor dogging your every step as you make it. No one can dance like that.

And no one can write like that.

Writing systems like the ones I mention above are how you learn story craft and improve your knowledge, skill, and ability.

It's the equivalent of learning the choreography, running through it over and over.

But when you sit down to write your story, you have to let all that go. The reason you put so much time into studying any pursuit is so that when the time comes to *do* the thing, you can forget about all that training and let muscle memory and intuition take over.

That's the spark and the life of your creative product, honed by all the knowledge and experience you've accrued. But you have to let go and trust that you've done so. That it's all there, part of the fabric of who you are as an artist and a craftsperson.

Not long ago I interviewed bestselling author Barry Eisler for my How Writers Revise feature,[23] and among the many gems he let drop during our conversation was one that grabbed my focus: that mastering any skill or craft involves three different ways of acquiring the skill: theory, drill, and free practice.

To oversimplify Barry's explanation:

- **Theory** is *learning* the craft. In the case of writing, that means reading craft books, taking webinars and classes and workshops, attending conferences, etc.
- **Drill** involves what Barry calls "looking for the magic trick behind the magic": analyzing other stories to figure out how craft applies in action.
- **Practice** is doing it—butt in seat, words on page.

(You can see Barry's whole explanation in our recorded interview on my YouTube channel at 1:12:18.)[24]

FORGET THE CAT

All these many writing theories, systems, techniques—as helpful and insightful as they may be—are just step one: the foundation. They're how you begin to understand your art form and the skills you're trying to master: Narrative structure. Character development. Plotting.

Establishing and building stakes. Creating and maintaining suspense and tension. Point of view. Voice...and the countless other elements involved in weaving the complex tapestry of story.

Then you have to get out and see them in the real world, how they work—or don't. That's what I call "training your editor brain," learning to objectively assess *other* people's stories to see what works well and what doesn't, why or why not, and how the author did or didn't achieve their ends for the story.

This is where you start to hone your skill at not only diagnosing the problem, where there may be one, but how to address it to strengthen a story. This is some of the most potent, effective learning you will do for your craft.

And then you take all these skills—what you've learned academically and theoretically, what you've learned from analyzing other people's stories—and you write your own. But not by rigidly applying all these principles to your work as you're creating it. Instead, forget all that theory and *write*. Don't hamper your creative freedom by getting bogged down in mechanics.

Forget the steps. Just dance.

If you've put in the time and effort on steps one and two—theory and drill—you have internalized these concepts and they're now tools in your toolbox, ready to hand when it's time for practice: actually doing the writing.

When to Call in the Cat

There *is* a time to give those tools the spotlight, when you might focus more deliberately and consciously on the elements of craft and how to use them in your writing. But that's not in the drafting process.

It's in creating an outline, if you're a plotter, and making sure it's watertight before you start writing.

It's in diagnosing what may or may not be working in the story as effectively as it could, and troubleshooting those areas—a.k.a. editing.

It's in honing and fine-tuning to make sure the story on the page is conveying the version in your head—a.k.a. revising.

That's another reason the second step—drill—is such a valuable skill to develop. Learning to identify what's working well and what isn't in other people's stories—in which you have built-in objectivity that every writer lacks in their own work—is how you gain skill in seeing these areas in your *own* writing.

And learning to diagnose why something isn't working, and how it could be more effective, is how you gain skill in addressing the areas of your *own* stories that may not be working as well as they could.

As valuable as the various schools of thought, writing systems, formulas, and techniques may be, no single one of them is a how-to manual—not for every author.

That's what finding yourself as a writer and forging your writing career means: figuring out what tool you need when, and knowing how to use it when you do. And that's different for every writer, every story.

That third step—the practice of writing—is one the cat can't take with you. You have to shut the door on the cat—and all the other writing systems and theories and techniques you've learned—and find your own way, trusting that you've internalized what you may need of others' systems to be able to determine what works for you.

Learn your craft. Experience it through others' stories. Then create your own.

One final word about writing advice: So much of it is based on what writers absolutely *shouldn't* do, what you "can't" do in successful stories, long lists of "don'ts" that will tank your story or career:

- "Don't use adjectives or adverbs."
- "You shouldn't use semicolons because they seem pretentious."

- "You can't sell a book with a prologue."
- "Don't try writing multiple points of view or multiple timelines with your first full-length manuscript."

The list is long, and I'm betting you can fill in many others you've heard.

I'll go ahead and confess right now that "don't," "can't," and "shouldn't" are none of my favorite words. As soon as someone precedes any advice or instruction with one of these proscriptions, I start thinking about how I might get around them, or exceptions, or how I can do the exact opposite thing just to show that no one is the boss of me.

So many of these absolute "rules" wind up fettering an author's creativity and voice. It's a main reason I almost always use the word in quotes. And quite often, these "rules" and injunctions aren't valid or useful constrictions anyway:

- Descriptive words like adjectives and adverbs can add great color and depth to your story.
- Punctuation—*all* punctuation—is designed to aid in guiding readers fluidly through your story and to clarify meaning, and stratifying it is a ridiculous affectation.
- Good prologues rock and can powerfully set up an entire story.
- And any creative art should be about stretching your abilities in areas that are difficult and perhaps just beyond your current skills, like multiple storylines. Otherwise how do we grow as artists? As Vincent van Gogh said, "I am always doing what I can't do yet in order to learn how to do it."

The "rules" of writing can so often strap you down or cram you into a mold that simply isn't right for every author, every story, every circumstance. Finding your style and voice and the most effective approach to your writing means discovering what works best for *you*.

When to Consider the "Don'ts"

And yet, like the experiences of others that can help save us from unnecessary pain, some of these prohibitions may help you write a better story or reach your readers more effectively.

For example, that oft-repeated advice not to corner an agent or editor in a bathroom stall and vomit your entire plot upon them? Solid.

Don't start your story with a dream or your character waking up? Pretty good advice, given that many agents and editors will immediately tune out upon encountering yet another iteration of a device that has become a tired cliché.

Still other proscriptions aren't nearly as black-and-white as they may be presented:

- "You shouldn't head-hop in stories, because it makes readers doubt the author's authority and feel as if they have uncertain footing in the story." Yet watch Kevin Kwan rampantly do just that and rake in the millions.
- "Authors shouldn't write outside of their lived experience, because it may be perceived as cultural appropriation and make your book harder to sell." Yet a world of every author writing from only their narrow personal lives would be artistically barren indeed for both creator and audience.

The truth is, life (and art) is often made up of a fire hose of dos and don'ts streaming at us nonstop. Much of it is well-meant, a lot of it is probably hard-won by the advice giver, and the best of it is even quite likely to benefit you, as a writer and as a human being.

But as a creative (and as a human being), it's also our nature to have to find out for ourselves, to varying degrees.

Choose the "Rules" You Want to Break

Maybe you're a mostly rule-following but partial maverick. Maybe you're a by-the-book straight arrow. Maybe you're a complete renegade, eschewing all "rules" to forge your own path through the underbrush. It's all valid, and it's *all* right if it's right for you.

You may make mistakes. Seemingly stupid ones. Even major ones. Hopefully none you can't recover from. And in the process of that recovery, you will learn and grow. You will increase the experiences you have to draw on in the future, your knowledge, and your skill. And no lessons are as deeply learned as those from direct experience.

You may find in trying to write a multiple-POV novel that you've created a complete hash of a story and have two hundred thousand words of unusable manuscript. But is it wasted? No. You've learned, to paraphrase Edison, one of plenty of ways *not* to write a successful multiple-POV story, and you won't make those same mistakes again.

Maybe it's shown you another approach that might work better. Maybe it's helped you move the ball down the field just one yard line, but you'll try again with the next manuscript, and the next, and the next, and pretty soon you'll be writing *War and Peace*.

Or maybe you'll just wind up with a file full of harvest material that could find its way into other stories. You don't know yet, and you may not know for a long time. But nothing is wasted: no effort we make, no experience we have, no lesson we learn. Some of my most valuable experiences—in writing and in life—have been my "failures." They are, almost without exception, the precursor to and often the reason for my successes.

But that deep, foundational knowledge of your craft comes not from reading about writing, but from *doing* it.

Here are some "don'ts" that may in fact be universally applicable: Don't let yourself get buried in writing advice. Don't work so hard trying to learn your craft that you're never actually practicing it. The next time some "writing expert" tells you "don't do this," "you can't try that," "you shouldn't do this other thing," don't take it as gospel; just nod and thank them for their insight.

And then, if you really want to try that thing for yourself, do it anyway.

You may fail spectacularly and get knocked to the mat—but as long as you get up again...and again...and again, you're never down for the count.

Or you may succeed spectacularly and blaze a trail no one has yet walked. Being an artist, being a vibrant living being, means letting yourself experiment and try and live fully. And failure isn't the end. It's just a new beginning.

(But do trust me on the bathroom thing.)

Part Five

CAREER

Chapter Twenty-four

Caveat Scriptor: When Creators Become the Customers

Imagine pursuing a business where your chances of success and profit were small, but the overhead costs to operate it could be significant and ongoing. Where your vendors were doing quite well in their businesses, even while yours might be struggling just to break even, let alone turn a profit. Where even if you do sell your product, it's likely to yield less than a living annual wage. And that doesn't even factor in things like health insurance costs, sick leave, or retirement savings.

Most people would look at these P&Ls and step far away from this business model.

But these are the harsh facts of our industry, chiefly that most books do not sell well and most writers do not make a living from their writing, even as they are increasingly responsible for bearing the costs.

And yet in all my years working in the publishing business I have never seen the level of industry that's grown up in recent years around services and products marketed to authors.

Writers have become not only the product but the customer.

Dreams are powerful things, and artists are powerful dreamers. It's one of the most magnificent and sublime things about creatives. Not only do they stay connected to those most hopeful and tender parts of being human, but through their art they share it with others.

That can also make creatives uniquely inclined to follow their dreams—sometimes at the expense of reality.

We all hope we might be among that tiny fraction of authors who catch fire: become bestsellers, sell foreign and movie rights, reach—and make—millions. But the reality is that most won't.

There is no part of me that wishes to discourage writers or any other artists from their art. The value of art in our world is incalculable. But the cost of living *is* calculable. And it's a key consideration in how we run our writing careers if we want to build and sustain them for the long haul.

I wrote in chapter one about the upside of this knowledge in operating the *product* side of your business: how understanding the financial realities of the publishing business can give you more autonomy over your own writing career, rather than leaving authors feeling their success is at the mercy of the gatekeepers.

But let's look at operating the *customer* side of your career: you as a writer hiring other professionals and services for your business. I am not denigrating or dismissing those professionals or services or their potential value to writers. I'm one of them, making my living offering services to writers and publishers.

But I *am* encouraging you as an artist and a businessperson to be an informed consumer and make sound, practical investment decisions. That starts with asking yourself two essential but entirely subjective questions.

One: What do you need versus what do you want?

To be a writer the overhead is encouragingly low. The main requirements have always been simply a writing implement and something to record your thoughts on, whether that's a cave wall, a stone tablet, paper, or an electronic file.

To run a writing *business* there may be more costs involved. Your job is to determine what you need to operate your career, versus what you want.

You may desire someone to help you with the writing itself, like a writing coach or teacher. You may want to invest in classes, books, conferences, and other educational opportunities. You may want editing help, or to pay for critique or beta-reading services. You may consider hiring someone to assist you with design, marketing.

But how much of it do you genuinely *need*?

Here are just some of the many services and professionals you can pay for, and a few considerations in deciding whether they are "necessities" for your goals:

- **Do you need an MFA,** for instance, or an expensive writing program that claims to replace one? Nope. Many MFA grads are also not making a living from their writing, and many published authors do not have MFAs. That's not a requirement for or guarantee of success. There are other ways to learn your craft and your business.
- **Do you *want* an MFA?** That's something different, and that becomes a subjective cost consideration: Is that expenditure personally worth it to you, considering that it's unlikely to yield much measurable ROI?

- **Classes, conferences, retreats:** You can find excellent ones priced extremely reasonably, and mediocre or even poor ones priced exorbitantly, and vice versa. Price is not necessarily the indicator of value. Caveat emptor—do your research: Vet the offerings and those who are providing them, and look for ways to see what previous attendees have thought. Quality writing education and training don't have to cost a mint.
- **Writing/book coach:** Having someone to help in the process, to keep you motivated and focused, may be a lovely luxury, but is it necessary? This field has exploded lately, but since time immemorial writers have managed to write without them. Like hiring a personal trainer, it may make the work easier or more efficient, though, or encourage you to show up for it, and that may be a service you're willing to pay for.
- **Paid beta reading or critique services:** This is another field that has expanded in recent years, but the time-honored way of doing this—trading crits with other authors, enlisting educated readers, etc.—is free (or just the price of a thoughtful thank-you gift or dinner) and can be just as useful if you understand what you need from these other sources and how to get it. See my website's Editing Toolbox page (FoxPrintEditorial.com) for a free downloadable questionnaire you can offer your beta readers, for example, to elicit useful, actionable feedback.
- **Editing:** A good, experienced developmental editor can be a marvelous luxury, someone who can offer you objective, actionable input to help you make your manuscript as strong and competitive and marketable as it can be, and push your writing and your story to the next level. But if you are contracted with a traditional publisher a dev edit is generally encompassed in-house, as are copyediting and proofreading.

  But authors have long succeeded without hiring an independent developmental editor. If you can find good, solid crit partners and/or beta readers, often they can help offer the objective input that will help you see whether your intentions are on the page and show you where the manuscript may need more development or clarification. Editors often make this process much easier and more focused, but I'd still qualify this as a "want," not necessarily a need.

For authors self-publishing, or with small or hybrid pub houses, I often suggest at least a copyedit may be a "need," as readers can be brutal about mistakes and typos, and you're competing with every polished professionally published title out there.

- **Formatting and cover design:** Personal choice. I know many self- and indie-pubbed authors who do this for themselves, and there are good programs to help you with both (which can be an investment, FYI). But you can also hire this done if you need it and worry that your abilities won't match your expectations; professionals bring expertise, artistry, and knowledge of the market that can help your book look more polished.
- **Audiobook production** can also be done with little overhead (if you're willing to sacrifice part of your royalties for it), or you can bear these costs yourself if you decide to self-publish your book in this format, which is also a matter of personal choice. Those expenses usually involve equipment to record with; a space to record in, whether you create that or rent it (I created a very affordable and effective version of my own recording studio in my closet with shower rods and moving blankets); hiring voice talent if needed; and an engineer/editor if you want that done professionally, or the software to do it if you choose to tackle it yourself.
- **Marketing, publicity, and advertising services** can similarly be as much or as little as you choose. Know that spending more does not always guarantee more exposure nor more sales. Spending less may not get the results you want either, though. And there are plenty of marketing/outreach

efforts you can do on your own without needing to hire a publicist or other pro. This one is, again, a "want" item.

Depending on your career and personal goals, you may weigh which of these services feel necessary to you. With a traditional publisher, most will be provided in-house, to varying degrees. If you choose to go with a small or indie press you may deem more of these services "needs." If you go hybrid you may still be financially responsible for a great many of them, if you or your publisher deem them necessary. (Make sure you fully understand what you're getting in return with a hybrid publisher—the costs can be exorbitant and the benefits uncertain. Publishing expert Jane Friedman has some excellent info about hybrid publishing on her website.)[25]

Adding all these services up, you could be looking at a very significant investment well into five figures.

Will you make that back? Many don't.

I'm leaving that statement as stark as it seems because I think it's important that authors understand the realities and likelihoods in this business.

Which leads us to the second question: Knowing the uncertain chances of fully recouping those investments, are they still worth making to you?

Two: Is it worth it?

It's important to define "worth it" by metrics specific to *you*:

- Your personal goals and desires
- Your career/business goals and your needs/wants
- Your financial situation

These considerations will help you decide whether what money you do decide to spend is a worthwhile investment. That means vetting what you're getting, and the ROI (return on investment) for each—and this is a subjective equation.

In deciding what's worth it to you, ask yourself some key questions:

HOW IMPORTANT IS THIS TO YOU?

This is a purely subjective assessment of where this expenditure/service falls on your priority list for your personal and career goals. The more specific you can be in defining what those goals are, the better. Are you seeking a traditional publishing path? Self-pubbing? Do you want to hit bestseller lists? Garner X number of reviews? Just share your work with an audience of any size?

Earlier I told of how I once paid several thousand dollars to buy my rights back from a small publisher to whom I had sold them for zero dollars. Think about that: It cost me money to own a story I had written.

When I did so, though, it felt worth it to me for important personal and professional reasons, even not knowing whether I would recoup those costs. But I took into account several other considerations in determining that as well:

WHAT WILL YOU GET OUT OF IT?

This isn't always a tangible product—like a formatted book, for instance. You might decide to spend money for an opportunity: to meet with your dream agent one-on-one in a paid consultation, for instance, or to learn from an expert you admire in an intimate setting like a retreat. You might do it to level up your story and writing by working with a professional.

But be clear about what you are and are not getting. Consider that paid services are just that. Because you've paid to add in a private crit consultation with an agent, for instance, that doesn't mean they will sign you. The best editor or educator in the world can't guarantee you'll be offered a publishing contract. That fancy writer's retreat won't necessarily result in a finished or polished manuscript or key industry contacts.

Those things *may* happen as a result, but there are no guarantees, no magic formula. If anyone is promising you miraculous or foolproof results, you're likely getting hustled. No one has the secret sauce or a magic wand.

Judge whether an expenditure is worth it to you by what you *know* you'll get from those services: An agent you've paid for a consult is likely to provide valuable professional input on the marketability of your story, or whether it's ready to submit, in greater depth than if you'd simply queried them. A good professional edit will likely help you level up not only your story, but your writing and craft skills and knowledge. That fancy writer's retreat with published authors or industry pros probably at the least offers a wonderful, writing-focused vacation with like-minded creatives, and connections made with other authors.

Consider what you're spending, and what concrete ROI it will yield—not the possibilities, but the realities.

IS THIS MONEY YOU CAN COMFORTABLY AFFORD TO SPEND?

I hope it's evident by this point, but given the financial realities of this business, do not spend money that isn't discretionary for you. Don't gamble that you'll make back money you need or want for other important areas of your life, including paying bills, savings, and other expenses and personal priorities.

Decide how much you can/will budget for this type of service—and for how long, based on what it may yield in terms of income—and stick within that.

WHAT IS YOUR TIME WORTH TO YOU?

Many of these services are things you can find "workarounds" for with less expensive ways of accomplishing them, or by learning to do them yourself. Weigh the costs of that—in your time, effort, peace of mind, and the quality you hope for—in deciding what's worth paying someone to do, and what you might accomplish in other ways.

With *Intuitive Editing*, which is self-published, I spent a pretty good chunk on my book designer, graphic designer, audio engineer, marketing, and other overhead costs. However these were all services I did not want to learn or to perform myself, or that would cost me more in time and lost income than it would save, or that I worried I wouldn't be able to do myself to the level of professionalism I wanted—and I was fairly confident I would at least recoup those costs. That made these expenditures worth it to me.

Your writing career is a business—operate it that way

I keep an extensive spreadsheet of all my business expenses and my income, and I regularly track it in ascertaining how much it makes sense to spend on what services for my personal goals and financial situation, and often against what the time commitment of doing it myself—including learning a skill—costs me in income, effort, and mental stress, as opposed to what it would cost me financially to hire someone else to do it.

The expenses I'm willing to incur for my editing business are substantially higher than what I was willing to incur when I was writing fiction, both because editing is my main passion and focus and because it makes up the core of my income, a more profitable venture I'm willing to sustain higher operating costs for.

I strongly recommend authors keep spreadsheets year on year to track their operating costs and income. That lets you see growth as well as gauge what expenditures are worth it, not just financially but for your personal goals. It's essential that you have a realistic idea of what those goals and expenditures are if you want to sustain and build a long-term career.

You should also vet the professionals and services you hire carefully. I offer a free thirteen-page "Get It Edited" guide on the Editing Toolbox page of my website (FoxPrintEditorial.com) to help you do that with editors, and the tips I suggest there can also apply to vetting most any other service or professional. Victoria Strauss investigates complaints about professionals in her wonderful Writer Beware feature through the SFWA (Science Fiction & Fantasy Writers Association, www.sfwa.org).

The beauty of this business is that the overhead for product development, as Flo Rida says, is low, low, low, low, low, low, low, low.

And yet judging by the marketing for some of these services, authors can't properly do their work without whatever they're offering. Be cautious of those who make you believe you "need" to hire any service, that writing is best done by committee, that writers can't write without external guidance and accountability and motivation—all of which they're happy to provide to you for a price.

Your day job should support your writing career, not your writing staff. Make sure that you carefully consider where you're spending your money, and for what, in creating the career path you want.

Chapter Twenty-five

Advocating for Your Writing, Your Career, and Yourself

At his keynote speech at the 2023 Writer's Digest conference in New York, author Chuck Wendig talked about his journey as a writer leading him to writing for the Marvel and Star Wars universes, a collaboration that notoriously ended badly, in no small part thanks to the company's response to internet trolls objecting to his diverse characters.[26] (Spoiler: They fired him.)

Working in Hollywood, Wendig said, made the publishing world feel like a great big hug.

But even if ours is a kinder, gentler industry than the Hollywood machine, a big part of writers taking their place at the table is not only advocating for ourselves as authors, but protecting our creative output: in other words our work and our rights to it.

And you must be your own champion and gatekeeper and guard.

Those of us who create often want so badly for our work to be shared, to have the chance to be meaningful to others, and because of that we are uniquely in a position to be taken advantage of.

While our field's main writers' union, the Authors Guild, has done wonderful and much-needed work in advocating for authors—like establishing that agents should not charge to read submissions, offering guidelines for more author-favorable agency/publishing contracts, and protecting the rights of writers—to a very large degree it's up to authors to advocate for themselves.

But how do you protect yourself on a practical level in an industry where authors are often those with the least powerful seat at the table?

When to Advocate for Yourself

ADVOCATING FOR YOUR WRITING TIME

The first way you can advocate for yourself as a writer is by daring to claim the time you want to dedicate to your art.

That sounds almost remedial as a concept, but it's easy to feel guilty about taking time for your creativity, especially if it's not yielding an income. All of us have so many calls on our time, and it's tempting to relegate writing into the category of luxuries that can be cut when it's scarce.

But I'd argue that creating is essential to our well-being, and even our humanity. There are many "reasons" you could use to justify why it's important: that you're building a career, that you're honing your skills, that you want to set an example for your kids of pursuing things that are important to you.

But I'd like to suggest that you *need* no justification, and that the desire you have to write is sufficient all on its own as the reason: You want to do it because you want to do it, and that's enough.

Honor your creativity, honor the stories that are inside you, and honor yourself by carving out what time you can to dedicate to the craft that matters to you.

ADVOCATING WITH CRITIQUE AND FEEDBACK

Feedback is a necessary and important part of honing our skills and our stories, and soliciting feedback that will be constructive and useful to you is often within your own hands, as is what you do with it. Know how to ask for the kind of feedback you want when offering your story to beta readers and critique partners, and even editors and coaches.

Once you receive feedback, there may be varying types and degrees of it, with varying insightfulness and resonance for you, and advocating for yourself and your work means knowing how to decide what fits your story and your vision and what may not serve you. It means understanding that in a subjective business like art, anyone's feedback, including that of professionals, is only an opinion. And it means knowing and honoring your own opinions as well.

Yes, it's very valuable to see how what you have on the page may be coming across to readers, but ultimately this is *your* story, *your* vision, and it's up to you to know what that is and be the one championing that. (Read more about soliciting and navigating feedback in chapters nineteen and twenty.)

ADVOCATING WITH PROFESSIONALS

There are basic considerations every writer should be mindful of in sharing, selling, and marketing their writing. **A disclaimer**: I'm not any kind of legal professional, nor an expert on these matters, but I'll try to point you toward resources to help you educate and inform yourself so you can safeguard your own intellectual property.

Hiring a pro

Hiring an expert to help you in the areas where you're *not* an expert can help elevate your writing and your stories and be more competitive in a crowded market. But while these folks may have extensive knowledge in their fields, ultimately it's up to you as the work's creator to advocate for what you want to achieve.

When I published *Intuitive Editing*, I had a very clear and specific idea what I wanted the cover to look like. I chose an expert and very experienced designer, the marvelous (and marvelously named) Domini Dragoone, who sent me an extensive cover questionnaire and then offered five different mockups of potential covers as part of her services for me to choose which most closely matched my vision, which she would then hone and fine-tune from there with my input.

None of them was the specific image I had suggested. It wasn't that they weren't good—Domini is the best, and any of her ideas would have made smashing book covers. I just had a concept in mind that reflected what I felt the book's spirit was and I wanted to convey that on its cover.

Domini was kind enough to design several more covers, but when I still wasn't feeling the vibe of any of them, she was confident enough to advocate for herself and point out that several of them contained the specific elements I had asked for, just not in the exact image I'd suggested. She rightly reminded me that I had hired her not only for her abilities but also her aesthetic and knowledge of the industry, and delineated why the covers she'd created would be more effective in the marketplace than the image I had requested.

She was entirely right to advocate for her work. But I was right too in advocating for the elements and the feel that mattered to me. Together we created a cover I love every time I see it and that I feel is striking in the marketplace.

Conversely, author Joni B. Cole in an interview we did[27] talked about how radically wrong her publisher got the initial book cover design for her craft book for writers, *Good Naked*. Despite that others at her publishing house said they shared her concerns, Joni was the only person willing to stand up and insist on a different cover. She knew what she was selling, and she was right to ensure that her cover reflected that.

With anyone you hire to help with any aspect of your writing—editors, formatters, cover designers, coaches, etc.—it's important to be able to speak up for what you want, even as you respect the expertise and skills they bring to the table, and their own artistic vision based upon it.

Another important part of advocating for yourself, though, is taking the time and energy to make sure you're hiring experienced, reputable experts who understand your work and your vision and will do the work on time and as promised. Yes, it can be time-consuming and tedious to vet these professionals thoroughly, but it's part of honoring yourself and your work and standing up for it.

Once an author and I agree to work together, I offer a contract for professional services spelling out our scope of work, which includes an intellectual property clause. If your contract with a professional doesn't specifically offer a similar clause (or they don't offer a contract at all—in which case I recommend not working with them), it's okay to ask for it. If they balk…so should you.

Submitting and selling your work
When submitting to agents and editors, as long as you've done your research into whom you're submitting to, you don't generally need to worry about your rights to your work being pilfered in the submission process. With established, reputable professionals and companies, you don't have to copyright a manuscript before going out on submission. (More on copyrights in a moment.)

Nor may it be a great idea to ask an agent or publisher for any type of nondisclosure agreement. Doing so may make you look like an amateur at best, mistrustful of the professionals and companies you're submitting to at worst, and may deter them from even considering your story.

But do make sure your name, a contact, and the manuscript name are in the header or footer of every page, and add a cover page with that info and any representation information. And make sure that you're carefully considering the people you submit to.

Advocating for yourself professionally also includes advocating for yourself with the people who represent and buy your work—agents and editors. Yes, most authors are thrilled to receive an offer, but it's okay—and I'd argue crucial—to take time to ascertain whether the person, company, and terms are the right fit for you and your career.

- **Know who you're signing with.** Does this agent or editor seem to genuinely understand your work and your vision for it? Does their view of it match yours? Are they enthusiastic about it? Do they have a solid track record—and with work similar to yours—that matches your goals, whether that's the editors and publishers you're interested in or the market for your story? What resources do they have and how much of them do they seem willing to invest in you, your story, and your career?
- **Know what you're signing.** How much commission does the agent take? Under what circumstances? (Consider areas like subrights, future work, adaptations, etc.) What rights are you signing over with a publisher, exactly? For how long? For how much money? How will that money be disbursed to you—and when? What limitations does the contract entail? Some contracts are draconian in their "noncompete" language, even curtailing authors from submitting or publishing other material elsewhere.

Writer's Digest offers an excellent overview on their website of what to consider when signing a publishing contract,[28] and author Cynthea Liu has a good blog post on her website with insightful tips on how to interview agents—though I don't recommend asking every single question.[29]

Signing an agency or publishing contract can be a coveted milestone in an author's career. But take care to read what you're signing, and thoroughly understand the terms.

With agents, make sure you understand and agree with the terms of representation and that it matches what you've discussed: the commission and how royalties are paid to authors, the duration of the contract, which work(s) of yours are encompassed by the agreement, the scope of representation, termination clauses, and more. The Authors Guild has an excellent guide to agency agreements on their website.[30]

When you sign a publishing contract you are essentially signing over certain rights to your work. While even a $10,000 or $15,000 advance may sound wonderful for an author who's never been paid for their creative work, along with the opportunity to have it on the market, realize that you may be selling major rights in all or most media (now known or yet to be invented) throughout the world for the life of copyright, which is 70 years past your own life.

Obviously the calculus of our careers means that selling our rights is the product we're offering, but consider the scope of it when you're negotiating a price. Understand exactly what rights you're offering and what the terms are, your royalty rate, payment structure, etc. (The Authors Guild offers a clause-by-clause model trade book contract with clear explanatory commentary on their website.[31]) If anything feels unclear, it's okay to ask about it. It's okay to negotiate the terms regarding the amount they're offering or what specific rights and to ask for changes (but realize you may or may not get them). It's okay—and in fact can be an excellent idea—to hire an IP lawyer to go over the contract to make sure you're signing what you want to sign. (We'll talk more about how to value your work in the next chapter.)

And be sure to do your due diligence before submitting or signing with anyone. There are bad actors in every profession, and publishing is no exception:

- I'm a big fan of Victoria Strauss's Writer Beware feature with the SFWA (www.swfa.org); she investigates complaints into industry professionals and shares her findings.

- The open-forum site Absolute Write Water Cooler (AbsoluteWrite.com/forums) is another good place to search before submitting or signing.
- Jane Friedman has a free Sunday Sermon on her YouTube channel about being savvy about spotting less-than-ethical business dealings and scams that I highly recommend watching.[32]

Contests

Winning writing contests can be a feather in your cap, and it's enticing to consider being able to add "award-winning author" to your bio, but they come with their own set of considerations.

Many contests are moneymaking prospects for the organization or individual running them. That doesn't necessarily mean the contest isn't worthwhile, simply that you should keep in mind that this is a business proposition and protect yourself accordingly.

Research the contest to see who's offering it and make sure it's a reputable organization, and one that will mean something to industry pros or readers if you cite it as a credit. The fact of winning a contest may not carry a lot of weight if agents, editors, or even readers have never heard of it.

But most important, make sure you read the terms and conditions of the contest. Some specify that winners or even all entrants are offering publication rights to their work, sometimes onetime rights in conjunction with the organization running the contest, but sometimes broader rights that can rob you of your own intellectual property and the chance to do something else with it beyond the contest. Authors and pub-industry veterans Anne R. Allen and Ruth Harris offer a great summary of red flags on their blog.[33]

Advocating for your assets

Finally, not to be morbid, but it's worth thinking about and proactively advocating for what becomes of your intellectual property after you're gone. What rights you retain and any income from it, such as royalties or future publication, are part of your estate. They can be rolled into the rest of it in your bequeathals, or you might want to consider an intellectual heir who can assume or manage these rights.

Misappropriation of your work

Many authors dream of seeing scores of their own titles on bookshelves one day. But what if you found out that there already were—but you hadn't written them?

That's essentially what happened to publishing expert and author Jane Friedman.[34] In 2023 a reader emailed her about Jane's newest books.

The trouble was, she hadn't written any.

Jane discovered a handful of books for sale online geared toward her area of expertise—helping authors launch and sustain successful writing careers—purporting to be written by her.

But they weren't. When Jane checked them out, she immediately suspected they were AI-generated fakes from a huckster trying to trade on her brand and reputation: Their text was consistent with results from what she calls her own AI "vanity" prompts, e.g., "What would Jane Friedman say about…?" (As a consistent blogger for many years, Jane suspects there's plenty of her own material for these large-language-model AI engines to cannibalize into plausible knockoffs of her work.)

Naturally she immediately contacted the sites to tell them of the fakes so they could take them down.

Except they didn't. One asked whether she had copyright on the impostor books, which of course she didn't, and whether her name was trademarked, which of course it wasn't. And then they closed the case, leaving the books both available and falsely attributed to her.

The other merely pointed her toward a comment thread in a group for reporting violations, run by volunteer "librarians."

Luckily Jane has a strong enough following and reach that when she started posting about the issue on social media and the story was quickly picked up by multiple major media outlets (including the Daily Beast, the *Guardian*, CNN, and BBC Newsnight), the problem was resolved and the impostor titles removed from the sites.

But Jane and many others in the industry are concerned that this is just the first volley in a likely slew of impostor books trying to trade on other authors' reputation and hard work. And not every author has Jane's power and platform.

In an industry already riddled with ways of taking advantage of authors and infringing on their rights, this one may be the most chilling. Initially concerned about whether AI would replace authors across industries from journalism to screenwriting to publishing and more, writers now have to worry that it might be plagiarizing them and stealing their identities.

And despite the preternatural growth of artificial intelligence and the speed at which it's advancing and expanding, both government and business have been slow to take meaningful measures to regulate it. As of this writing, what happened to Jane doesn't even seem to be technically illegal.

And when an author's rights *are* violated, it's difficult to have these impostor books removed. Jane is backed by a major publisher for her book *The Business of Being a Writer,* the University of Chicago Press, and she's a member of the Authors Guild, yet still it wasn't until she took to social media with her significant following there that the books were removed.

What about authors without her backing, reach, or high profile? When you've spent years building up name recognition, reader trust, and a reputation and following, a single poorly executed AI-generated hash of a book can contaminate an author's brand and undercut a career's worth of good work and goodwill—not to mention misappropriating your profits. And pirated books also steal compensation that belongs to the author.

With few guardrails currently in place to prevent abuses like this, what can an author do to protect themselves and the work and career they may have spent significant time, energy, and money developing?

Join the Authors Guild if you're eligible
If the 2023 Hollywood strikes taught authors nothing else, it should be the incalculable value of having a union with the collective strength and resources to effectively protect and advocate for creators. The Authors Guild (AuthorsGuild.org) offers access to legal advice and guidance, along with the power of a union to advocate for members—plus resources like web-building guidance, educational events, even insurance and discounts.

Talk to a trademark/IP lawyer about protecting your work
Not everything is trademark/copyright eligible—or practical—and the laws and rules are vast and hairy. But consider speaking to someone who may be able to at least advise you on which assets can and perhaps should be protected.

And I always advocate hiring an IP attorney to look over any contract an author is considering signing, if that's financially feasible for you. It's a relatively small investment in safeguarding yourself against obscure or sneaky language that can cost you a lot more down the road.

Another Authors Guild benefit is access to legal advice in areas of contract, copyright, etc., and there are good, reputable online sites like Legal Zoom (LegalZoom.com) and Zen Business (ZenBusiness.com) that offer legal resources a lot less expensively than most typical practices.

Piracy and fraudulent AI appropriation
Piracy is a vexing and complicated problem that admittedly I, too, am often overwhelmed by. So many sites pop up all the time offering

free downloads of material you may be selling, and trying to find and snuff them all can feel like an endless game of Whac-A-Mole.

But there are a few basic things you can do to try to safeguard yourself. Create Google alerts for your name and your book and series titles. That will send you notices of any internet mentions, including when your book is being illegally offered for download.

The process of stopping online piracy is a little complex (and sadly only varyingly successful), but there is legal protection against this type of theft, the Digital Copyright Millennium Act, DCMA. The Copyright Alliance offers specific procedures for filing a DCMA takedown notice with a site that is pirating your work or otherwise infringing on your copyright, along with templates for the notice.[35]

Specific to fraudulent AI-generated work, get into the habit of checking major bookselling sites like Amazon, as well as Goodreads, periodically to see whether all the books identified as yours really are. Keep in mind that other authors may legitimately share your name (there are at least two other Phoebe Fox authors I know of, besides my own pen name), so you also want to make sure their works aren't being misattributed to you.

As Jane Friedman points out, this kind of appropriation is a far greater threat to authors' livelihoods and careers than simple piracy of their work.

If you see an AI fake for your work—or any other author's—report it: to the site, and to the author if possible. Go as public with it as you can. Squeaky wheels get the grease. The more complaints companies hear, the quicker they'll act.

How to effectively advocate for yourself

Knowing when you should advocate is important—but the *way* you do so is crucial. Let's look at some tips for yielding the best results possible.

BE CLEAR AND SPECIFIC ABOUT WHAT YOU ARE ADVOCATING FOR AND WHY

As an editor, sometimes my feedback butts up against an author's original intentions for their work. I strive to offer feedback based on what I see on the page and glean of their intentions, but there are times when I feel that something the author has chosen is not serving their story effectively and may in fact be hampering it.

My general rule of thumb is to state my opinion, support it with specific reasons, and make clear suggestions on possible ways to address it. In multiple-pass edits, where I see the work more than once, I'll push twice on any element I feel strongly about, but after that I defer to the author, as it's their story and their vision.

You won't convince anyone of your point of view if you can't articulate it clearly and support it with convincing reasons.

ALWAYS TAKE THE HIGH ROAD

This is a small industry, and word gets around about authors who are rude or high-handed. You don't want to work with someone like that, and nobody else does either. You can advocate for yourself and still be civil, polite, and respectful.

Some of my favorite books on conversation, conflict, and negotiation:

- *Getting to Yes*, by Roger Fisher and William Ury
- *Negotiating the Nonnegotiable*, by Daniel Shapiro
- *Influence*, by Robert B. Cialdini
- *We Need to Talk*, by Celeste Headlee

KNOW WHAT YOUR DEAL-BREAKERS ARE

No matter how strongly you may advocate for yourself, in a mercurial and diversified business like publishing, which is often replete with many people's input and opinions, you will not win every skirmish. Know what hills are worth dying on.

I've already shared how I pulled the rights from a publisher when I realized that our visions for my work and my career had diverged. Because I felt so strongly about the issue—and partly because writing fiction has never been my main passion or pursuit—I was willing to take that risk. Another writer might not be, although I have spoken with many authors who have done just that, perhaps most famously Barry Eisler, who walked away from a half-a-million-dollar traditional publishing deal because he objected to the way the book was being marketed.[36]

Allison Winn Scotch was told to write under a pen name when her book sales floundered. She'd spent years building a writing career under her own name and was not willing to sacrifice that.[37] Other authors have done so to make it easier to write in different genres or to garner a publishing contract.

Whatever choices you make for your own career are entirely valid, depending on your goals and preferences. But make sure you clearly define what yours are—and then find the fortitude to speak up on your own behalf.

In any creative business, an essential part of the skill set creators must develop is the ability to advocate for themselves, their rights, and their work. Remember you are your number-one champion—or should be.

Advocating for yourself and your career also applies to how you value your work and how you price it, so let's talk about that topic in the next chapter.

Chapter Twenty-six

How Do You Value Your Creative Work?

In 2023, global financial behemoth Goldman Sachs valued the online creator economy at $250 billion and predicted that it would *double* in the next five years. That figure doesn't even factor in the $2.3 trillion dollars generated by the global media and entertainment industry—and yes, that's *trillion*—which is forecast to grow in the next three years by more than 25 percent.[38]

To put that into perspective, the entire sports industry generated $512 billion globally in 2022, and is forecast to grow by a compound annual growth rate of a comparatively meager 5 percent by 2027.[39]

Artists—creators—are the indispensable source of much of the content insatiable consumers watch, read, listen to, wear, and look at. The work of creators drives both the evolution of creative industry and its economy, which relies almost entirely on their creative efforts.

Creative products are in high demand, and that demand is only growing across almost every sector of entertainment. One of the main reasons Hollywood finally was forced back to the table to negotiate with striking writers and actors in the summer of 2023 was because stockholders demanded it, as the lack of creators providing the product on which the industry is based ground it to a halt.

With revenue-driving product like that, who run the world? Artists.

And yet who often financially benefits least from the sale of that product? Same answer.

Frankly, the logistics of the business of art boggle my nonmathematical mind, but here's what every artist should take away from these facts and figures: Never forget the value of your art.

Putting a Price on Your Work

Forging a viable, sustainable writing career is a combination of the two prongs inherent in the term: art and commerce. The latter demands we find a monetary way to value the former, a concept that's easy to stumble on in a nonstandardized, variable, subjective area like creative work.

How much should you charge for your writing and other creative work? How do you determine what your art is worth?

Part of the calculus of how to value your writing and other creative work is external and largely out of an artist's control: how the work is valued in the current market, whatever that is specific to your situation and artistic product, and what that market will bear.

But the other side of that equation is personal to each author, based on her situation and goals. Determining and considering each of these prongs can guide you in putting a monetary value to all aspects of your creative work.

DETERMINE MARKET VALUE

As a creative, you may be selling your product in a number of different markets. The buyers in that market may fall into a variety of categories; for instance:

- **publishers**, who will be buying rights to your fiction and nonfiction, including journalistic outlets like newspapers and magazines both online and IRL, and other online outlets and blogs;
- **writers' organizations and conferences,** which rely on creatives in various fields to offer programming that draws registration or membership;
- **readers and fans**, to whom you may sell your product directly, as in self-publishing, paid-newsletter models like Substack, or with subscription models like Patreon and others;
- **other creatives**, to whom you may market classes, services, or presentation programming you create.

In each case, understanding the realities of your target market and the buyers within it will help you set realistic parameters for the value you may expect or negotiate for.

A large publishing house may be able to offer more money than a small press, for instance—in fact the latter may even offer no advance at all, in exchange for the author receiving a higher share of royalties than traditional publishers. With indie/self-publishing, the author bears all costs of publishing and keeps 100 percent of net sales (minus the percentage distributors like Amazon and Ingram take for selling the book).

"Hybrid" publishers usually require payment from the author—often significant sums—in exchange for their services, and can take rights or a share of profits.

A publication with higher circulation may have a bigger budget for content than more specialized or modest ones (although depressingly frequently that may not be reflected in the rates they offer content providers).

You can likely expect and negotiate for more money from a for-profit organization than from a nonprofit, from a larger one than from a smaller one, and a higher-priced event or venue than from a more modestly priced one.

Direct to consumer, you may need to do some market research and testing to determine what your particular market will bear. For instance, many sources suggest Patreon-type contributors are more willing to offer small regular amounts to a creative whose work they appreciate than larger fewer or onetime contributions.

Pricing your self-published work, classes, presentations, and other direct offerings will depend on preparation, production, printing, and presentation costs as well as what people will pay for your work, and part of your math may include whether fewer sales at a higher price suits your business model, or it's a numbers game of selling high volume for low unit cost. You may *want* to factor in the costs you bear, but those matter only insofar as the market is willing to absorb passing along those costs.

If you don't learn or know what these market realities are, then you don't have a solid basis of consideration to determine how to value your offerings when considering the second prong of valuation:

DECIDE ON THE WORK'S VALUE TO *YOU*

Any business market consists of supply and demand. In the previous section we considered the second half of that equation, the external part beyond your control. What you do control is the supply, and the costs and subjective values associated with it for *you*. That doesn't mean what you feel or hope your work is worth, but rather what makes it worth doing to you, worth the time and energy it requires, worth surrendering certain rights to it, if applicable. That question has both tangible and intangible answers, which are unique to every writer.

For instance, in the current market the average book advance with a traditional publishing house is commonly said to be somewhere between $5,000 and $20,000.[40] After that, if you "sell through" in your contract—meaning you sell a specified number of copies, which most authors do not—you will make a percentage of the profits, which is usually small, generally between 7.5 and 15 percent.[41] Of that, if you are agented, you will pay another percentage to them—usually 15 percent.

That's average market value, and of course results may vary, but it's a starting place to consider whether that feels worth it to you considering the personal costs and value of your art if you choose a traditional publishing path.

Considerations for that metric may include what the time and energy demands of creating that product are worth to you. If you can assume the likelihood that you will get something close to the average advance and royalty rate if/when you sell your manuscript, that helps you plan a business model that works for you, considering your personal "production costs."

For example, if this is your only income stream, clearly you will need to find other ways to support yourself in addition to selling this story. Does your balance sheet allow sufficient time for you to do that as well as create this work? Do those time demands suit your other personal goals, like time with your family, or for other pursuits, or rest and downtime? Are there value-adds beyond the monetary valuation that may influence whether it's worth it to you, like exposure or credits?

You can do similar math with the financial realities of whatever path you choose for your work: small press, indie/self-publishing, hybrid, journalistic outlets, paid newsletters, etc. Calculate the initial payment you receive (if any); any additional royalties you may receive (if any); consider nonmonetary compensations as well; factor in associated costs and benefits in producing the work; then determine what it's worth to you in light of that.

With market realities being what they are and the surfeit of creative product available, both to publishers and to readers, you may not always (or often) have negotiating room in market value. But you can determine how you value your own time and energy. Beyond money, what are the other considerations, the value-adds for your personal career goals?

A publishing contract with a major house, for instance, may not offer the money you hope for, but may come with other benefits worth considering, like marketing, distribution, exposure, or even perceived cachet that may open up other related avenues of income, like garnering you higher speaking or teaching rates, or broadening your platform.

Self-publishing can require a significant personal outlay of funds up front, and more if you choose to market heavily, but you also will generally keep the lion's share of revenue generated by your work (minus the portions retained by the distribution outlets where you may sell your books, like Amazon and Ingram, or the fees to e-commerce platforms for direct sales), and you maintain control of every element of your book and its marketing and sales.

Offering workshops and presentations for free for a writing conference may not meet your financial goals, but might offer other intangible values: exposure, résumé credits, legitimacy, contacts, the chance to learn from others and build your writing community.

Keep in mind also that your personal and business goals will probably shift over the course of your career. Early in, when you're building a reputation and résumé, for example, you may be more willing to accept less value for your work than you might be as you begin to establish yourself, and nonmonetary considerations may be less important to your business model at that point. The content you once offered for free or low cost may no longer be worth what it costs you in time, effort, or lost work.

That doesn't make you a prima donna or too big for your breeches. It simply denotes a change in your career goals and priorities. This is a business, and it is not incumbent upon you to devalue what you feel your product is worth.

Take Ownership over Your Work's Value

Which brings up my last point, and one of my personal pet peeves. In businesses that grow up around creative product, it's often the creators who see the least financial benefit from that work, and are often asked to provide it for far less than it may in fact be valued.

This type of lowball offer may come in the guise of several seemingly persuasive points from potential buyers: that costs have skyrocketed, or there have been budget cuts, or an organization is a nonprofit or is barely breaking even in an event, for instance.

If you *want* to accommodate some of these concerns, that is a personal choice. In my career I have been happy to donate countless hours of my creative efforts to give back to a community I love or an organization I respect or simply want to work with.

But do keep in mind that other product and service providers would probably not be asked nor expected to cut their rates to accommodate. Even a nonprofit will likely face fixed market-value costs for things like printing or AV equipment or space rental, and those are simply line items in the budget that they plan for. You are also a value-add—these buyer markets don't exist without the product you're providing.

You may not be able to come to a middle ground where the price you want for your efforts fits what a particular market will pay for them. But that doesn't mean you have to adjust how you value your work unless you want to, for reasons that suit your priorities and goals. There comes a point where you may say no—and that's okay (see chapter eight, "The Power of 'No'"). That's how writers create a sustainable, viable business and take ownership and autonomy over their own careers.

But don't be afraid to negotiate. One of my favorite author negotiation stories was told to me by Jason Stanford, a former political journalist and speechwriter as well as an author. One of his books, *Forget the Alamo*, is a meticulously researched reexamination of the "white heroism" myths surrounding the infamous standoff with General Santa Anna in Texas.

He and his coauthors, Bryan Burrough and Chris Tomlinson, received a decent offer on the book within two days of pitching the idea to their publisher—who then *doubled* the offer in negotiations when the three authors asked for more money.[42]

Jason also offers my favorite advice about negotiating: "One, pretend you're worth it, because you are. And two, they're not going to fire you—they've already tried to *hire* you."

This addresses some of the most common reasons authors may shy away from asking for more money, which are often rooted in fear: fear that our work isn't good enough, or that no one else will want it. Fear that we're being greedy or arrogant for asking for more compensation or better terms, or that if we have the temerity to do so, whoever is offering for our work will change their minds or offer to someone else instead.

Think of it this way: By making an offer, a potential buyer has already shown their hand to some degree—they want your work. You are now in the power position of getting to see how *much* they want it.

If one of your goals for your writing career is to make money—which is fully legitimate and valid—then you have to approach selling your work like the business it is. Not only is it fair to negotiate—it's common, and often expected.

An offer is an opening sally, an exploratory effort for a buyer to see how little they can spend to obtain this product they want: your work. For you as the creator of that product, it's a starting point to see how close you can get the buyer to the value *you* have put on that work. No one wants to leave money on the table.

If you've educated yourself as much as possible about the market for what you're offering and determined whether it will bear what you think the work is worth, and if you know your own bottom line of what it's worth to *you*, then you have a clear idea of the leeway you have to negotiate. Ask for what you'd like to get, know what you would settle for getting, and be willing to walk away if their offer never rises up to the latter.

That sounds terrifying, I know. But if we don't value our work and champion it, who will? And why would anyone else value it? More often than you would imagine—and perhaps counterintuitively—asking for more money can make a potential buyer want your work *more*. Rather than making you seem difficult or undesirable, your confidence in the product may serve as assurance to a potential buyer that it's worth having, even if it costs a bit more than they initially offered.

It helps, too, to not think of negotiation as a hostile battle or a zero-sum game. It's neither. In its best form negotiation is a type of diplomacy: You're simply two parties whose interests align, trying to find acceptable common ground for both to get at least part of what they want. Chances are good that neither of you will get exactly what you ask for—but in a healthy, good negotiation, both parties will still feel they've walked away with a win.

And remember that there are ways to negotiate beyond asking for more money up front. With writers' organizations that have asked me to present, for instance, I've negotiated for a split of registration proceeds, or an escalating percentage after a certain number of registrants, rather than a higher flat rate. I've asked organizations to carry more of my books for sale during the event, or buy them outright for attendees, or partner with other organizations to meet my fee.

In publishing contracts I've asked for higher advances, but also negotiated rights back that I didn't want to include, or to lower the royalty threshold or raise the royalty percentage, or to change restrictive verbiage that might have curtailed my ability to sell other projects elsewhere.

In fact, literary agent Kristin Nelson of the Nelson Agency goes so far as to say an author should never sign a boilerplate contract (meaning the standard initial terms businesses often send out, which tend to skew heavily toward favorable terms for the company) without negotiating certain points more in their own favor: "All boilerplates are terrible," she says. "That's why agents negotiate the heck out of them."[43]

The Authors Guild has made its model book contract public so anyone can access it, whether they are a member or not, along with explanations of each clause and suggestions for what to look out for and what you might ask for, an invaluable resource for authors you can find on their website.[44]

You should read every single contract you're ever offered before signing—in any arena, even if you have an agent representing you—and make sure you clearly understand its terms. If you don't, ask your agent or another adviser, like an IP attorney; it's worth it to make sure you aren't signing away more than you realize and devaluing your work.

There are plenty of good resources available for learning how to negotiate, and it's a skill every creative should learn whether or not you have a representative negotiating on your behalf, as a crucial part of valuing your own work.

While many authors hope to sell their writing, there will be plenty of times you may be writing for free, from all the writing you'll do to learn your craft, to establishing yourself as a writer, to promoting your work with blog posts, newsletters, and other adjunct writing. That writing is equally valid as any that yields you a paycheck.

Writing has many inherent rewards whether you're paid for it or not: from the pleasure of pursuing your passion and doing the writing itself, to expressing and sharing something of yourself through your work, to forging a powerful invisible connection with people who respond to it.

That's not to say you shouldn't want to be paid for your work, and ask to be. But remember that its monetary value has nothing to do with its worth. While the former may respond to the vagaries of the market, the latter is decided by *you*.

Chapter Twenty-seven

Build Your Community, Not Your Network

My introverted husband likes to tease me about the way I plunge into meeting new neighbors whenever we've moved. He jokes that I want to make *them* casseroles to say hi and introduce ourselves to the neighborhood, and he's right: I've always made strong efforts to get to know the people who live in my community.

Rather than showing up weirdly on people's doorsteps with lasagna, though, I do it organically, little by little over months and years.

We walk our two giant dogs twice a day, and invariably encounter other neighbors out walking theirs, or jogging, or strolling with their kids, or working in their yard. I always say hello, and sometimes stop to chat and introduce myself. Our Great Pyrenees thinks himself the neighborhood ambassador, and will pull toward anyone we encounter to offer his magnificent self up for petting. (Nearly everyone obliges. That giant white fluffball is a charmer.)

I say hello at the mailboxes, wave at neighbors driving by, attend neighborhood block parties. Our fairly small neighborhood will share recommendations for local services and businesses and restaurants on our Facebook page. We exchange recipes and names of plants we've succeeded in keeping alive in the Texas weather extremes. We buy mulch and Girl Scout cookies and gift wrap from the neighborhood kids when they're selling them, or sponsor them in their tournaments to raise money for their schools.

We collect mail for neighbors when they're out of town, right fallen garbage bins or retrieve stray trash and pop it back in, or toss newspapers onto their driveway if the delivery person misses the mark (like if she's throwing them from the 1980s).

I've brought cookies and toffee to neighbors for the holidays or when they aren't feeling well, or for no reason—just as a fun pick-me-up. I've brought meals when neighbors had a baby. We've given saplings and plants to other neighbors who wanted them when they weren't suitable for our yard, returned wandering dogs home when they got loose, helped pull dead branches to the curb after a storm.

Neighbors don't necessarily become your closest friends (though in one delightful case they happen to have done just that). But little by little you learn people's names and their families and a little bit about their lives. You create community ties.

So when a bit of a crisis came up in my neighborhood not long ago that required quick community action and we needed to reach out to as many people as possible, I wasn't starting from scratch.

When I knocked on neighbors' doors or accosted them in their driveways or yards or on their walks, many of them already knew who I was. They were happy to chat with me for a few minutes. They were willing to give me their email addresses and phone numbers so we could continue to communicate about what was going on. They reached out with questions or concerns or to discuss the matter more deeply, and many of them asked how they could help.

Within an incredibly short period of time we had assembled a large grassroots network of neighbors who were able to come together and take effective action to solve our issue.

Would that have happened so readily and quickly if I'd been a complete stranger approaching people? I don't think so. Over the years we've all accrued a certain amount of social currency together, simply by socializing—not with any eventual end goal in mind, but just for the sake of being neighborly.

But when the time came, it turns out that community was an invaluable, in fact indispensable way of approaching an issue where we genuinely needed community engagement in order to be able to tackle it effectively.

Stop Networking

As authors and creatives, we're so often preached at to create a network, a platform, a "street team" to publicize our work. To schmooze with more accomplished authors and agents and editors and anyone else who can help our careers. To me this always feels transactional, and I think it's why the idea of networking puts such an icky taste in people's mouths. In this scenario people seem to be regarded as commodities, tools for gaining an author what she wants and needs.

A lot of us don't care for that approach, and so we resist those exhortations.

But the truth is, to use a hopefully forgivable cliché, it takes a village. And "it" is everything: from living in a community to raising a child to creating to reaching people with your creations, and every other element of life. Human beings do not live in a vacuum, and no one is an island (as long as we're rampantly throwing around clichés). We are an interconnected larger organism, one made up of individuals, but (and let's just go all in on the clichés) stronger together.

Authors do, in fact, need a "network," a "platform" to create a successful career. We need "connections"—people to support, encourage, and inspire us to keep us motivated and catch us when we falter. To help us see our own work clearly as we're writing and revising so we can make sure we're sharing our vision effectively on the page. Our support network can help us find the right help when we need it, build connections that help further our careers, spread the word about our work to help us reach readers, and countless other benefits that enrich our work, our spirits, our careers, our lives.

So how can you create yours, while not doing it in a way that feels inorganic or smarmy?

Don't try to create a network. Create your community.

My way of doing this in my field includes a lot of different endeavors:

- It includes my blog, something I do that doesn't pay off in any material way, but which allows me to share perspectives and insights I may have as a longtime publishing industry insider with authors who may benefit from it, and lets us connect directly through the comments. I also interview authors on my YouTube channel about their career, writing, and revision challenges and advice.
- It involves community outreach—speaking, teaching, and presenting.
- It involves taking time to respond to any author who may reach out to me with inquiries, questions, concerns, or areas they struggle with, and give them as complete an answer as I can—and pointing them toward others who can help where I may not be able to.
- It involves mentoring newer editors, and always making myself available to share insights, tips, and information with industry colleagues.
- It involves fan letters I regularly write to authors and industry professionals whose work I've found meaningful or helpful, or reaching out just to connect with colleagues whose names I may know, but we haven't yet met directly. I also create and participate in occasional online events with other editors and industry pros I admire.

- It involves commenting on people's blog posts and social media posts, supporting and celebrating others' successes and wins.
- It involves sharing with my own community the work and resources of colleagues that I admire and find useful.

I don't do these things to build a network. I've never been mindful of doing that. Instead I've simply spent the span of my publishing career developing relationships with people gradually and organically, because in the same way that it's what makes my neighborhood feel like home and my life feel like a connected community, it makes my career feel like one too.

There are also some things I don't do. For instance, I don't leave reviews online of books that I've been involved with, because it feels a little ethically gray to me. I don't have time to read every single book or article by every writer or publishing pro I know. I'm a sporadic user of social media and not always the best about commenting on others' posts, and I don't fill my feed with marketing or promotional reposts.

I may not be able to support authors and colleagues in that way, but I do it however I can. For example I may send a personal note of congratulations or appreciation for their work, or feature them in an interview, or share a photo of myself with their book. Building and supporting your community doesn't mean you have to go beyond what you have bandwidth for or comfort with; it just means doing what you can, when you can, to help the people you're sharing this writing journey with.

That also applies to social media. In an industry that relies so heavily on awareness, outreach, and engagement, social media can be a valuable tool to help you connect with other authors, readers, and colleagues who will help you build your career. But doing it halfheartedly, by rote, or with a hard-sell approach won't net you those results any more than not using it at all. Numbers of followers don't matter if they aren't genuinely engaged with you and/or your work.

Social media can be a wonderful way to connect with people you might never have developed relationships with otherwise, to learn from them, to commiserate and bolster and share and build community. But it can also thrust before your eyeballs a whole toxic realm of nasty trolls, ideological poison, bot-generated propaganda and lies, and even just create the corrosive effects of seeing others' carefully curated feeds and gauging our own real-world lives against those highlight versions.

How does all that affect your personal and creative state of mind? How much of your day do you lose to scrolling, posting, and creating "content"? And is that time you're taking away from other, more important values to you, like your writing, or your loved ones, or your other pursuits?

There's no "right" way to use social media, just as there's no one "right" way to write. You have to weigh what it offers you in terms of building your writing community against what it costs you: in energy, creativity, and time, and mental and emotional well-being.

Building Your Writing Community

Maybe you're already a multipublished author and think you don't need to build your network anymore. Or maybe you're earlier on the timeline of your career and feel you're years away from your first book launch and don't need to worry about it yet.

I agree. In fact, I encourage you *not* to build your network, not now and not ever.

Instead, involve yourself in your *community*—in this case the community of writers and other folks in our field—from the moment you decide to pursue your creative impulse to write, and continue to do so throughout your career. And give more than you get.

There are so many ways to do this, but just a few ideas:

- Take time to write reviews of books you've read and enjoyed on outlets like Amazon and Goodreads and others.

- Help spread the word about friends' books through word of mouth, or your social media, or your book club.
- Celebrate joys and triumphs with your fellow writers, and commiserate with and support them amid the setbacks and challenges.
- Write emails or talk to authors or presenters or speakers whose words and work affected you and tell them what you liked or how it helped your own writing or career.
- Offer feedback to your fellow writers if they ask for it, and make it constructive and positive.
- Join a writers' group or organization and participate. Volunteer to help. Partner with or mentor newer authors.
- Make an introduction between people you think might benefit from knowing each other; connect an author friend with your agent or editor or a conference organizer. Share your resources—both people and information. You don't diminish your stockpile of these values by sharing them; you increase them exponentially with every person you reach out to.

Don't do these things because it builds currency you can cash in at some future point, but because it develops strong community ties. And because it feels good—for the people you reach out to and connect with, and for yourself. And because it's good for you, as studies repeatedly show.[45]

And then just maybe, when the time comes that you could use the support of the people in your community, as with my neighbors, you will find that they're there for you...in an overwhelming way.

Part Six

LIFE

Chapter Twenty-eight

The Wisdom of William Shatner

The hubs and I were watching TV one morning not long ago and saw a trailer for a new show called *Stars on Mars*, where almost- and onetime celebrities apparently compete to survive in an atmosphere created to mimic that of Mars. It's hosted by William Shatner.

As I do almost involuntarily each time I see Shatner, I said to my husband after the ad, "William Shatner is a marvel. He has created one hell of a career out of an average level of talent."

Now, I have nothing against Mr. Shatner. In fact I'm very Shatner-positive. I feel as warmly inclined toward Bill Shatner as it is possible to feel toward a famous person who intersects my life very little, but I'll always be fond of him because I was an original Trekker and he by God was the captain of the *Enterprise*.

That's the thing about Shatner—he's likable. More than that, he has a certain presence. Even though he does basically William Shatner in every single thing he's in, that's an okay guy to spend time with. He's not necessarily flashy on-screen nor particularly innovative, and I don't know that anyone would describe him as a chameleon.

But he's traded on his charisma and likability (and one wildly successful cult hit) to create a steady stream of work across a very long career—and what seems to be a deeply contented life.

What Shatner Can Teach Authors

Creating a successful creative career is not about talent. If you are a human and have experienced life, you have plenty of talent for creation. Skill is a different matter, but that's something you can learn and hone. So why sit there twisting yourself up staring at your blank page and wondering if you're good enough? You *are* good enough. I'm telling you that right now with 100 percent certainty.

Here's why I bring up Shatner to you, my reader friends, who are likely not clear what a midlist actor has to do with your writing career. Perhaps you are Shatner-neutral or, God forbid, even Shatner-negative.

William Shatner doesn't matter and nor do your feelings about him. What does is that he has parlayed his average amount of ability in his chosen field into—by any measure—an enormously successful career.

BILLY MAKES BANK

If you gauge success by money, Shatner's net worth is $100 million. Why? Because he works. But it wasn't the original *Star Trek* series that set him up for financial success—it was canceled after just three seasons and afterward he was unemployed and living in a camper van,[46] wondering how to support his family. The show became a cult hit only later, and he makes no royalties from it.[47]

Shatner takes a lot of roles, though: He has 249 acting credits, per IMDb, not just starring in films and TV shows, but hosting reality shows, documentaries, and docuseries; voicing cartoon characters; and making plenty of guest appearances on other shows (including a credit as Big Giant Head on *Third Rock from the Sun*).

And that doesn't even count his ad work, another sixty-plus credits, most recognizably as the Priceline spokesperson, but he has also shilled for the Medicare Coverage Helpline, Planet Fitness, and a company called SoClean.

I think we can safely say, judging by his body of work, that William Shatner is not precious about the projects he accepts. He's just a worker bee, doing what he's offered, banking his bucks and living his life.

I'm not saying Shatner has no talent. He was an indelible Captain Kirk, a credible T. J. Hooker. His portrayal of Denny Crane netted him an Emmy for a guest-starring role, in *The Practice*, and a whole spinoff series for the character, *Boston Legal*—and another Emmy—and I've never *not* liked him in anything.

Bill Shatner just wants to work—and so he does. And he supports himself by taking what work he is offered.

But money isn't really all that life is about. If you're like many creatives, I'm guessing you also value your creative spirit. I'm guessing you value the ability to indulge it as you see fit and explore it to the fullest reaches of your imagination. I'm guessing that while you might welcome stacks of money and the freedom to not have to work at other jobs to support your art, your main creative goal is to be able to pursue it on your own terms.

Shatner works all these various "day jobs" that may not speak directly to his highest creative goals, but that pay the bills. Which brings us to his next life lesson for authors:

SHATNER BUYS HIMSELF CREATIVE FREEDOM

If you measure creative success by the ability to express yourself fully and pursue any creative avenue that calls to you, Shatner is clearly blazing a trail.

He feels the freedom to explore his creativity in any way he chooses, as evidenced by the dozens of books he's written, both fiction and nonfiction. By his many spoken-word albums, including wack, you'll-never-unhear-it covers of "Mr. Tambourine Man" or "Lucy in the Sky with Diamonds." Or his starring in a horror movie filmed entirely in Esperanto.

Shatner does what the hell Shatner wants to do.

William Shatner doesn't care if you think that stuff is nuts. Shatner going to Shatner. He is living his best life for nobody but William T. Shatner. (I have no idea if his middle initial is T, but I like to imagine that perhaps he and James Tiberius Kirk share a middle name.)

(*Side note*: Wikipedia adds "OC" after his name, which I wanted to believe was a typo for OG, like Shatner is the original gangsta, but apparently it stands for the honorary title Officer of the Order of Canada, which he is.)

Sure, when I was an actor my dreams were about a career like Meryl Streep's. But I'm thinking I would have been awfully happy with Shatner's career path too. He's spent a lifetime working in the craft he loves. He's translated that into the ability to pursue myriad other avenues of creativity that interest him, and he seems unhampered by what anyone else thinks of it. That's something I've spent my life striving for.

Shatner knows Captain Kirk will always be his major legacy, and he leans in, attending countless *Star Trek* conventions, and even sending up his own image in a classic 1986 *Saturday Night Live* sketch[48] about those appearances where he hilariously exhorts avid costumed fans to "Get a life!" Bill Shatner doesn't take himself or his career too seriously. Which may be why he exemplifies yet another lesson for authors:

SHATNER PERSISTS

If you measure a successful career by its longevity, Shatner began his career in his twenties and seventy-plus years later he's still going strong, including an appearance for the Discovery Channel's Shark Week—swimming with sharks at age ninety—and that 2023 *Stars on Mars* TV series. Dude is ninety-three years old and he's still out there Shatnering his ass off.

He just doesn't stop—despite the ups and downs of his (or any) creative career. He stays in the game. He perseveres.

SHATNER IS HAPPY

This, to me, is the most important measure of a successful creative career—and a successful life: Did we live life on our own terms? Were we comfortable in our own skin? Were we *happy*?

Possibly the greatest TV interview I've ever seen was one where Shatner was being interviewed on a late-night news program when he decided to go into space—William Shatner, Captain Kirk, at age ninety decided to GO INTO SPACE, kids!—and I shit you not he sat there during the interview going to town on Chinese takeout straight from the container, with chopsticks. *Throughout* the interview.

I was mesmerized. And yes, I've tried since to find the clip and cannot for the life of me, but it one day will be shown as a relic of the golden era of television.

William Shatner feels so free in his own personality and skin that he will by God enjoy his dinner while it's hot even if he's doing a live national television program, because Shatner don't care.

That is a man who feels pretty damned good about himself and his life.

One of the most common last regrets of the dying compiled by nurse Bronnie Ware from her twelve years working in palliative care with patients at the end of their lives is not living a life true to oneself.[49] Do you think Will Shatner is going to die with that regret? Hell, no. On his deathbed Shatner's going to be like, "Fuck, yeah, I lived *every damned inch* of my life to the max." (Excuse the language—it's not me; it's Shatner.)

People, all we get is this one ride, so far as we know. Don't waste it worrying about what anyone else will think about how you saddle up your pony. Channel BillyShat, auteur, visionary—the OC. Write the stories of your soul, your wildest imaginings.

Pour one out for the Shats and forge the life of your dreams.

Chapter Twenty-nine

Give It a Rest

My dog Gavin has a profound passion for his chew toys. Chewing is his gift and his calling. Gavin and his "chewies," as we call them, share the love that dare not speak its name.

He can chew for hours—to the point where my husband cannot bear the squeaky rubber noise. To the point where guests comment upon it, with a tepid smile that wants to suggest it's adorable, but which is shaded with pity for our poor obsessive furry son, and sometimes not a little bit of superiority about their own no doubt well-adjusted pets.

Gavin likes to nap with the chewy. He likes to lick the chewy. After a game of fetch he likes to carry the chewy home. If he cannot get to a chewy, for instance in his kennel, he will ruck up his rug and shove it in his mouth—his other obsession—and just sit there like it's his binky.

There is much to admire in my dog's single-minded devotion and focus on his chewies. But sometimes he gets so worked up it seems as if it's taking over his life, and he seems constitutionally unable to give it a rest and focus on other things until we take the chewy away.

314 🐾 THE INTUITIVE AUTHOR

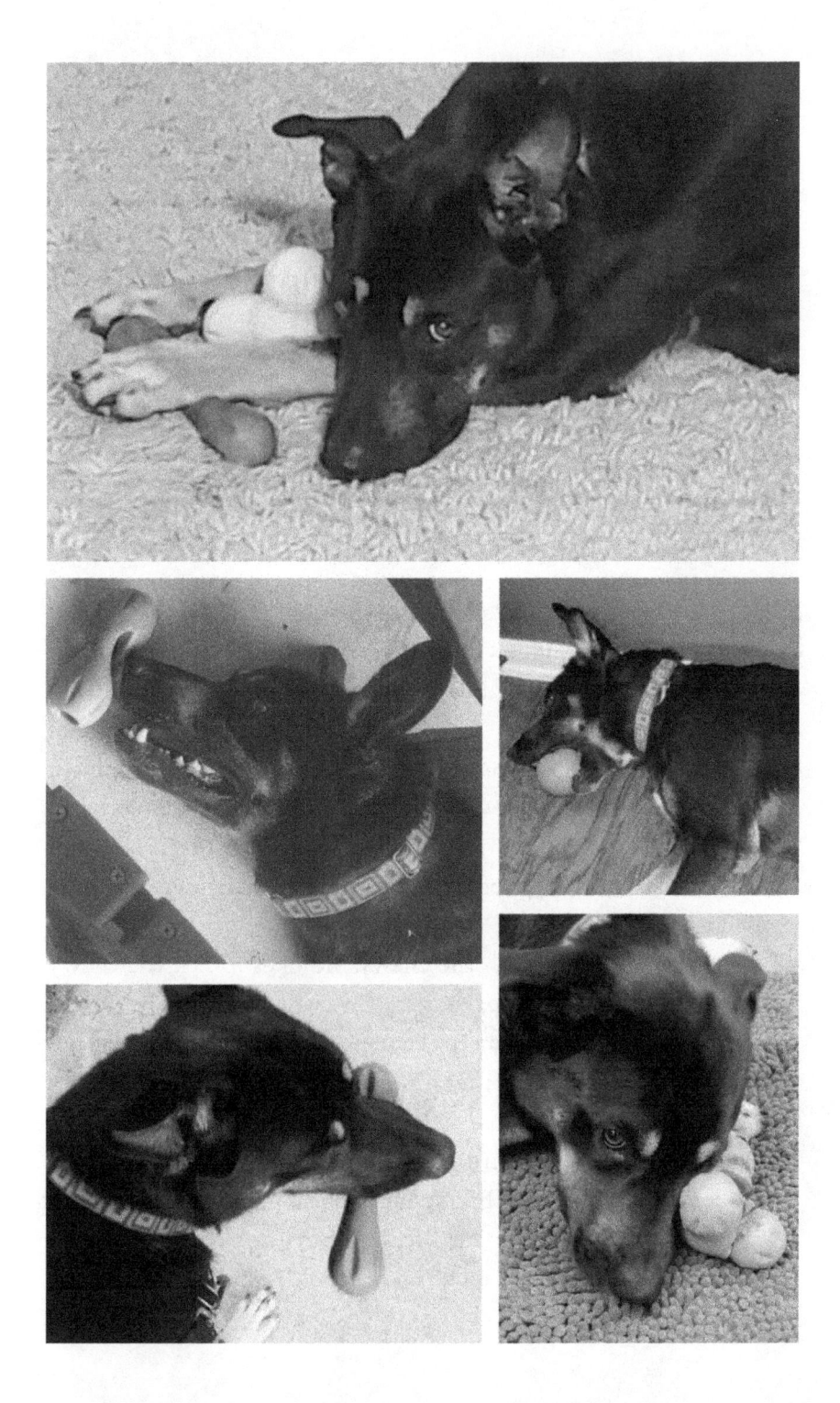

Sometimes our writing can become like Gavin's chewy.

Creativity is such an intrinsic part of who creatives are, it can feel as if it's our whole identity. Common writing advice leans into that: "Real writers write every day, no matter what"; your stories are your "book babies" for which you must endure months and sometimes years of labor; writing is easy—just open a vein and bleed.

It's become a common joke that writers are constantly thinking about their stories: in the shower, on a walk, at work, most soberingly while with family and friends. It's a comic cliché that we lie sleepless for hours with our heads spinning with ideas, the necessary notebook ever ready beside the bed to write them down before they flee in the night.

Friends, I do these things. I can't count how many articles and blogs I've written on my dog walk or in the middle of the night; how often I'm distracted by working through some new concept I want to teach or thoughts about an author's manuscript I'm working on. How many nights and weekends and holidays I've given up to work.

This kind of passion and dedication aren't bad in and of themselves. But just like Gavin's chewy, we need to know when to put our creative work down and focus on other parts of life.

Writing Shouldn't Be a Slog

I started writing almost from the moment I knew how, wanting even as a little kid to give voice to the worlds that lived in my head, to emulate the stories I loved, and to see myself in print. My first finished manuscript still lives in a keepsake drawer, a remedially illustrated autobiography entitled *My Book about Me, I Wrote It Myself* (I cringe at the comma splice). It's more of a short story, given my tender age at the time, written on construction paper and bound with yarn and a three-hole punch, and contains such literary gems as "I like eggs."

Like a lot of us who grow up to love words and story and writing, I found a lot of pleasure in creating my own, making up whatever reality I wanted. Back then it was the *doing* of it that I loved. Autobiography aside, I wasn't writing to create a finished product. I wrote for the joy of it, the sheer delight of creation on the page. It was just another kid's game, the way I entertained myself, just like my sister created elaborate working stables with Barbies and model horses, or my younger brother created cityscapes with LEGOs and blocks.

It was imagination and entertainment. It was fun. It was *play*.

I think most of us start our writing journeys this way. We pick up a pen (or sit at the keyboard) for the sheer enjoyment of freeing our imagination, of creating. It's the process that's the point, not the product.

But at some point that feeling of total freedom gives way. It gets crushed under self-consciousness, self-doubt, comparisons, the judgments of ourselves or others. It gets lost amid responsibilities: school and chores, work and family. It gets buried under an avalanche of stress, worry, fear, and uncertainty when the inevitable pressures of life bear down on it, whether that's personal issues and struggles or professional ones; individual or situational or even global.

Suddenly writing feels frivolous, or pointless, or like a chore. One more pressure, one more failure, one more expectation weighing us down. Craft books and articles exhort you to create a writing routine and stick to it no matter what. Self-pub gurus churn out a book a month and tell you that's what's needed for success in this field. Stephen King writes that in his decades-long career he's written *every single day of his life* except maybe one Christmas and that time he was in a life-threatening accident.

And you slide further into self-castigation as you find yourself dreading sitting down at your computer to write, or feel more and more inadequate with every day you fail to.

This, my friends, is when you should give your writing a rest.

Not forever—unless you want to, of course. And then by all means, put the pen down and never look back.

But writing, no matter what anyone says, including the venerated, gifted Stephen King—whom I adore, let me just say, even as I tell him to *STEP OFF, Mr. King*—should be exactly what you felt it was when you first felt the urge to do it: a fun exploration of your imagination, a nourishing creative outlet, a fulfilling use of your finite time here on Earth. Even when it's hard.

And it is hard—if you've written a word you already know it as well as anyone. But it's hard in the way that most rewarding things are, like learning to ride a bike or drive a car. These aren't product-oriented pursuits any more than writing should be. We don't learn these skills so we can say, "Check! Done." We learn them so we can open up our world beyond the borders of where we can travel with only our feet—just as writing widens our world beyond our own lived experiences.

And most of us probably aren't beating ourselves up when we're not using our wheels. Our vehicles will be there for us when we're ready for them.

So will your writing.

Art Is Not Life

The most affecting book I read this past year was called *Rest: Why You Get More Done When You Work Less*, by Alex Soojung-Kim Pang, and I urge you to treat yourself to it as your gift to yourself.

Pang presents the (to me) revelatory concept that rest is not the opposite of work—it's an intrinsic part of it, the other side of the coin, like breathing out and breathing in are both part of respiration.

Lest you dedicated creatives take that as permission to use your rest time to consciously percolate ideas, that's not what he means. Yes, that kind of passive creativity is crucial. But it too should be stepped away from sometimes.

We are more than our productivity or even our passions. *Life* is more than that.

When Gavin steps away from his chewies for a while, or has them taken away, he has the chance to work on obedience exercises, which we both enjoy. He's able to have love sessions with me and my hubs on the floor. We go on long walks where he can sniff every single spot where every dog in a five-mile radius has ever peed. He gives his jaw a rest and avoids TMJ.

But much more important, he has time to unwind and relax. To unspool himself from the tightly wound ball he can become and learn to self-soothe. To rest. To stretch out in a pool of sunlight and simply enjoy the warmth seeping into his black fur.

The creative impulse is, to borrow a concept from entrepreneur Paul Jarvis in one of his newsletters, "like having an electric car. Sure, it can go super fucking fast, but it also needs to recharge. If you don't charge it, it doesn't go at all. Both things are useful (going fast is exhilarating, but charging is required)."

I keep a very brisk, tight roster of activities in my day-to-day work. I edit for publishers and authors full-time. I write a weekly blog and contribute to several writers' publications and outlets. I maintain a fairly robust schedule of speaking and teaching engagements, many of which involve travel, in addition to a series of online self-directed recorded workshops I make available to authors as part of my Working Writer Courses on my website. I write my own books as well, formerly fiction, lately nonfiction guides for authors.

All of this is my passion and my life's work, and usually I get recharged from the doing of it just like the regenerative braking in our electric car while it's in motion—but even then I have to take my foot off the accelerator to recharge.

But it's easy to forget that amid what always feels like an endless and regenerative to-do list, and when I do, the joy and enthusiasm and *flow* I usually take from all these pursuits start to seep away. Instead of exhilarated and inspired, I feel stressed, frustrated, inadequate, feelings made worse by the sense that my creative well has dried up, as it tends to do at these burnout times.

That's when I need to take my foot off the pedal.

As soon as I realize I've gotten into a worker-bee mentality and it's taking a toll on me and my work, I ease off my schedule; reclaim any nights and weekends I've slid into working; deliberately seek out more of the things that charge my batteries: my husband and friends and dogs, nature, baking, physical activity, gardening. I give myself permission to *take time*, literally—to take it back from the obligations and strictures I sometimes put on myself to CREATE, CREATE, CREATE that rob any sense of the joy I usually get from the doing of these things.

Those projects will all be there when I'm ready. And I will bring more to them at that time not *despite* stepping away from them, but *because* of it. As I create mental and psychic space for myself again, I start to notice the juice trickling back in. Ideas come back, along with the pleasure of noodling on them. This downtime makes me more effective.

Unfortunately our instinct at these times of overwhelm is often the opposite: Do more! Work harder! And yet flogging ourselves to be "better" doesn't lead to increased productivity or creativity. In fact, just the opposite: It shuts us down, the body and psyche eventually taking the rest they desperately need in unhealthy ways, like illness or exhaustion, burnout and self-castigation and despair. This is when we may get the dreaded "writer's block"—dead-ended in our creative work or spinning our wheels and going nowhere. Yet it's not some mysterious blockage that afflicts us, but an obstacle we create for ourselves by draining our batteries too far into the red zone.

It may feel counterintuitive, but at these times when you're feeling overwhelmed by your looming expectations and obligations, whether imposed by others or your own ruthless inner drive, take your foot off the accelerator and recharge. Say no to your writing and put your WIP down—even mid-NaNo if that's what you need.

Even if you're on deadline. These are artificial pressures we put on ourselves—useful only if they help you, not if they harm you. NaNo will be there next year, or you can create a writing challenge of your own when you're ready, alone or with friends. Deadlines are mutable. Ask your publisher for more time if you need it, or delay your own indie-pub timeline. The world won't end if you have to shift your production schedule or release date (trust me—it happens all the time...).

Remember Paul Jarvis: "Going fast is exhilarating, but charging is required." Take time to recharge, even when—especially when—life feels like a hectic crush or a series of pressing obligations we have to get through. Give yourself permission to not worry about your writing so much and how well it may or may not be going at the moment, and just let go—no pressure, no guilt... no obsessive chewing.

Chapter Thirty

What Are You Working Toward?

Friends, authors...kids (I feel like I can call you that as I am edging gently into the realm of the elders)—lately I'm noticing that a bunch of my friends have been moving toward retirement.

I'm a bit younger than they are, but watching them frolic at their leisure as I continue to keep my regular work schedule is starting to feel like seeing all your friends in the neighborhood playing outside during summer vacation while you're in summer school.

To combat this, I've been doing something that for some reason it took me thirty years of freelancing to implement: taking advantage of the flexible schedule being self-employed allows me to play hooky on weekdays with my husband and friends, when activities are less crowded.

And it's been great. I can work-shift and swap out a weekend day or make up the time in other ways, or just occasionally schedule myself a little more lightly to allow myself a four-day workweek.

It was on just such an excursion recently, at the Lady Bird Wildflower Center one uncrowded Tuesday to see the finest display of

Texas wildflowers I've seen since moving to Austin seventeen years ago, that one of the friends we were with, retired for several years, started pressing me to do more of this kind of thing: working less and playing more.

"Right now my business is in strong growth mode," I countered. "While I have the momentum and all the energy I currently have, I need to keep building it."

"For what?" she asked as we trekked up the stairs of the center's turret to get a panoramic view of the surrounding fields of flowers and the Texas hill country and the stunning array of clouds at the horizon.

Friends, authors…kids (I feel I can call you that as a Gen Xer, which I suddenly realize no longer connotes the plucky, independent youth that it did when I once was one, but the middle-aged)—I was floored. I stopped right on the step where I was and realized I had no answer for her question.

For most of my life I've been an ambitious little thing, whether I was pursuing acting or journalism or my editing career. No lie, when I was in middle school my favorite game to play with my best friend was what we loosely called Corporations, where we created imaginary companies and all their branding, correspondence, and made-up transactions and employees. When most kids were playing Barbies or cowboys or house, I was playing entrepreneur.

And in some ways my career still feels like play to me. I love almost every aspect of running my business and continuing to look for ways to expand it. It's not unlike how many writers begin writing for fun, as a game or play, long before they decide to pursue it as a career.

I've always understood that I am *not* my career and that it's only one prong of what makes my life satisfying—and yet my friend's question made me try to concretely define a clear endpoint I hadn't thought about. I've been building for building's sake, just taking every next step and opportunity that opens up as long as it seemed fun and helped expand my career, my business, my reach.

I don't have some overarching master plan for world domination or to build a dynasty or leave a legacy. I have no children to whom I want to leave a family business, nor even any intellectual heirs who might be interested in assuming mine when I'm gone. As my husband and I begin reexamining and updating our estate planning documents, I've begun looking at how to disperse (and disburse) my intellectual property after my death.

If you ask me what motivates me and my career, it's how much I enjoy the process, and that it helps allow us to live the lifestyle we want to live.

And this last point is what my friend's question made me think more deeply about.

I just finished reading a book called *Die with Zero,* by Bill Perkins, whose basic premise is that rather than the common mindset of socking away savings and building a fortune you can leave behind after your death, why not do as much as possible with the money we work so hard to earn, so that we enjoy the fruits of our labors while we're alive?

The book's message can feel a little privileged in the sense that not everyone has the luxury to rack up savings, retire early, or disburse accumulated wealth.

But the central nut of it has had me thinking a lot, in line with my friend's question that stopped me in my tracks: What eventual reality am I working so hard toward…as opposed to fully enjoying the reality I'm *in*? What more do I want?

Among many goals writers may have for their writing is often one about becoming part of the literary canon, creating a classic that lives on after we're gone, that leaves our words and our mark in the world.

Leaving aside the unlikeliness of this outcome—of the hundreds of millions of books published throughout the course of history, only a tiny fraction of those endure—it also feels to me like it keeps the author focused on an unknowable, uncontrollable future for their writing, rather than the part that *is* within their power to affect: the doing of it. I wonder if worrying about our artistic legacy may rob us of the simple joy we take in making our art.

Or maybe your goal is about amassing that fortune you can "die with zero" on, getting to the point in your career where your whopping book advances allow you the travel and adventure, leisure and pleasure you dream of having "one day."

Even if that were a likely outcome (spoiler: It's not), "one day" may be a lot closer than you think.

Perkins offers an exercise in his book he calls "time bucketing." Basically, using average life expectancies for your health and demographic, you divide your expected remaining time to live into five-year buckets, and then figure out which of your goals and dreams need to happen in which buckets, based on your age, ability, health, cognition, ability to afford each item, etc.

For me and the hubs, it was sobering to realize that we probably have just two or maybe three time buckets left to do some of the highly active or ambitious items on our list before our age and health may preclude them. Our "one day" isn't just right around the corner. It's now. It has to be.

Your Life and Your Art

In our culture, and particularly in creative careers, it's very easy to internalize the message that we are defined by what we do. Especially with artists, our creativity is so much a part of who we are that it's tempting to believe it is who we are.

But not defining that as my total identity has been key for me to be able to keep my career in perspective and realize that old cliché really is true: I work to live; I don't live to work. As much as I adore editing and it nourishes my soul, at the end of my life I don't think I'm going to bask in all the manuscripts I've been privileged to work on, but rather in the experiences I had and the people I shared them with.

That doesn't negate the meaning and fulfillment I derive from doing that work now. It just means that I understand its place in the bigger picture of my life. Editing and writing—my creative callings—are a key piece of the pie, but they are not my pie.

To a certain degree success in a competitive field like writing and publishing will always involve choices between personal and professional goals. Those choices may shift and evolve, and each of us has to decide where that line is for ourselves, but our metric for deciding that must strive to keep the larger scheme of our lives in mind.

Actor Martin Short, in his autobiography *I Must Say*, talks about how he developed a way of prioritizing his life years ago, when he spent two miserable months between jobs worrying he'd never work again.

He thinks of his life in nine categories, like courses one might take in school. Even if he's flunking out in one, he says, he can keep his overall GPA high by excelling in the others. So if he flags in category six, for instance—creativity—he may focus harder on category one, self, or category two, partner/family, or friends, etc.

I love this idea because it puts more eggs into our baskets as creatives. It means that even if we're struggling creatively—or in any other area of life—it's not the end of the world. You can still give your attention to other areas where you may be thriving more at any point in time, and overall maintain your equilibrium and joy.

That seems pretty healthy to me. And it also feels essential for nourishing the parts of ourselves that we draw on in our creative efforts and that often allow us to achieve them: the experiences we have, the people we know and relate to, our feelings, and our own core well-being.

If your identity is not fully wrapped up in your writing, then all the many challenges and setbacks inherent in our creative field—or any field—won't shatter you. Yes, there may be disappointments and failures, but they comprise only part of your well-being. They don't define you, so they can't crush you.

WHAT WILL YOU REGRET?

Maybe it's a function of getting a little older, but these days I find I frame much more through the lens of, What will matter to me, looking back at the end of my life, about how I lived it?

I don't think I'm going to be thinking about the books I've been privileged to work on, as meaningful as they've been to me, or the ones I've written, or the classes I've taught. I don't think it's going to be the goalposts I hit, the accomplishments I achieved.

I expect that when I'm facing the imminent end of my existence, what's going to matter to me won't be the days I spent ticking through my to-do list, but rather with whom I shared the time I was given, and who is around me when I'm living my final days. I suspect what I'll treasure will be the memories I made, the joy I found, the laughter I shared with the people who mean the most to me.

If I have regrets, I don't think it will be for the tasks I've left undone, but rather for the opportunities I turned down. The times I conformed to what others expected of me, rather than being authentic to my truest self. I won't be thinking about all the words I wrote or edited, but the ones I didn't say to the people I care about, and should have.

These ideas seem so ordinary, commonsense even, and yet how easy is it for us to lose sight of our core values in the hustle atmosphere most of us live in?

I try to remember these principles when I'm making decisions about my career in the context of my life, to use them as a framework for prioritizing my time and my energy. And so far it has stood me in good stead. I love my work and derive enormous satisfaction, enjoyment, and purpose from it. I'm comfortable with my level of success, even though it may not reach stratospheric heights. Those are choices that I've made deliberately, knowing what I am and am not willing to dedicate and sacrifice to work that may carve my time away from living life in a way that I also find deeply satisfying.

I may never fully retire, I've told my husband. I will likely work in some fashion as long as I'm constitutionally able to do it. But I'm going to try hard to do it *less*, starting right now, in this time bucket, when I am fortunate to be healthy and financially stable and fully compos mentis, so that I can more deeply enjoy what I'm lucky enough to have.

I'm not suggesting any certain path for anyone. We all have to find our own balance wherever we are in our lives for what we personally value. But knowing what that is—really thinking about and concretely defining it—can allow us to have meaningful, fulfilling work along with a meaningful, fulfilling life in a way that may insulate us from the many vagaries of this career.

Don't waste a moment of "your one wild and precious life," in the words of poet Mary Oliver. Write for the joy and fulfillment and delicious artistic challenge that brings value to your now. But also remember to fully live…freely love…frequently laugh.

Chapter Thirty-one

Reclaiming the Creative Spark in Troubled Times

By many measures, people have more reason to feel optimistic about the state of the world today and the future than ever before. In the long arc of history, overall humans are healthier, live longer, there is greater literacy, less poverty and hunger, more freedom and equality (yes, really) than at any time in the past.

And yet given headlines in recent years—pandemic, war, racism, increasing tribalism, rising antisemitism and racial violence, gun violence, accelerating global warming, fraying democracy, concerns over artificial intelligence, attacks on civil rights—for many people lately the world has felt like the world's worst make-your-own-sundae bar where every available topping is toxic, creating a corrosive, angry atmosphere that seems to play out in world events, politics, even in snarky neighbor exchanges on NextDoor.

Add to that everyday stresses and pressures like family concerns, money worries, health matters, mental health issues, and other challenges, and life's stream of trials great and small can threaten to derail our peace of mind—and our creativity.

In the face of all the real and weighty concerns in the world, we may wonder, why does our writing even matter?

Writing Amid Suffering

The first time I cried after Russia attacked Ukraine was a few days after the initial invasion in early 2022—when my husband and I went to see the film reboot of *Cyrano de Bergerac* with Peter Dinklage.

As for many of us, the Ukrainians' plight had been chewing a hole in my gut since Russia began their unprovoked aggression. But their situation hit me with visceral immediacy when I watched soldiers in the film, on the eve of what they know is a doomed suicide mission, write letters to their loved ones back home—not because the scene was so well executed (though it was), but because it put me, directly and empathically, inside the skin of a people determined to fight together for their homes and country and freedom against an unjust attack and an army that far outguns and outnumbers them. It made me *feel* Ukrainians' fierceness, their incredible resourcefulness and grit, their heroism.

That's the power of story.

Ideas and information may be the necessary elixir of life, but *story* is the delivery device that gives them potency. There's a reason propaganda is one of the world's most powerful tools.

Stories are what make ideas palatable and digestible. They draw us intimately in and engage our emotions. We filter them through the lens of our common human experience. And storytellers are the ones who bring these human stories to life for us.

European leaders initially dragged their feet on putting economic and political pressure on Russia as Putin's forces pressed down on Ukraine...until an emotional phone call with Ukrainian president Volodymyr Zelensky telling the stories of his people—their situation, their suffering, their heroism—moved them to literal tears and almost immediately prompted action.[50]

Story has such power that those who fear dissent for their ideas burn and ban books—like the Nazis during the Holocaust, or more recently the growing efforts across the United States to remove books that a small segment of special-interest groups find dangerous because they deal realistically with darker issues of America's past: slavery, land theft, racism, brutality. Because they offer views of a world and of people that may not conform to a particular group's narrow definitions of what is "acceptable"—stories that deal with issues of health and sexuality, that feature LGBTQ themes and characters, that include any material they disagree with or find personally threatening, like religious issues, political viewpoints, even language.

Think about that: The potency and impact of words is such that some people are terrified of the influence they may have to inform, educate, and expand people's thinking. To empower them and spur them into action. They know the power of story and want to silence it.

And yet even knowing the influence our words and thoughts and stories may have, it can be hard to create them when we're feeling grief, rage, helplessness, hopelessness at headlines that too often focus on negative, sensationalized click-bait and source suffering from across the world, funneling far too much of it into our consciousness. At the loss of loved ones, or financial fears, or worry for our children's futures and whether they will even have one.

But these times of tribulation and adversity, when our creative efforts may feel futile or trivial or escapist, are when our writing might play the most important role of all.

WRITING HELPS PROCESS PAIN

Whether your own pain or the empathic pain we feel for others who suffer, finding an outlet for it, a way to let ourselves feel what we're feeling, to try to relieve some of the pressure of that pain that may be bottled up inside, unarticulated, can help leach out the poison. It's the very foundation of healing methodologies like talk therapy and journaling.

Before we can process anything, before we can heal, before we can turn our pain into something potentially positive, we have to know what we're feeling, let ourselves feel it, find a way to understand our own reactions. As writers we often do that through our writing.

And in navigating and sharing our own deepest and most vulnerable, raw emotions, we may help others find a way to do the same for their own.

Even if its effect is only to entertain and offer escape, story holds power to mitigate suffering. How many of us binge-watch "comfort shows" like *Ted Lasso* or *Schitt's Creek* or *The Golden Girls* for relief and solace during uncertain and unsettling times?

WRITING MAKES SENSE OF THE SENSELESS

There is no reality where something like the slaughter of children or the shooting of unarmed people or terrorist attacks could ever make sense. But if we remain lost in our fury, our pain, our bewilderment, our frustrated helplessness, or whatever emotions are overriding everything else at any moment in our lives, then we cannot find the distance to fully understand what happened…and what people and society might do to keep it from happening again.

Story illuminates the world, a lens through which others may find some measure of understanding of their own tragedies, their own pain. It frames our world through a perspective that allows us to see our own lives more clearly—to reassess, to rethink, to consider. Working through difficult and painful things in our writing may offer insight and aid to ourselves and others amid their own struggles.

WRITING CONNECTS US

It's easy to feel alone in our suffering if we hold it corked up inside us—and that feeling of isolation almost always makes our pain keener.

But sharing it is a form of connecting with others in similar situations. We may not recognize our exact *experiences* in someone else's, but there's every chance we might connect with the resultant *emotions*, those near-universal connective fibers among us.

Author Michael Lewis tells a deeply poignant story in a *SmartLess* podcast interview of the loss of his nineteen-year-old daughter and her boyfriend in a car crash. In the immediate aftermath, author Dave Eggers, a neighbor and friend, appeared on his doorstep with food and said, "I'm not leaving.... I'm going to sit outside in my car and I'm not leaving." He simply gave the gift of his presence, and that created a connection Lewis didn't realize he desperately needed—and one he says he will never forget.[51]

Sharing another person's experience, in whatever way, unites us and makes us feel less alone.

WRITING GIVES VOICE TO THE VOICELESS

Not everyone will tell their story, and not everyone may have the reach you might have, as an author. Many people have been—and are—so marginalized that their stories may not have had opportunity to be heard.

Your writing can serve as an amplifier, a way to give a voice to those who may not have a voice: to draw attention, to share your reach and your readers and help spread their stories.

WRITING CREATES HOPE

The world can feel damned bleak at times—especially, it seems, in our times lately. Writing can help people find their way out of anguish and hopelessness as you create worlds that *might* be possible, progress that *could* happen, triumphs of people's better nature over our worser ones.

To paraphrase author and political pundit Jason Stanford in his essay written in response to hearing a friend say she had decided not to have children because of climate fears, every dystopian story starts in bleakness and despair...but the story isn't about that. It's about the human transcendence of such hardships.[52] Give us a model for that, and a reason to believe it's possible.

WRITING CAN CHANGE THE WORLD

Story's power lies in its ability to affect people: to make them feel, to make them think, and ideally to make them act. It's why politicians and media outlets and advertisers rely on it: It spurs people into action, and story has the power to influence their thinking and behavior—for both good and ill.

You can write to be the good in the world. Harriet Beecher Stowe's *Uncle Tom's Cabin* is often cited as a major societal influence in the fight for the abolition of slavery; *Will & Grace* helped set the stage for laws guaranteeing equal rights for marriage; the movie *JFK* led to the release from the National Archives of long-sealed records about the Kennedy assassination a mere year later.

Story can make sure we never forget the lessons of history, the way that *The Diary of Anne Frank* brought home the horrors of the Holocaust to an entire world and generations of people who didn't live through them firsthand, or Toni Morrison's *Beloved* makes visceral and real the horrors of slavery.

Story has the power to change the world because it has the power to change *people*, who drive change in the world.

And yet in such heated and polarized times, should we introduce controversial concepts into our writing? If we color our art with our personal views, do we risk alienating readers, diminishing the market for our stories? Should art be neutral, or take a stand?

Writing Safe or Risking Your Readers

That we're living in polarized times has become a cliché for the reason so many clichés do: It's true. There seems to be a heightened sensitivity in the world these days, and even words and ideas that may not once have been seen as controversial can be perceived as incendiary.

Story's noblest purpose is to get to the heart of some of the deepest and most complicated human emotions, thoughts, topics. To forge a path through the thickets of thorny ideas. To reflect and hopefully shed light on our society, human nature, and readers' lives.

Yet in times like these, doing so can inflame some of your readers, even alienate them. There are differing schools of thought on what that means for authors, as well as to agents, publishers, and marketing people. Some writers choose to walk the middle of the road in the interest of not limiting readership or risking a slew of angry reviews. Some decide to carry their torch off the trail and into the darkness despite the risks of all that may lie within it.

There's no right path. As with so much of writing, the right approach is the one that's right for *you*, as a person, as an author, and as a creative professional. But every author should consider this question for themselves and make deliberate choices. A sort of life and creativity mission statement, if you will.

In my own writing I look for stories to help illustrate and spark ideas, and often find influence and inspiration from what's going on around me. It may be a podcast I've listened to, an article I've read, a concept I've been thinking about—or current events in the world. Because my purpose and conscious intention with my work is to find ways to help writers, I tend to examine all of these prompts through that lens.

I am not a political pundit, nor do writers seek out my work for my personal ideology and views, so I keep everything focused on that core mission of helping authors.

But I am a human being, as we all are, and I'm a creative, both of which mean that I'm profoundly influenced by the events around me, as are we all. None of us exists in a vacuum, and just as writers must be mindful of the world our characters live in and their place in it as key elements of what shapes them and their behaviors, we can't isolate any part of ourselves from all the richness that we are as full humans.

Much of my thinking and formulating of ideas in my field of expertise, writing and editing, is in fact drawn from and influenced by everything in the world around me. That's a key part of my process. And I've made the choice to share that in my work. To be my true self, while still honoring writers' purpose for seeking it out and trying not to muddy my focus on that.

That may result in some people not being receptive to my work and central message. I've carefully considered that and it's a risk I'm willing to take because it makes my work feel more organic and whole to me, and I consider that important.

But some authors may feel that doing so is not a risk they're willing to assume, or that it unnecessarily limits their audience, or that it's not their place to weigh in on topics outside of their specialty. I recently saw a reader comment on one industry pro's post about a current event that they appreciated that this person "stayed in their lane" for the most part, meaning not venturing outside the parameters of their work. It's not everyone's cup of tea.

But the writer's job is not necessarily to be everyone's cup of tea.

Who are you as a writer? What do you want to say? What's important to you? These are the kinds of questions you might deliberately ponder, if you haven't already, in determining how far out on a ledge you want to go with your writing. How personal you want to be. How definitive you want to risk being.

There is no right or wrong answer here, and no path is better than any other. But it's part of finding your voice as a writer, as an artist. It's about knowing what drives you creatively. It's about knowing your purpose—with every story, and for your entire career and art. These are not casual choices. They will shape you as a writer. They will form your artistic voice. They will define your message and your readership. They will define *you*.

My personal decision was based on the fact that I wanted to be able to fully express who I am even in my writing about craft, and that I wanted to be cohesive in my career with who I am as a person.

Despite that this may narrow my potential audience, I love the fact that those who do vibe with me are my people and comprise a writing community that nourishes me. It lets me feel more authentic, and it frees me. And I cherish a deeper hope of perhaps offering a perspective that could help to bridge divides.

That may not feel right to another editor or writer or agent, who may prefer more of a separation of church and state, so to speak—their business pursuits entirely separate from their personal lives. And that's an equally valid choice, as is anything in the full spectrum in between.

The key is to make whichever path you're traveling your deliberate, thought-out choice, one that best fits your personality and purpose, your goals and values for your career and your life.

And then commit to that with your whole unbridled heart and mind. That's how you create your individual style and voice—and how you build a career with meaning.

But how do you actually *write* amid turmoil, anguish, or despair?

How to Create in Troubled Times

Writers, I think, are more than usually affected by the darker phenomena of life. Do a search on existential depression (as I in fact recently did) and what repeatedly pops up near the top of the results are articles that link it to those who are "deep thinkers" or highly sensitive—two common traits of writers and other creatives.

But even knowing the good your art may do for yourself and for the world, how can you do it amid all that angst that you, as a creative, as an extra-sensitive, deep-thinking, hyperaware artist, may be roiling with at various times of your life?

You use it.

Though it may feel unfathomable while you're enduring them, these powerful, uncomfortable emotions can make your writing even more relevant and impactful. Many of us are wrestling with how to cope in the world, whether that's a result of our current increasingly poisonous sociopolitical, ecological, and too often intimate environment, or life's everyday speed bumps: financial, health, personal struggles that can derail even our strongest creative desires.

Art that "leans in" to this unrest many of us may be feeling in troubled times can tap into that zeitgeist and hit a chord with many others, whether it's novels like Margaret Atwood's powerful, disturbing *The Handmaid's Tale*, which paints a picture of gender inequality and oppression of women so terrifyingly realistic and timelessly relevant that it became a touchstone for a protest movement against modern sexism twenty-five years after its publication; or popular songs that become anthems of social justice, like Edwin Starr's "War" or Marvin Gaye's "What's Going On" or Beyoncé's "Freedom"; or shows and movies grappling with pervasive issues like the corporate greed and social inequality of *Succession*, or *BlacKkKlansman*'s sharp, timely look at racism, or *Barbie*'s ruthless spotlight on gender inequality.

The power in letting these struggles inform your work is that they're universal. Whether or not all your readers may be feeling all the same things now, or have faced the same challenges and setbacks, chances are good they've wrestled with common suffering at some point: rage, betrayal, loss, regret—and also share common longings for forgiveness, acceptance, love...peace.

The marvelous thing about spinning struggle into art is that, counterintuitively, it can make your struggles a bit easier. Letting your characters wrestle with a problem you're wrangling not only lets you channel all those difficult emotions into your work, thus infusing it with intimate, visceral feeling and passion, but frequently it also helps you work through it yourself at the "safe" remove of helping/watching your protagonists do the same. Their battles will help you understand and work through your own—and help readers recognize and transform their own challenges.

You can use your struggles to help create and inform the story. Author Laurie Frankel created her affecting novel *This Is How It*

Always Is, about the challenges and joys of a trans child and her family, in part by drawing on her own experiences with her trans daughter.[53] Bestselling author Allison Winn Scotch wrote about how the current state of the world was affecting her as a writer—essentially shutting down her creative font for two years, until she looked straight into the face of the monsters tormenting her and channeled all that into her 2020 novel *Cleo McDougal Regrets Nothing*, which poured out of her in just six weeks.[54]

Do you remember poet Amanda Gorman standing up on that stage during the 2020 presidential inauguration speaking the truths of her heart with all the passion and conviction of her soul? Do you remember the impact of that—perhaps on you, and certainly on so much of the world as the power of her ideas came through in her words and her delivery?

Gorman spoke of her own thoughts and her own experiences and her own perspective, and yet it became universal, resonant to so many. She has spoken of her fear of public speaking, her doubts about that poem, and the fact that she almost even canceled this historic appearance. But she found her courage, and her story mattered and it made a difference.[55]

It's easy to discount our own stories. To discount our voice. It's easy to lose faith in ourselves, or to compare our writing to panoramic, epic, world-altering stories and think, *What's the point of mine? What do I have to say?*

Your story may not spur a revolution. It may not spark a wave of social justice. It may not change anyone's life.

But it can have an impact—an important one. It may make people think. It may make them reconsider an entrenched belief. It may help them understand or cope with something going on in their own lives. One of the most meaningful letters I ever received about my novels was from a woman who told me that my books got her through chemo. That single reader *experienced* something in response to a story I helped put into the world. We shared a connection.

I'm writing this book while the Ukraine war rages on in its third year. While brutal war is waged in Gaza. Amid deadly conflicts in Myanmar, Sudan, Afghanistan. By the time it's published I don't know what will have happened to those who are fighting for their country, their homes, their freedom, and their lives. By the time you read this they may have lost all of it.

But Lin-Manuel Miranda had it right in *Hamilton*: Despite who lives, who dies, it's who tells their story who will keep them alive and make sure the world knows the meaning of their fight, their valor, their sacrifices.

There are heroes on the front lines who fight the literal fight in their effort to change the world. And there are the warriors who help those stories reach the world.

You are the storytellers. You have the power to affect the world no matter how small or grand your story. Tell it. It matters.

Chapter Thirty-two

Lessons from an Unexpected Wedding

A few months ago, while staying with my mom in Georgia for the wedding of my niece, the morning after the ceremony I overheard my mom say quietly in the next room to her longtime partner, "Do you think we should get married?"

This was startling to hear: Though they've been together for twenty-one years, so long and so happily that her partner is part of our family and we call him our fauxther (our fake father), they'd always said they had no need to get married. They met in their sixties, having already created families and full lives of their own, and are both in their eighties now.

But it took me only a microsecond to grab my phone and hustle into the adjacent room, to find my mom standing in front of the desk where my fauxther was grinning like a fool.

"Should I be recording this?" I asked excitedly. "Is this a proposal?"

Reader, it was.

One Wedding and Five Lessons

I learned a lot from this unexpected and wonderfully joyful event that applies in life and in writing.

IT'S NEVER TOO LATE FOR SOMETHING THAT MAKES YOU HAPPY

Later in the afternoon of the unexpected proposal, my mom and I were out shopping together when she asked hesitantly, "Do you think it's ridiculous to get married at our ages?"

"Hell, no," I said. "I think it's awesome."

My brother agreed, and we got busy quickly putting together a wedding for them, which we celebrated over the holiday.

Whether you have begun writing yet or just dream of it, whether you've finished something or not, shared it with others or not—whether via traditional publishing or any other way—there's no such thing as too late. If you want to write, write. If you dream of publishing, dream it—and then do it, regardless of how old you are when you start. There is no expiration date on creativity.

ASK FOR WHAT YOU WANT

My mom is a traditional lady, not one you would expect to buck convention and propose.

But she'd also realized, seeing the joy and celebration of my niece's wedding, that she wanted to be married to my fauxther before they died, as she puts it. He wouldn't have asked—she'd told him years ago that she had no interest in marrying again. And so she did the asking.

If you don't ask for what you want, you may never get it—and you may never know how others might feel either. When Mom asked, Fauxther lit up like a candle and gave her an instant yes. "I never thought this would happen," he confided to me later.

Ask for the time and support you need for your writing. If you don't you may never find out that your family and friends might be eager to help you achieve your goals. Ask for the representation you want, the publishing path you want, the contract terms you want, the money you want. You miss 100 percent of the shots you don't take.

MAKE MEANING IN A WAY THAT IS MEANINGFUL TO YOU

My parents wanted to keep the ceremony small, intimate, and personal. They didn't want a huge event or a giant group of people, just a handful of family at their home, with a simple "reception" afterward that my brother and I put together. We repeatedly offered fancier options, but this was what they wanted, what made them happy. And that was the only thing that mattered.

The same goes for your writing and your writing career. Write the stories that are meaningful to you. Pursue the path that feels right for you: trad publish, small-press or hybrid publish, indie-pub, or don't publish at all. No other yardsticks for your writing matter other than what fulfills you and makes your work meaningful to you. Ultimately it's the only thing about this pursuit within your control.

TAKE TIME FOR YOURSELF AND THE PEOPLE YOU CARE ABOUT

I tend to keep a brisk work schedule, but this holiday season, especially with the wedding and all the planning that went into it, and even the "postproduction" work of creating a wedding album and editing their video, I let myself do less work-wise without guilt or trying to frantically make up for it. These are the memories I'm creating that will matter to me when I look back on my life, not whether I fit in a little more work or made a little more money.

Your writing matters, but so does your health, your mental well-being, time to recharge, people (and animals!) you care about, and activities you love. Make time for those even as you regularly set aside time for your writing. They are just as important—perhaps even more so.

There were loved ones missing from the ceremony because of distance, death, and even family rifts. But we focused on those who were there and the joy we found in sharing the occasion. World events rage on, with war and violence and suffering, polarization and rancor, political strife and danger to democracy, and despite the feelings of grief and pain and even despair these current events may engender, for that weekend we simply celebrated hope and light and love.

Remember what really matters. My family and I are diametrically opposed ideologically and politically, and it's created tension and distance in the past. But none of that mattered over the weekend, when we gathered together and celebrated not just my parents' long-delayed vows, but the holidays and the many December birthdays in our family. We genuinely took joy in all the things we love about one another and celebrated this unique and happy event, and the thought of our differences didn't even enter into any of it.

At one point on her wedding day, my mother said in wonder, "Except for the days when you children were born, this is the happiest day of my life." The smile on my fauxther's face when he heard it was luminous. After the ceremony we presented him with a signed "Certificate of Official Family Status," formally conferring the title of stepfather, and I don't know whether we kids, my mom, or my brand-new stepfather enjoyed the gesture more.

We will surely face hard times again. But for those magical few days, we simply relished the unmitigated pleasure of the occasion and one another's company. We were there together. We were healthy. We were happy.

The world may be scary, uncertain, disturbing. It can be dark sometimes. Let what you create bring the light.

Don't dwell in perceived shortcomings or "failures" from the past, or anxiety about the future. Celebrate where you are now, all the wins in your writing, big and small. You published your novel? Became a bestseller or won an award? Made your day's word count? Sat down at your desk and opened a WIP file? Huzzah, bring the champagne for all of it. Every step along the path is farther than you were before, and you created something today that didn't exist yesterday.

That's all we can do in the world, just try to put something good into it day by day, a little at a time, as best as we're able. It matters, and it's enough.

Endnotes

1. Alice Speilburg, "Author Advances: An Update for Your Expectations," Science Fiction & Fantasy Writers, May 25, 2021. https://www.sfwa.org/2021/05/25/author-advances-an-update-for-your-expectations/

2. The Authors Guild, "Key Takeaways from the Authors Guild's 2023 Author Income Survey," Sept. 27, 2023 (updated Oct. 25, 2023). https://authorsguild.org/news/key-takeaways-from-2023-author-income-survey/

3. Business Wire, "Hagens Berman: Booksellers Sue Amazon and Big Five Publishers for Alleged Monopoly Price-Fixing the U.S. Print Book Market," March 25, 2021. https://www.businesswire.com/news/home/20210325005940/en/Hagens-Berman-Booksellers-Sue-Amazon-and-Big-Five-Publishers-for-Alleged-Monopoly-Price-Fixing-the-U.S.-Print-Book-Market

4. Directory of the Global Publishing Industry, https://www.publishersglobal.com/

5. Tiffany Yates Martin, FoxPrint Editorial blog, "How Writers Revise" feature. https://foxprinteditorial.com/category/how-writers-revise/

6. Jessica M. Goldstein, "Have you noticed that everyone's teeth are a little too perfect?" *Washington Post*, Sept 14, 2023. https://www.washingtonpost.com/style/interactive/2023/teeth-celebrities-veneers-tiktok

7. TED Radio Hour podcast, "The Artist's Voice," May 14, 2021. https://www.npr.org/programs/ted-radio-hour/996497783/the-artists-voice

8. TED talk, "The Pride and Power of Representation in Film," Jon M. Chu, April 2019. https://www.ted.com/talks/jon_m_chu_the_pride_and_power_of_representation_in_film

9. TED talk, "A Powerful Poem about What It Feels Like to Be Transgender," Lee Mokobe, May 2015. https://www.ted.com/talks/lee_mokobe_a_powerful_poem_about_what_it_feels_like_to_be_transgender

10. TED talk, "A Visual History of Social Dance in 25 Moves," Camille A. Brown, June 2016. https://www.ted.com/talks/camille_a_brown_a_visual_history_of_social_dance_in_25_moves

11. TED talk, "Using Your Voice Is a Political Choice," Amanda Gorman, November 2018. https://www.ted.com/talks/amanda_gorman_using_your_voice_is_a_political_choice

12. Gabe Ulla, "Chef Gerardo Gonzalez Perfects the Art of Collaboration," *Vanity Fair*, July 21, 2021. https://www.vanityfair.com/style/2021/07/chef-gerardo-gonzalez-perfects-the-art-of-collaboration

13. Sylviane Gold, "Camille A. Brown Choreographs Once on This Island, Her First Broadway Musical," *Dance*, April 30, 2018. https://www.dancemagazine.com/camille-a-brown-choreographs-once-on-this-island/

14. Jelisa Castrodale, "Entire Shipment of Cookbooks Sinks to the Bottom of the Ocean Causing Release Date Delays," *Food & Wine*, January 27, 2022. https://www.foodandwine.com/news/cookbooks-sink-shipping-delay

15. *Diners, Drive-Ins, and Dives*, "Mega Meats and Sweet Treats," March 29, 2019. https://www.dinersdriveinsdives.com/Pieous-Austin-TX

16. For a laugh, you can check out my video of Me Now interviewing Baby Writer Me from fifteen years ago on Facebook (https://www.facebook.com/1454365816/videos/2090499517769578/) and Instagram (https://www.instagram.com/tv/CWEDE33lpke/?utm_source=ig_web_copy_link).

17. Kathryn Magendie, "Royalties: What This Writer Made, Once Upon One Time," Writer Unboxed, December 1, 2020. https://writerunboxed.com/2020/12/01/royalties-what-this-writer-made-once-upon-one-time/

18. *Dead Eyes*, Episode 31, "Tom," March 10, 2022. https://headgum.com/dead-eyes/31-tom

19. James Clear newsletter, "3-2-1: On weaknesses, the secret to happiness, and what you want but haven't said," May 9, 2024. https://jamesclear.com/3-2-1/may-9-2024

20. Emilia David, "George R.R. Martin and other authors sue OpenAI for copyright infringement," The Verge, Sept. 20, 2023. https://www.theverge.com/2023/9/20/23882140/george-r-r-martin-lawsuit-openai-copyright-infringement.

21 Jane Friedman blog, "Ask the Editor," Oct. 15, 2023. https://janefriedman.com/how-can-i-set-aside-the-cacophony-of-writing-advice-and-just-write/.

22. Reyes Ramirez, "Artificial Intelligence Raises Questions on Intellectual Property And Ownership," Texas A&M Today, Oct. 25, 2023. https://today.tamu.edu/2023/10/25/artificial-intelligence-raises-questions-on-intellectual-property-and-ownership/.

23. Tiffany Yates Martin, "Barry Eisler and Pioneering the Path," FoxPrint Editorial blog, May 4, 2023. https://foxprinteditorial.com/2023/05/04/barry-eisler-and-pioneering-the-path/

24. Barry Eisler Interview, Tiffany Yates Martin YouTube channel, May 4, 2023. https://www.youtube.com/watch?v=B2oQX0n9a_0.

25. Jane Friedman blog, "What Is a Hybrid Publisher?" first published December 7, 2016; updated June 24, 2024. https://janefriedman.com/what-is-a-hybrid-publisher/

26. Abraham Josephine Riesman, "Why Did Marvel Fire Comics Writer Chuck Wendig?" *Vulture*, October 12, 2018. https://www.vulture.com/2018/10/why-did-marvel-fire-star-wars-comics-writer-chuck-wendig.html

27. Tiffany Yates Martin, FoxPrint Editorial blog, "How Writers Revise: Joni B. Cole and Toxic Feedback," July 6, 2023. https://foxprinteditorial.com/2023/07/06/how-writers-revise-joni-b-cole-and-toxic-feedback/

28. Brian A. Klems, "Book Contract: What's Negotiable and What's Not," *Writer's Digest*, Jan. 11, 2013. https://www.writersdigest.com/contracts-and-legal-considerations/book-contract-whats-negotiable-and-whats-not

29. Cynthea Liu, "How to Interview a Literary Agent," Writing for Children and Teens blog, June 2, 2007. https://www.writingforchildrenandteens.com/agents/how-to-interview-an-agent/

30. The Authors Guild, "An Author's Guide to Agency Agreements," June 12, 2018. https://authorsguild.org/resource/an-authors-guide-to-agency-agreements/

31. The Authors Guild, "Model Trade Book Contract," March 12, 2020. https://authorsguild.org/resource/model-trade-book-contract/

32. Jane Friedman, "Spotting Publishing Scams and Bad Deals," YouTube, July 23, 2023. https://www.youtube.com/watch?v=gkuYs8t-H8Y&list=PL81aMcw0YOtLbwkDRJPX4wxL3U_dhQVSE&index=9&t=3911s

33. Anne R. Allen and Ruth Harris, "Beware Bogus Writing Contests! Look for These 8 Red Flags," May 5, 2019. https://annerallen.com/2019/05/beware-bogus-writing-contests/

34. Jane Friedman, "I Would Rather See My Books Get Pirated Than This (Or: Why Goodreads and Amazon Are Becoming Dumpster Fires)," August 7, 2023 (updated August 20, 2023). https://janefriedman.com/i-would-rather-see-my-books-pirated/

35. The Copyright Alliance, "Copyright Owners Only: Stop Online Piracy of Your Work by Filing a DMCA Takedown Notice." https://copyrightalliance.org/resources/report-piracy/

36. Tiffany Yates Martin, "Barry Eisler and Pioneering the Path," FoxPrint Editorial blog, May 4, 2023. https://foxprinteditorial.com/2023/05/04/barry-eisler-and-pioneering-the-path/

37. Tiffany Yates Martin, "Allison Winn Scotch and Creating a Career on Your Own Terms," FoxPrint Editorial blog, Nov. 3, 2022. https://foxprinteditorial.com/2022/11/03/how-writers-revise-allison-winn-scotch-and-creating-a-career-on-your-own-terms/

38. PriceWaterhouseCoopers, "Entertainment & media revenues rebounding strongly from pandemic slump; shift to streaming, gaming and user-generated content is transforming industry: PwC," press release, July 12, 2021. https://www.pwc.com/gx/en/news-room/press-releases/2021/global-entertainment-media-outlook-2021.html

39. Statista, "Sports industry revenue worldwide in 2022, with a forecast for 2028." https://www.statista.com/statistics/370560/worldwide-sports-market-revenue/

40. Best Seller Publishing, "How Much Do Authors Make Per Book? Your Realistic Guide to Author Income," July 25, 2023. https://bestsellerpublishing.org/how-much-do-authors-make-per-book/

41. Publishing.com, "What Are the Average Royalties for a Book in 2024: Current Rates Explained." https://www.publishing.com/blog/average-royalties-for-a-book

42. Tiffany Yates Martin, "How Writers Revise, Jason Stanford," FoxPrint Editorial blog, July 6, 2021. https://foxprinteditorial.com/2021/07/06/how-writers-revise-jason-stanford/

43. Kristin Nelson, "If You Remember One Thing, It Should Be This: Never Sign an Unnegotiated Boilerplate Contract With Any Publisher," The Nelson Agency, Oct. 23, 2012. https://nelsonagency.com/2012/10/if-you-remember-one-thing-it-should-be-this-never-sign-an-unnegotiated-boilerplate-contract-with-any-publisher/

44. The Authors Guild, Model Trade Book Contract. https://go.authorsguild.org/contract_sections/1

45. The Mayo Clinic, "Friendships: Enrich your life and improve your health." https://www.mayoclinic.org/healthy-lifestyle/adult-health/in-depth/friendships/art-20044860

46. Hadley Freeman, "'Take It Easy, Nothing Matters in the End': William Shatner at 90, On Love, Loss and Leonard Nimoy," *The Guardian*, May 20, 2021. https://www.theguardian.com/culture/2021/may/20/william-shatner-interview-love-loss-and-leonard-nimoy

47. Dan Zinski, "William Shatner Does NOT Get Royalties from Star Trek: The Original Series," Screenrant, November 3, 2020. https://screenrant.com/star-trek-william-shatner-no-royalties-details/

48. "Get a Life!" Daily Motion. https://www.dailymotion.com/video/xmagzq

49. Bronnie Ware, "Regrets of the Dying." https://bronnieware.com/blog/regrets-of-the-dying

50. David J. Lynch, Michael Birnbaum, Ellen Nakashima, and Paul Sonne, "Historic sanctions on Russia had roots in emotional appeal from Zelensky," *Washington Post*, Feb. 27, 2022. https://www.washingtonpost.com/business/2022/02/27/russia-ukraine-sanctions-swift-central-bank/

51. Michael Lewis interview, *SmartLess* podcast, episode 91, April 11, 2022. https://podcasts.apple.com/us/podcast/michael-lewis/id1521578868?i=1000555975206

52. Jason Stanford, "Every Dystopian Story Starts This Way," *The Experiment*, Substack, May 22, 2022. https://jasonstanford.substack.com/p/every-dystopian-story-starts-this?s=r

53. "*This Is How It Always Is* Was Inspired by Its Author's Transgender Child," NPR, Jan. 30, 2017. https://www.npr.org/2017/01/30/512030431/this-is-how-it-always-is-was-inspired-by-its-authors-transgender-child

54. Allison Winn Scotch, "Writing in the Chaos," Writer Unboxed, July 30, 2019. https://writerunboxed.com/2019/07/30/writing-in-the-chaos/

55. Amanda Gorman, "Amanda Gorman: Why I Almost Didn't Read My Poem at the Inauguration," *The New York Times*, Jan. 20, 2022. https://www.nytimes.com/2022/01/20/opinion/amanda-gorman-poem-inauguration.html

Acknowledgments

These won't be short, because no writer—or editor—works alone, and I am indebted to many.

This book and my entire career don't exist without writers, so first and foremost I thank *you*: every author I've worked with, known, spoken to, read, and all the writers who have ever believed in themselves and their voice and vision and picked up a pen (or other writing implement) and committed their soul to paper (or other medium) and shared it with others. Creativity is a courageous, naked, deeply personal act, but one that has the power to change lives, change the world. Everything I've learned about the craft, as well as the creative business and life, I've learned from you. Your work gives my work purpose and meaning. There are no words for how grateful I am.

I asked a handful of friends and colleagues for support in the production of this book, and without exception, each of them leaped to the ready with not just a yes, but an almost instant, warm, and enthusiastic one. Each of you touched me more than you know with your response and kindness:

For my beta readers: Karin Gillespie, you're always at the ready with encouragement, support, commiseration, and such insightful, on-point feedback on my books. I so value your friendship—by far the best thing to come out of the turbulent origins of our creative partnership! ;) Lainey Cameron, you're a marketing and keyword genius. You fill in blanks I don't even know I have and make me look much better than I ever could on my own, and your perspective broadens mine and makes my books better. Thank you. Laura Drake, I can't even remember exactly how our paths first crossed, but I'm so glad they did. You're a staunch supporter of writers, an inspiration as an author for your gifts and grit, and a lovely human I'm happy to call friend. Your feedback added much clarity. Richard LeMay, we've been roommates, creative partners, and for better than half my life, close friends. Thanks for your always honest feedback and genuine encouragement and support of my work.

There are many others to whom I owe a debt of gratitude, beginning with Jane Friedman, publishing Yoda, fellow "dream crusher," and boon to writers everywhere. Jane, you know I've made you my secret mentor, even though you didn't volunteer for the position. Thank you for all you've done and continue to do to support my work and career, and for all that you give to the writing community. You are a bright light in our industry. (Mark Griffin, I'm lifting a doughnut to you as well!)

Rochelle Weinstein, I'm so grateful that all those years ago I was lucky enough to be introduced to you, and for the warm and nourishing friendship that has resulted. Your resilience, adaptability, passion, and talent have been in no small part an inspiration for so many of the ideas in this book.

Amy Collins, every time we talk you somehow make my day. Thank you for the steady stream of validation since we first met, for your very early feedback on this book that brought into bloom the first hopes that I'd hit the mark I was aiming for, and for your warmth and genuineness—with me and with writers.

Erin Flanagan and Sharon Short: I have to pair you together because I found you together (or you found me). I've come to value you both so much as artists and as friends, and finally getting to meet in person only cemented that. Why can't we do that all the time? Thank you both for your perpetually positive words that always make me feel like my work matters.

Amy Jones, it's weird I didn't know you a few years ago, because I feel as if we're constantly eddying in each other's orbit now—to my delight. Thank you for bringing me into the wonderful *Writer's Digest* community, and for your sharp (yet tactful!) eye that makes me a better writer.

Stephanie Storey, who would have imagined what would grow

from a single pandemic video interview? I'm so grateful for such a meaningful friendship that resulted, and love that we get to do our talks IRL now. Thank you for always being the perfect sounding board, demon commiserator, and such a key part of my creative—and personal—support system.

Therese Walsh, you created something magical with Writer Unboxed and the OnConference, and it's my privilege to be a part of it. Thank you for allowing me to be! And thanks for your always positive, enthusiastic reception to my work.

Peter Cox, I'm in awe of the Hydra of support you offer the writing community through your work as an agent and through the online writers' community Litopia and your Pop-up Submissions online program (and will never cease to be dazzled by your production values). Thanks for inviting me into your community, and for your generous support of my work.

Ann Garvin…grrrlll, you feel (and maybe kind of look?) like a separated sister; your humor and energy and openness of spirit delight and inspire me. Thanks for making me better in every way.

Rachael Herron, your smile is impossibly infectious, and so is your warmth and energy. I so respect all you offer to the writing community, including your own writing, which you know I love. I love shop-talking with you, and I'm so grateful for the ways you amplify my work with your own.

Kelly "Champagne" Harrell, you saved the day with this book when I needed it, but your friendship nourishes me on the daily. Thanks for letting me glom onto you all those years ago and pluck you away for myself.

Domini Dragoone, thank you for always bringing my books to life even more vividly and richly than they live in my head. You're truly an artist—and possibly a mind-reader—and your work makes me even happier with my own.

Tony Di Piazza, you take what by rights should intimidate and overwhelm me and make it understandable (I was going to say "easy," but I'm still tech-challenged me) and even fun. Thanks for your expertise and skill, and your generous approach.

Camille LeMoine—also known as the gifted and prolific author Camilla Monk—I'm grateful for your giant brain and design skill in creating my websites and all my branding. You somehow crawl up inside my head to extract a vision I didn't even know how to articulate, and make me look better than I have any natural right to. Plus I get to call you friend!

Finally, for my husband, Joel, my lobster. Despite avowing that you aren't the creative type, you constantly create time and space for me to work on what I love (even when it's too much and too long); and more than your 50 percent share of the happy life I get to live with you. None of this means anything without you (and the boys!).

About the Author

Tiffany Yates Martin has spent more than thirty years as an editor in the publishing industry, working with major publishers and *New York Times, Washington Post, Wall Street Journal,* and *USA Today* bestselling and award-winning authors as well as indie and newer writers. She is the founder of FoxPrint Editorial (named one of *Writer's Digest*'s Best Websites for Writers), and author of *Intuitive Editing: A Creative and Practical Guide to Revising Your Writing.* A regular contributor to writers' sites and publications like *Writer's Digest,* Jane Friedman, and Writer Unboxed, she is also a frequent presenter and keynote speaker for writers' organizations around the country. Under the pen name Phoebe Fox, she's the author of six novels.

Also by
Tiffany Yates Martin:

INTUITIVE EDITING:
A CREATIVE & PRACTICAL
GUIDE TO REVISING
YOUR WRITING

It's hard to look at your own writing with the objective eye needed to shape it into a tight, polished, publishable story—but just like writing, self-editing is a skill you can learn.

Packed with practical, actionable techniques to help authors evaluate how well their story is working, where it might not be, and how to fix it, this indispensable guide doesn't offer one-size-fits-all advice or rigid writing "rules." It helps authors discover what works for their story and their style—to find the best version of their vision—and gives you the tools you need to edit and revise your own writing with inspiration, motivation, and confidence.